TWAYNE'S WORLD AUTHORS SERIES

A Survey of the World's Literature

SWEDEN

Leif Sjöberg, State University of New York,

Stony Brook

EDITOR

Vilhelm Moberg

TWAS 584

VILHELM MOBERG

By PHILIP HOLMES

The University of Hull

TWAYNE PUBLISHERS

A DIVISION OF G. K. HALL & CO., BOSTON

Copyright © 1980 by G. K. Hall & Co.

Published in 1980 by Twayne Publishers,
A Division of G. K. Hall & Co.
All Rights Reserved

Printed on permanent/durable acid-free paper and bound
in the United States of America

First Printing

Library of Congress Cataloging in Publication Data
Holmes, Philip, 1944-
Vilhelm Moberg.

(Twayne's world authors series; TWAS 584: Sweden)
Bibliography: p. 183–187
Includes index.
1.   Moberg, Vilhelm, 1893–1973—Criticism and interpretation.
PT9875.M5Z68   839.7'372   80-11523
ISBN 0-8057-6426-7

Dedication: For my wife and children.

Contents

About the Author

Philip Holmes was born in Birmingham in 1944 and educated at Magdalen College School, Oxford, at High School in Sweden and at King Edward VI Grammar School, Camp Hill, Birmingham. He took a degree in Geography and Swedish at the University of Hull in 1967 and spent a year reading Scandinavian languages at the University of Uppsala. Since 1969 he has been a lecturer in the Department of Scandinavian Studies at the University of Hull. His doctoral dissertation was on "Narrative Technique in the Novels of Vilhelm Moberg," and he has previously published articles on Moberg's novels, and written on Strindberg, Harry Martinson, and postwar Swedish novelists in general.

Preface

Vilhelm Moberg is recognized primarily as a novelist who has documented and dramatized the life of the rural peasantry of one corner of Sweden at various periods in its history: his characters are the small peasant farmers, crofters, soldiers, and emigrants of the province of Småland. Unlike most earlier Swedish writers who have portrayed rural life, Moberg was himself born into a crofting family and is able to describe this world with detailed knowledge and, therefore, total conviction.

Moberg first made his mark as a playwright and throughout his life produced a steady stream of plays for stage and radio, but his reputation rests largely upon eighteen novels written between 1927 and 1967, and in particular upon the tetralogy collectively titled *The Novel about the Emigrants* (1949–1959), which deals with emigration from Sweden to America in the 1850s. A critical analysis of Moberg's novels is the main concern of this book, and readers wishing to discover more about the author's fascinating life are referred to the biographies listed in the bibliography.

Moberg acquired a considerable reputation as a political figure, an aspect of his life that is closely linked to his work as a writer. By becoming involved in several national controversies and by supporting the cause of individuals at odds with established authority, he gained a name as a people's tribune and champion of popular liberties. This book begins with a brief account of both his formative provincial background and his career as a writer and public figure.

My grateful thanks go to my colleague, Gavin Orton, who has provided help and advice during the writing of this book, and to my wife who has read the manuscript.

Translations from the Swedish are my own and page references are to the first Swedish editions.

Philip Holmes

University of Hull

Chronology

1898   Karl Artur Vilhelm, son of Karl Gottfrid and Ida Charlotta Moberg, born August 20 in Algutsboda Parish, Småland.

1909   Begins work at Modala glassworks.

1916–   Attends Folk High School in Grimslöv and Katrineholms
1918   Praktiska Skola.

1919–   Journalist on local newspapers in Östergötland and Värmland.
1922   Publishes numerous sketches and tales with local settings.

1921   Military service in Växjö, Småland. Publishes *In Tunic and Linen Trousers*, comic tales, under pseudonym "Ville i Momåla."

1922–   Local correspondent in Alvesta, Småland, for *Nya Växjö-*
1928   *bladet*.

1922   *The Princess of Solklinten*, romantic novel.

1923   Marries Margareta Törnquist. *Within the Bounds of Baggemosa*, local tales.

1925   *Embezzlement* performed in Stockholm, Moberg's first success as a dramatist.

1927   *Raskens*, novel, an important breakthrough.

1928   Becomes a professional writer and moves to Stockholm.

1929   *Market Eve*, radio play, published, as well as the dramas *The Wife* and *Wedding Salute* and the first part of *The Novel about Adolf at Ulvaskog*, entitled *Far from the Highway*.

1930   *The Clenched Hands*, the second Adolf novel.

1932   *A. P. Rosell, Bank Director*, novel.

1933   *Man's Woman*, novel, and *Violation*, drama. Moberg's breakthrough as a serious dramatist.

1935   *Memory of Youth*, first part of the trilogy *The Novel about Knut Toring*.

1936–   Vice-chairman of the Swedish Society of Authors.
1937

1937   *Sleepless Nights*, second part of the Knut Toring trilogy.

1939   *The Earth is Ours!* third part of Knut Toring trilogy. Dramatization of *The Clenched Hands*. Campaigns in support of Finland against the Soviet invasion.

1940– Writes articles condemning Nazi tyranny and Swedish
1945 appeasement of Hitler.

1941 *Ride This Night!*, novel, and *The Swedish Struggle*, pamphlet. Becomes vice-chairman of the Association of Swedish Dramatists.

1942 Dramatization and film version of *Ride This Night!*

1943 *The Truth Emerges*, pamphlet, and dramatization of *Man's Woman*.

1944 *Soldier With a Broken Rifle*, novel.

1945 *Our Unborn Son*, drama, and *The Segerstedt Controversy*, pamphlet.

1946 *The Brides' Spring*, novel.

1947– Researches into emigration in Sweden and USA. Lives at
1948 Carmel, California.

1949 *The Emigrants*, first part of tetralogy *The Novel about the Emigrants*.

1950 *The Unknown Relations*, factual account of Swedish emigration.

1950– Involved in controversies over indecency in literature and
1951 corrupt justice.

1952 Second emigrant novel, *Unto a Good Land*.

1953 *The Ancient Kingdom*, novel, and *On Being Vigilant of the Authorities*, pamphlet.

1953– Swedish Radio broadcast thirteen of Moberg's dramas. The
1954 dramas *Wife of the God* and *Leah and Rachel* now published.

1955 *Why I Am a Republican*.

1956 Third emigrant novel, *The Settlers*, and *The Conspiracies*, pamphlet.

1957 *The Judge*, drama.

1959 Final part of the emigrant tetralogy, *The Last Letter to Sweden*.

1961 *The Night Waiter*, drama.

1962 *The Fairy Tale Prince*, drama.

1963 *A Time on Earth*, novel.

1965 Moberg attacks American involvement in Vietnam.

1967 *Land of Traitors*, novel, and dramatization of *A Time on Earth*.

1968 *Tales from My Life*, autobiographical essays.

1970 *A History of the Swedish People. Part I. From Odin to Engel-*

brekt. The emigration tetralogy filmed in two parts by Jan Troell.

1971 *A History of the Swedish People. Part II. From Engelbrekt to Dacke.*

1973 *At the Time of Writing,* newspaper articles, and *Articles of Faithlessness.* On Wednesday, August 8 Moberg is found drowned in the sea near his cottage at Väddö.

CHAPTER 1

Life and Work

I Origins

VILHELM Moberg was born in a cottage in Algutsboda Parish in
Småland on August 20, 1898. The province of Småland lies in
south-central Sweden, and Värend, where Moberg was born and
grew up, occupies its southeast corner. Värend has a distinct and
ancient heritage: in earliest times a tribe of obscure origin, the Wirds,
settled here and established a kingdom long before the founding of
the Kingdom of the Swedes to the north. Moberg was always deeply
conscious of his roots among the people of Värend and its landscape,
and various periods of the area's history provide the setting for almost
all of his novels and a number of his plays. In his fiction, and later in
his writing of factual history, he aims to bring his forefathers to life, to
create a place for them in the history and literature of his country. Yet
Moberg's Värend is both more restricted and much more extensive
than any particular area. Like Thomas Hardy's Wessex it includes
many clearly recognizable locations and yet becomes an independent
world, distinct from geographical or historical reality.

The real Värend is a remote corner of a remote province, for
centuries one of the poorest parts of Sweden with a landscape dominated by great brooding forests and dotted with tiny farms and crofts
at the very margin of cultivation. The local people have always had to
struggle to wrest a living from the poor rock-strewn soils of these
uplands, and the miles of stone walls and giant mounds of stone which
lie like islands in the fields bear witness to the patient labors of the
peasants down the ages in clearing the land. For six hundred years
the forest wildernesses of Värend marked the border between
Sweden and Denmark, and the area frequently became a battleground, pillaged by armies from north and south alike.[1] The
traditionally freehold peasants of the borders demonstrated their
independence of central authority on many occasions by resisting the

15

Swedish monarch's calls to arms against their neighbors the Danes,[2] and several times rose in revolt against their own king.[3] For these reasons the peasant farmers of Värend gained a reputation for being hard-working, stubborn, and independent-thinking folk.

It is into this area, with its distinct culture and history, that Vilhelm Moberg was born, and his character and the nature of his writing are to a marked degree shaped by his origins. Moberg has provided us with the following account of his childhood world:

I was born in a little soldier's croft in an out of the way part of Småland which was then still completely untouched by the blessings, or if one prefers the curses, of civilization. None of the so-called technical advances had reached it. There was a railway admittedly, but that was some miles away . . . otherwise we had only narrow country lanes, and the horse and wagon was the most rapid form of transport. No one hurried in my childhood. They did a great deal of work, usually very hard work, but they never appeared to be in any hurry. When I eventually left this environment and later returned to my parents' home on a visit, my father noticed my restless nervousness and asked: "Why are you in such a rush, lad? You'll reach the grave soon enough, you too." . . . The croft where I came into the world consisted of a few small fields which had been cleared in the middle of a forest of mixed coniferous and deciduous trees, and a small stream flowed past only a stone's throw from the cottage. Here nature seemed untouched since the day God had created it, and in the midst of this virgin wilderness I awoke to human consciousness as one life among the many of this earth.[4]

Moberg's father came from a long line of soldier-crofters from this part of the country.[5] Carl Gottfrid Moberg served in the Kalmar Regiment under the long-established militia system by which each parish recruited an infantryman for the ranks and furnished him with a cottage and croft on which to support himself and his family. In return for the tied smallholding the militiamen attended maneuvers for a month each autumn. The militia system was phased out after 1901 but Vilhelm Moberg later lovingly recreated the world of these part-time soldiers and their families in the novel *Raskens* (1927). Moberg's mother, Ida Charlotta, also came from a local farming family, and in 1907 his parents were able to buy a small farm of their own in Moshultamåla with money provided by relatives in America. Moberg has painted a detailed picture of his early years both as fiction in the novels *Memory of Youth* (1935) and *Soldier With a Broken Rifle* (1944) and in a collection of autobiographical essays, *Tales from My Life* (1968). Included in this last work is the essay "Brodd"

("Germination") from 1932 in which he writes of his home environment:

I was one of seven children in a little soldier's cottage consisting of a single room. A present-day sanitary inspector would presumably condemn the tumble-down, more than hundred year-old cottage, as unfit for human habitation—at least for such a large family—and no doubt the seven children's daily diet lacked a great deal which wealthy parents would have considered essential for *their* children's health and well-being. But these circumstances can now be passed over as insignificant. As for material advantages, one cannot miss what one is not aware of. . . . Beyond the threshold of the soldier's cottage we had a clear view. Nothing obscured the sun; the sky was a great vault above us, always at its highest point directly above where we were standing, almost the first thing in the world that aroused my wondering attention. A gooseberry bush, a crab apple tree with a magpie's nest, a stream where the pike swam gaping sleepily between the weeds, a sandpit where the stones rattled, a bushy spruce with baby crows in its branches—these were things of wonderment for the child's keen, newly opened eyes.[6]

In many ways Moberg's was a deprived childhood, and it lasted only a few years before he had to work to earn his keep. Nevertheless, he returns to the images of childhood repeatedly in his novels and especially to the wonderful summers when he wandered barefoot along forest paths and went fishing in the local streams and tarns.[7] Later in life Moberg felt a great sense of loyalty toward the people he had encountered in his childhood. They were his own people in a very special sense, and he always belonged in part to them, regarding it as his duty to record their vanishing culture for those future generations who were not fortunate enough to have shared his experiences.

But the idyll of childhood was a prelude to an unsettled youth. Moberg's basic education was very restricted as the school year lasted for only four months, and apart from reading and writing the children were taught only biblical history and Luther's catechism. Moberg's parents were devout, and he read the Bible from cover to cover at the age of ten.[8] Although he lost his Christian faith when still a young man, Moberg's interest in the Bible as a literary work continued unabated, and its influence upon motifs and style is noticeable in a number of his works and grew stronger over the years. He was always impressed by the Old Testament stories and observed that "The greatest writer in world literature is the author of the Pentateuch."[9] As a child his hunger for reading matter other than the spiritual works

which surrounded him at school and at home became a major source
of frustration and conflict. It was especially painful as his parents and
neighbors showed a total lack of comprehension for his craving for
books, which was considered quite unnatural in a farmer's son. He
had to go to extreme lengths to satisfy his needs.[10]

From the age of nine Moberg had to help his father on the farm,
and when he was eleven he began work with other lads his own age at
the nearby Modala glassworks, carrying in wood to fuel the furnaces.
There is a marked schism between the two worlds in which he moved
in his teens, between the old peasant community with its values of
conservatism, self-reliance, and religious conformity, and the new
world of his workplace with its modern ideas of atheism and radical
politics.[11] The formative influences of this period upon the young
Moberg were later carefully recorded in *Soldier With a Broken Rifle*
in which he stresses the importance of the socialism he encountered
at the glass factory. Some caution is, however, necessary in reading
the novel as autobiography as its hero, Valter Sträng, is more politically active than was his creator at this time. Moberg became politically conscious during a period of social ferment in Sweden.
Organized labor demonstrated its newfound strength in a General
Strike in 1909, and a long struggle was waged for reform of the
franchise. There was also growing tension between the two wings of
the labor movement: the fiery Young Socialists favored direct action
as a means to attaining political power and a socialist state whereas the
more moderate Social Democrats preferred a constitutional course.
The Socialist ranks later split along these lines. In 1913 Moberg
joined the Algutsboda branch of the Young Socialists, but he soon
changed his allegiance to the Social Democrats. His socialist beliefs
always remained distinctly individualistic ones, however, and in later
life he became one of the party's most vociferous critics.

For a while Moberg found sanctuary in the local branch of the
Temperance movement, whose "temple" he joined because of its
much-coveted library. Valter Sträng's words express Moberg's own
acknowledged debt to the temperance lodge: "It had been his second
home and it had been like a school at the same time: all the books
he had borrowed and read, how he had learned to express himself in
the temple, to write minutes, to chair a meeting. He would never
forget what the temple had meant to him" (*Soldier With a Broken
Rifle*, 341).

By 1916 Moberg had become acutely aware of the limitations
which his surroundings placed upon his development and decided to

take the well-established escape route for young Swedes and emigrate. With a group of friends he intended to settle in Minnesota where he had relatives, but at the last moment his parents managed to persuade him to remain in Sweden, and it was to be another thirty-three years before he first saw America. The war years were good ones for the farmers, and Moberg's father found he could afford to send his son away to school for the winter, to Kronoberg County Folk High School at Grimslöv. The Folk High Schools had been founded with the aim of providing free tuition for those with no secondary education, and were (and still are) run by local authorities and a number of idealistic organizations. In his education Moberg's development followed a pattern common to a number of Swedish writers from peasant backgrounds including Dan Andersson, Ivar Lo-Johansson, and Artur Lundkvist. [12] Moberg actually learned little from the formal teaching at Grimslöv, but he did make fruitful use of the school library and took part in amateur dramatics. When the course ended he applied for various jobs but had to settle for work as a lumberjack, and from this work saved enough to return to school. He attended Katrineholms Praktiska Skola, a crammer where he studied day and night but never reached the goal of "Realexamen" ("Middle School Examination"). Weakened by overwork and a poor diet, the result of wartime food rationing, he contracted Spanish influenza during the pandemic of 1918 and the complications were nearly fatal. It took him six months to recover. Now, at twenty, he felt he was too old to be sitting at a school desk, and set about finding a career in earnest.

II *Beginnings as a Writer*

"It was a long drawn out beginning. [writes Moberg] I began early and developed slowly. I traveled long, meandering paths before I entered upon the path of the writer as a profession and livelihood. The period of preparation stretched over all of fifteen years, the years 1912 to 1927." [13] At the age of thirteen Moberg won a newspaper competition with a moralizing tale entitled "Svens hund" ("Sven's dog") and, by the age of seventeen he was a regular contributor to the radical idealistic paper *Såningsmannen* (*The Sower*) with pieces on nature and folk customs. Writing was a pastime for him, a way of spending his evenings after a day laboring on the farm, felling timber, or cutting peat. After his illness, in May, 1919, he took an unpaid position on the newspaper *Vadstena Läns Tidning* in Östergötland

where he was taken under the wing of the eccentric editor Pälle
Segerborg who was to become a close friend. Segerborg taught
Moberg journalism and encouraged him to observe closely the world
around him. But the editor was also fascinated by the other-worldly;
he dabbled in spiritualism and the occult and when Moberg wrote
some horror stories in the style of Poe, Segerborg was warmly enthusiastic and published his protégé's work as a regular feature in the
paper. He also introduced Moberg to Margareta Törnquist, whom
Moberg married in Vadstena in September, 1923, and who remained
his lifelong companion.

Vadstena Läns Tidning published more than sixty of Moberg's
stories, and Moberg estimates his total production during the next
ten years at more than five hundred tales, many of them published in
the provincial press under the pseudonym "Ville i Momåla." These
early tales have been carefully examined by Gunnar Eidevall.[14] They
show the writer exercising his narrative skill, gradually developing
his own style and finding the subject matter of the mature works.
Among them are many comic tales with local settings and colorful
dialogue. The characters are often familiar rustic types, mean
peasants and simple farmhands, gossips and maids, churchwardens
and crofters, yet personal observation plays an important part, for one
frequently discovers an underlying realism. A collection of these tales
was published as *Within the Bounds of Baggemosa* (1923). Lyrical
sketches and realistic depictions based on his experiences of local
people and places gradually come to dominate in the tales, some of
which were later expanded into incidents and scenes in the novels.
Eidevall shows, for example, how a pike-fishing scene in the story
"Hemlängtan" ("Homesickness") is adapted for use in no fewer than
four novels.[15]

In May, 1920, Moberg moved to the paper *Västra Östergötland* in
Motala as assistant to the editor, and in the autumn obtained a more
remunerative post in Värmland as assistant editor on *Arvika Nyheter*
whose editor also gladly published his stories.[16] At the turn of the
year he succeeded Segerborg as editor of *Vadstena Läns Tidning* at
the age of twenty-two and stayed until April, 1922, when disagree-
ments with his superiors led to his resignation. He then returned to
his home province as local correspondent for *Nya Växjöbladet* in the
small town of Alvesta, and here he stayed for five years. A similar
small town forms the setting of the novel *A. P. Rosell, Bank Director*
(1932) in which a major character is a local journalist.

Moberg's first published book was *In Tunic and Linen Trousers*

(1921). It is also his only wholly comic prose work and is based on a brief period of compulsory military service in Växjö in that year. Moberg did not make a good soldier. He detested the infringements that military life placed upon his freedom and frequently went absent without leave. These stories were in fact written while he was serving six days detention in the guardhouse.

The years in Alvesta must have been difficult and frustrating for him for, although he wrote several novels which were serialized in local newspapers, none of them gave him the breakthrough he now looked for. His first published novel was *The Princess at Solklinten* (1922), a love story of the romantic folktale variety. The strong but poor crofter's son Gottfrid loves the beautiful Karin but is prevented from winning her by her rich and unpleasant father. Moberg wrote later of this book: "I have not reread the novel in the last forty-five years. I do not indulge in unnecessary masochism, but I do know that it consists of a most unpleasant blend of Bjørnstjerne Bjørnson and Selma Lagerlöf, with an added ingredient of my own: an immature youth's infatuation with girls."[17] Nevertheless, at the time bad reviews of the book annoyed him, and he determined to write a literary work which would bring him recognition as more than a hack writer of romantic serials. But a number of similar disappointments followed.[18]

Although in the early 1920s Moberg suffered setbacks as a novelist, he did have some successes as a playwright. It is significant that he approached drama by way of the stage, and the provincial stage at that, rather than through literature. He had indeed never seen a play performed before 1920, and his experience was limited to the melodramas and rustic comedies performed in the open air in the local parks. His first play to be staged was a traditional rustic farce entitled *Marriages shall be made by a Matchmaker*, performed by an amateur group in 1922. As a result of this he became fired with enthusiasm and soon completed several plays for traveling companies. They neglected to pay him any royalties, but he has acknowledged a personal debt to them nevertheless: "Now, long afterward, I realize what great benefits I derived from seeing my first dramatic works in the revealing stage lights. I served my apprenticeship as a playwright; I heard how lines sounded from the stage; my eyes were opened to the need for concentration; I realized how easily a lull can occur in a play; I discovered numerous technical stage secrets which a dramatist ought to acquire. It was not me, therefore, who lost out—except in financial terms—from my contact with the provincial 'theater bands.' "[19] In the novel *A. P. Rosell, Bank Director* Moberg paints a vivid picture of a touring theatrical company of this kind facing financial ruin in a small town.

In 1924 Moberg's work reached the Stockholm stage. A comedy, *The Doctor at No. 18*, played at several theaters in the capital that year, and the following year he achieved his first success with the social satire *Embezzlement* which followed the contemporary trend toward topical drama. Use of the theater as a forum for debating social issues later became an important part of Moberg's work as a dramatist.

At this time, then, Moberg thought of himself primarily as a dramatist but was still publishing stories of folk life in the provincial press. Among these were several stories about the world of the soldier-crofter in the late nineteenth century which built upon his experience of his father's life as well as stories he had heard told of his forebears. Having earned some royalties from his plays, he was able in 1926 to take three months' leave from his newspaper and spent the time reworking these stories about soldier Rasken, his wife Ida, and their children, into the epic novel *Raskens: The Story of a Soldier's Family*. Bonniers published the book the following year, the first novel published under Moberg's real name.

Raskens is an astonishingly mature work and far superior to the works that had preceded it. It is a generation-novel which traces a soldier's life with his family on a small croft in Småland during the last decades of the last century. Moberg provides a carefully researched and detailed reconstruction of a rural way of life which had continued unchanged for hundreds of years and which by the 1920s was becoming unfamiliar to most Swedes. He displays great understanding and compassion for his characters and yet strives hard to avoid the temptation of portraying them in a sentimental or overly romantic guise. The desire to raise a monument to this forgotten class, the rural poor, is tempered by an objective realism which is at times brutal, and the even rhythm of a life regulated by the seasons is frequently punctuated by dramatic incident and strong effects. *Raskens* is technically an old-fashioned novel, built up from a number of independent stories which illustrate different facets of rural life and together make up a rounded picture, but the novel received good notices from the critics who praised its authenticity and realism. This was the breakthrough Moberg had been hoping for, and with this novel a major strand of Moberg's authorship is established which remained unbroken throughout his career: the authoritative chronicling of rural life.

III *The 1930s and World War II*

In the six years following the publication of *Raskens* Moberg consolidated his position as a writer of rural novels and also made a name for himself as a dramatist. His output is astonishing. Between 1927 and 1933 he published five novels and completed fourteen plays, although many of the latter now seem of doubtful quality. During this period it is possible to discern a gradual shift away from the minute documenting of rural life of the recent past toward a more critical examination of various aspects of the contemporary social scene, and in particular the spread of urban civilization and the changing countryside. The two predominant features of his work, social history and social criticism, are sometimes found in the same work and are often tempered by humor and satire.

The period in which several of these works are set, the three decades before and the three after the turn of the century, saw a rapid transformation in population distribution and social structure in Sweden—in effect an agricultural and industrial revolution. As late as 1870 nearly three quarters of all Swedes earned their living from the land, but by 1920 this figure had fallen to less than half, and farming methods had to change in order to maintain and increase the production of food.[20] At the same time there was a tremendous growth in industry and in the size and number of towns. The flight from the land, the increasing domination of an urban life-style, and the changes in rural society all figure prominently in Moberg's novels from the 1930s.

Both the chronicler and the social commentator are seen at work in the two-part *Novel about Adolf at Ulvaskog*. In *Far from the Highway* (1929) Moberg employs a narrative method similar to that of *Raskens*, dovetailing a dramatic plot into a minutely observed account of everyday life and work on a farm in the last century, thereby providing a comprehensive survey of the old social order. *The Clenched Hands* (1930) is a rural tragedy of classical dimensions in which the psychological portrayal of Adolf Bengtsson is set against a wider social perspective: the sweeping changes of rural depopulation and the influx of new ideas into the countryside. Moberg displays an ambiguous attitude toward his main character, seeing him as a reactionary but also as a tragic figure who stands alone against the tide of change.

Moberg's years in provincial journalism provide the material for *A. P. Rosell, Bank Director* in which he satirizes in an unusually bitter tone the life of a small provincial town whose foremost citizen is threatened with exposure as an embezzler. Bourgeois solidity and respectability are stripped away in a Strindbergian manner to reveal corruption and hypocrisy. Moberg's use of satire, begun earlier in *Embezzlement*, continues through the 1930s in plays such as *Chastity* (1937) and *The Maid's Room* (1938) which are lighthearted comments on the debate concerning modern morals.

As a dramatist Moberg's career in the late 1920s and early 1930s went from strength to strength. In 1929 his folk comedy *Market Eve* was a great success as a radio play and signaled the beginning of a fruitful collaboration with Per Lindberg, the head of Swedish Radio's drama section. In the same year Moberg published the volume *Allmogedramer* (*Dramas of the Common People*), a dramatic counterpart to the first three rural novels; it contains two three-act tragedies, *Wedding Salute* and *The Wife*. *The Wife* was also broadcast on radio. These plays all deal with the theme of marriage in a rural setting, but the major dramatic work of this period is set in an urban middle-class household. *Violation* (1933) deals with the sacrifices of personal freedom which the bond of marriage entails. This powerful social drama, produced at the Dramatic Theater in Stockholm, established Moberg as a serious playwright with the theater public. It is a feature of Moberg's career that he chose in his writing to alternate between genres, sometimes seeking alternative solutions to a problem in different works. This is perhaps most marked in the 1930s and can be seen, for example, in the novel *Man's Woman* (1933) whose classical tautness of structure and dramatic situation, with the wife torn between husband and lover, are similar to those found in *The Wife*, although the resolution of the conflict in this story of eighteenth-century Värend is rather different. In *The Wife* an attempt is made on the husband's life, while in *Man's Woman* the young wife, Märit, decides to run off with her lover to become an outlaw in the forest. *Man's Woman* is one of the finest love stories in Swedish, and its central character, Märit, one of Moberg's most remarkable creations. She is forced to choose between her freedom and a life within the community which she has made her home, and her dilemma is compellingly evoked. Moberg attempts to renew his narrative style in this work with its historical setting, lyrical prose with marked rhythms, and beautiful images of nature. He continued to write rural drama throughout the 1930s: a dramatization in five acts of *The Clenched Hands* came in 1939 and another popular comedy, *Widower Jarl*, in 1940.

From 1935 to 1939 Moberg published the massive trilogy about

Knut Toring. Knut is also torn between a feeling of solidarity with the community in which he finds himself and the need to make his own way in life. He has escaped from the village of Lidalycke in Småland and made a career in journalism in Stockholm. In *Memory of Youth* (1935) Knut has begun to find himself increasingly alienated from life in the city, and looks back to his roots to try to discover himself, thereby providing an account of his early life. *Memory of Youth* is a novel of development which in many ways reflects Moberg's own childhood, especially in the growing schism between the intelligent, bookish Knut and his philistine environment. Knut's schooling, spiritual development, hunger for books, and sexual awakening parallel Moberg's own experiences although, unlike Moberg, Knut makes a clean break with his childhood world and leaves for Stockholm at an early age. The autobiographical novel of childhood was a very popular genre among the group known in Sweden as the "Proletarian Writers," in other words, those of humble origins from the rural provinces who came to dominate the decade. Similar novels are Ivar Lo-Johansson's *Godnatt, jord!* (*Good Night, Earth!* 1933), Eyvind Johnson's tetralogy *Romanen om Olof* (*The Novel about Olof*, 1934–1937) and Harry Martinson's *Nässlorna blomma* (*Flowering Nettle*, 1935) and *Vägen ut* (*The Way Out*, 1936). These works all depict a problematical stage in the author's early development which, however, had long since been left behind, whereas the Knut Toring trilogy is firmly based in the present day and goes on to deal with the author's difficulties in coming to terms with the modern world.

Sleepless Nights (1937) continues the story of the mature Knut in Stockholm and explores the causes of his increasing discontent with his hollow existence. He finally leaves his job, his wife and family, and returns to Lidalycke to his roots and a life on the land. But the village has changed since he left; the flight from the land now threatens the future of the community, and in *The Earth is Ours!* (1939) Knut joins forces with Betty, a farmer's daughter of similar reforming zeal, in attempting to make Lidalycke a more attractive place in which to live and work. Everyday events in Lidalycke are set against the increasingly threatening international scene beside which they pale into relative insignificance. Moberg's attentions in this final part of the work are directed outward, and he appends to the novel an essay entitled "A Dream to Die For" in which Knut declares his willingness to lay down his life in defense of his country. The free and peace-loving Swedish people must be protected and the encroachment of an evil totalitarianism resisted at all costs. Moberg now felt compelled to abandon his earlier radical-pacifist views: violence must be met with violence.

This was by no means Moberg's first reaction to the growing threat of fascism and communism. From the time of Hitler's *Machtüber-nahme* he had been active with other writers in condemning National Socialism. They all supported the Spanish Republic and were actively engaged in soliciting aid for Finland against the Soviet Union, but the strength of their commitment can best be seen in the difficult years after the fall of Denmark and Norway in 1940, and before the tide turned against Germany in 1943. Moberg's opposition during this period took a number of different forms: he wrote a great deal in newspapers and magazines, spoke at public protest meetings, and in 1941 published a remarkable historical novel, *Ride This Night!*, which was dramatized in the following year and made into a film. The novel was an immediate best-seller and made a great impact. It may be seen as the most important single contribution to what is known in Sweden as "Beredskapslitteratur" ("The Literature of Mobiliza-tion").[21] Whereas Eyvind Johnson selected the world of contempo-rary Stockholm as a setting for the *Krilon* trilogy, his allegory of Sweden in World War II, Moberg chose a historical setting not unlike that of *Man's Woman*. The atmosphere of seventeenth-century Värend is established by means of archaic language and the use of telling cultural details. The period was chosen because Moberg found similarities between the situation of the Swedish people in 1940 and that of the Värend peasants in 1650, when Queen Christina of Sweden allowed German noblemen to impose a feudal despotism upon traditionally free men. The village of Brändebol comes in this way to represent Sweden, or perhaps all of Europe, and its villagers, who are forced to submit to the tyranny of a German baron, may be likened to the states of Europe falling under the yoke of Nazism. These men also seem to typify Swedish public opinion insofar as their reactions range from open collaboration through fatalistic acquies-cence to armed resistance. *Ride This Night!* was regarded at the time as a powerful and stirring encouragement to defend Sweden against foreign aggression, but its message is by no means so clearly chau-vinistic. The novel also contains an indictment of the Swedish govern-ment for its policy of appeasement toward Hitler. Because of book censorship Moberg was only later able to publish more strident criticisms of the Swedish coalition government's foreign policy. One concession which particularly appalled him was the granting of per-mission for German troops to use Swedish railways for access to

Norway. He wrote later: "The opening of Swedish railways to German troops, the so-called 'furlough traffic,' for more than three years was the most heinous infringement of neutrality and the most effective help to Hitler." [22] Moberg was also outraged by the use made of press censorship in the first three years of the war to stifle all reports of those concessions and of Nazi atrocities in the occupied countries, particularly in Norway. He was the first person to reveal the full extent of the concessions made, in a pamphlet in 1943.

The war also left its mark on Moberg's next major work. *Soldier With a Broken Rifle* (1944) is his second semiautobiographical novel, and he originally began work on it after completing the Knut Toring trilogy, which it complements in various ways. But he then found that he needed to express his concern at the national situation in a rather different form. In the course of writing the story of the soldier's son Valter Sträng from his birth in 1897 to 1921 he found parallels between the conduct of the right-wing goverment during World War I and that of the National Coalition during World War II. Allusions to the contemporary scene constantly break through the narrative, particularly in the last part of this massive novel where Moberg stresses the great ideals of socialism—among them freedom of the press—which the early comrades fought and suffered for, but which he feels have been betrayed by the present generation of Socialist leaders. This is Moberg's most political novel also in another sense, for he provides a fascinating picture of the rise to power of the Social Democrats in the early years of this century and the arguments and schisms within the party, all seen through the eyes of a participant. Primarily this is a novel of development which traces Valter's early life against a backdrop of Swedish social history. By means of a series of brilliantly painted interiors Moberg provides a panoramic view of provincial life at this time: we follow in Valter's steps to a glassworks, peat diggings, Temperance Lodge, Folk High School, and newspaper offices. The novel was for a long time neglected by critics, publishers, and public alike, perhaps because in wartime the reading public tended to reject realism in favor of escapism. It has recently (1972) been reissued in paperback and serialized on Swedish television.

In the early 1940s Moberg was also active in the theater. He was a financial backer and also chairman of Brita von Horn's new "Svenska Dramatikers Studio" ("Swedish Dramatists' Studio"), and it was largely at his instigation that the Studio put on plays that the larger theaters dared not stage in wartime. [23] Among these was one by Bertil

Malmberg (1889–1958), *Excellensen* (*His Excellency*, 1942), whose
anti-Nazi message provoked protests from the German government
and the Swedish Foreign Office. The Studio provided openings for
several new dramatists, among them Rudolf Värnlund (1900–1945)
and Josef Kjellgren (1907–1948), and it was here that Ingmar Bergman (b. 1918) made his debut as a stage director. Moberg also
agitated for the establishment of a town theater for Stockholm and
was instrumental in setting up a trade union for dramatists. When
"The Association of Swedish Dramatists" came into being in 1941 he
was its first vice-chairman. Moberg was always a staunch defender of
authors' rights, objecting to the low royalties paid to dramatists and to
the way directors frequently took liberties with an original text. His
own dramatization of *Ride This Night!*, produced at the Dramatic
Theater in 1942, won great acclaim, and its success must have encouraged him to dramatize *Man's Woman* in 1943. The impassioned and
lyrical drama *Our Unborn Son* (1945) finally established him as one of
the leading playwrights of his generation.

IV *Postwar Writing*

The postwar years saw Moberg once again deeply embroiled in
public controversy, but during these years he also composed his
masterwork, the tetralogy *The Novel about the Emigrants* (1949–
1959), a number of dramas and other works of fiction as well as two
volumes of *A History of the Swedish People* (1970–1971), a project cut
short by his death.

The immediate postwar years were a fairly quiet time with the
exception of a brief dramatic interlude in 1948 when the Communist
takeover in Czechoslovakia led to an ideological split in the ranks of
the Swedish Society of Authors.[24] Moberg took an anti-Communist
line which conflicted with that of the left wing of the society. In his
fiction and drama he now turned away from the contemporary world
to write more lyrical, historical works such as *The Brides' Spring*
(1946) and *The Wife of the God* (1954).

Moberg's masterpiece, the two-thousand-page tetralogy about
emigration to North America, was begun shortly after the end of the
war and took twelve years to complete. Research for this epic provided a welcome relief for him from the public forum in which he
involved himself during the first few years of its composition, and
unlike *Ride This Night!* and *Soldier With a Broken Rifle* this work
contains few allusions to the contemporary scene. Emigration also

figures prominently in the first part of *Soldier With a Broken Rifle*. The subject was part of Moberg's personal and social background, for Småland had been a major area of emigration and he himself had many close relatives in the United States. Yet he could find very little either in works of history or of literature about this, one of the most important social phenomena of the nineteenth century in Sweden as in other parts of Europe. He wrote of this discovery: "When in 1947 I began my novel about the first emigrants to North America, it became clear to me what I would do: I would write about people from Sweden whom the Swedish historians had forgotten."[25] Moberg began by gathering together material from letters written home by emigrants, from church registers in the areas hardest hit by emigration, and from the few published sources.[26] In 1948 he continued his researches in Minnesota where in St. Paul he discovered an invaluable source of information, the diary kept between 1854 and 1898 by Andrew Peterson, a Swedish emigrant who farmed at Waconia in southern Minnesota.[27] Moberg carried out extensive and painstaking investigations from the available historical documents as a basis for the novels, and this aspect of the work has attracted equally painstaking study by literary historians.[28] But he also succeeds in bringing history to life by dramatizing this material in a completely convincing way and at the same time underlines the timeless aspects of the emigration saga.

In *The Emigrants* (1949), the first part of the cycle, Moberg is careful to demonstrate the different causes of mid-nineteenth-century Swedish emigration: the inability of farmers to improve their lot on tiny crofts; religious intolerance; the inheritance laws which resulted in a growing number of landless sons. He achieves this by encapsulating each motivation in a dramatic and significant scene centered around a representative character. *The Emigrants* serves to introduce the main characters and shows how the group of sixteen men, women, and children leave their homes in Ljuder Parish in Småland in the year 1850 and take ship at Karlshamn for New York, which is reached only after an arduous sea journey. *Unto a Good Land* (1952) traces their journey onward across the American continent by rail and steamboat to the Minnesota Territory where they break new land in the wilderness and build new homes. The early part of the tetralogy is a collective depiction, but increasingly the focus is Karl Oskar and Kristina Nilsson and their children, and their struggle to make a new life comes to represent the experiences of all Swedish emigrants. *The Settlers* (1956) sees the emigrants establishing themselves and adapting to their new surroundings. The frontier settlement is gradually changing into a civilized community with church and schoolhouse. In this and the concluding volume, *The Last Letter to Sweden* (1959), the personal difficulties of Kristina Nilsson are highlighted, and the story is set against the backdrop of the Gold Rush, the Civil War, and a local Indian war.

In these four novels Moberg attains a breadth of vision unlike anything found in his earlier work. The theme of emigration struck a deep chord in him, and in presenting it in literary form he employs all his narrative and stylistic talents to the full. It represents the culmination of his career as a novelist. *A Time on Earth* (1963) is in some senses a sequel to the tetralogy. An aging emigrant, Albert Carlsson, lives out his last years in a hotel on the Californian coast. At the height of the Cuba Crisis of 1962 he reminisces about his life and in particular about his brother who died back home in Småland some fifty years before. Albert has a number of similarities with his creator, and the work is a very personal document which marks Moberg's restatement of his early pacifist beliefs.

While he was working on the tetralogy Moberg once again became involved in public affairs. "The 1950s was of course the decade of legal scandals," he wrote. "During the course of only a few years a number of remarkable so-called 'legal cases' occurred: the Unman case, the Kejne case, the Lundquist case, the Haijby case. . . . And it was during this period that the concept 'corrupt justice' arose."[29] The common element in all these cases was what Moberg saw as a blatant infringement of an individual's civil liberties, and he rushed to the defense of the individuals concerned, becoming personally involved in several cases. He wrote pamphlets, spoke at protest meetings, and even stole a secret document as part of a protracted crusade which angered the legal profession and embarrassed the government. What Moberg regarded as the corrupt state of Swedish justice also provides the material for two of his literary works: *The Ancient Kingdom* (1953) is a *roman à clef* set in the ancient kingdom of Idyllia which masks its savage criticism behind a Swiftian satire, and *The Judge* (1957) is a powerful dramatization of one of the cases involved. The name of King Gustav V figured in relation to one scandal which came to light in the early 1950s and Moberg, always a staunch antimonarchist, was moved to set out his beliefs in *Why I Am a Republican* (1955).

While all this was going on, Moberg was subjected to some abuse for the alleged indecency of *The Emigrants* and was drawn into a wider discussion of what constitutes indecent literature, sparked off on this occasion by Bengt Anderberg's novel *Kain* (*Cain*, 1948).[30] The mid-1930s had seen a similar controversy which centered around Agnes von Krusenstjerna's novel cycle *Fröknarna von Pahlen* (*The Misses von Pahlen*, 1930–1935) to which Moberg had added a comic rejoinder in his play *The Maid's Room* (1938).[31] The campaign begun against Moberg in the 1950s continued for several years in both Sweden and the Swedish settled areas of the United States.

In the 1950s and 1960s Moberg's dramatic production was smaller, but he did write a number of more experimental plays in different genres. *Leah and Rachel* (1954) is based on the Old Testament story, while *The Night Waiter* (1961) is a symbolist-expressionist drama about the problems of old age and death of a kind familiar from Pär Lagerkvist's works. *Woman's Man* (1965) is a problem play dealing with the social pressures on an older woman in love with a young man. Moberg's last completed dramatic work was an adaptation of the novel *A Time on Earth* from 1967.

The mid-1960s in Sweden were the years of the Vietnam protest campaign. In *A Time on Earth* Moberg had expressed his opposition to militarism, and his attitude to the United States had by then changed dramatically. The first edition of his factual work on emigration to America, *The Unknown Relations* (1950), ends with the words, "We can feel content that our countrymen were assimilated into that very people who today are prominent as the most powerful defense of human liberty on our earth." But for the 1968 edition he felt compelled to add an appendix in which he writes: "Twenty years later such revolutionary changes have taken place in world politics that the United States also stands out as an aggressive power."[32] In newspaper articles as early as 1965 Moberg had joined in urging American withdrawal from Vietnam and self-determination for its people. Though not as active in the movement as his fellow writer Sara Lidman, he did make an indirect statement with his last novel, *Land of Traitors* (1967). Moberg's attack on imperialism was less partisan than that of other campaigners and was veiled in the form of a historical novel as previously in *Ride This Night!* The plight of the people of the borders of Värend during the reign of the Swedish King Gustav Vasa in the early 1500s comes to represent that of other peoples divided by unnatural frontiers, whether in Berlin, Korea, Ireland, or other parts of the world. His condemnation of both great power blocks and his solidarity with those peoples caught in between them is never so clearly expressed.

Land of Traitors was Moberg's last work of fiction, for he then turned his attention to the factual writing of history, a subject he had always been interested in. In 1970–1971 he published the first two volumes of a projected series entitled *A History of the Swedish People* (the Swedish title means literally *My Swedish History Told for the People*) which deal with the mediaeval period up to and including the Dacke Revolt of 1542–1543. This remarkable work contains a series of personal essays in which, by using his great narrative talents, Moberg brings the history of this period alive and presents it in a largely fresh way. It is a tragedy that he completed so little of the work before his death.

Moberg was always highly skeptical of the literary establishment and especially so of the Swedish Academy and the institution of the Nobel Prize.[33] It is not surprising, therefore, that he was angered by his government's handling of the Solzhenitsyn case, and his displeasure was made very public in a memorable television debate with the then Prime Minister Olof Palme. Moberg writes of the case in terms which betray a deeply felt conviction: "Solzhenitsyn's cause is, of course, the cause of all writers who wish to act freely and without having to take regard of circumstances, who wish to write unobstructed by any power, political or otherwise, and only at the dictates of their own convictions. In him I see a symbol of that struggle which must be carried on in all countries for a free literature, a free social criticism unfettered by any interest."[34]

Writing was Moberg's life and he used it on more than one occasion as a cure for his depressions, notably after completing the emigrant tetralogy.[35] In 1957 he wrote: "When that day finally comes when I can no longer write, then I only hope that the door to eternity also closes behind me."[36] In the early 1970s he was beset by illness and often depressed by his own unproductivity. The work on the third volume of his history proved too much even for his considerable powers. On August 8, 1973, he was found drowned in the Baltic near his home at Väddö in Roslagen.

CHAPTER 2

Pictures from Rural Life

I A Soldier's Family

THE world in which Moberg grew up was to prove a lasting
influence upon his work, and he has outlined his relationship
with this world in the essay "Germination" from 1932:

A man can be transplanted any number of times but in a deeper sense he
cannot obliterate the stamp of his origins. He has permanent roots which
remain in the soil where he first began to grow, at least when his entire
childhood was spent in one place. A blood tie, a solidarity of feeling with these
people remains with me. However, I recognize clearly that this is no reason
for favoring these people in preference to all others. There were no doubt
individuals among them whom I would find it difficult to like if I could now
see them as they really were. But I own them as one owns those nearest to
oneself. . . . They are *my* people, and I react to the city-dweller's tourist
view of them in the same way one would react if those nearest to oneself were
put on display in some menagerie. On the other hand, they are ill served by
that old maidish sentimentality that makes them into angels and figures on
wall hangings, into improving illustrations for all those who love "nice
people." Conversely, I am in large measure *theirs*. They have given me
lasting impressions.[1]

Moberg's first three major novels, *Raskens* (1927), *Far from the
Highway* (1929) and *The Clenched Hands* (1930) all exemplify his
reaction against the tendency to overromanticize country people and
demonstrate his determination to provide a more balanced and realistic account of the people whose spokesman in literature he soon
became.

Raskens, the tale of a soldier and his family, has a firm basis in
Moberg's own background and in historical documents. Moberg's
father was a soldier in the Kalmar Regiment who left the army as late
as 1914, and soldiering had been in his family for generations.

Moberg's great grandfather, Nils Thor (1787–1872), is the earliest of his forebears about whom very much is known, and he served in the ranks for no less than thirty-six years.[2] Moberg was the fortunate recipient of a chest containing all of Nils Thor's important papers, documents concerning his inheritance, croft, and military service, which provide a glimpse of the life of a soldier some hundred years before the action of this narrative. As a child Moberg would sit listening to his father's comrades-in-arms spinning the broad yarns that were as much a part of all old soldiers' gatherings as were the drams imbibed, and some of these drastic and often ribald tales have found their way into the novel. Moberg had, on the other hand, no direct personal experience of a soldier's life at the autumn camp. The militiaman was first and foremost a man of the soil, and the narrative concentrates on soldier Rasken's life at home working the croft with his wife and family. (The title of the novel means "Rasken's family.") His intention in writing the book is to raise a monument over a forgotten social group, and he wrote later: "When in 1927 I published *Raskens*, it was my intention in this novel to provide a small place in our country's literature for the people from the tiny cottages, the rural proletariat. At that point in time I had not been able to find these people there." [3]

The narrative charts the course of one man's adult life from the mid-1870s until just after the turn of the century, and in so doing paints a picture of the kind of society in which he moves. The young farmhand Gustav is enrolled as Infantryman No. 132 for Momåla parish at a meeting held to recruit a successor to the previous incumbent, who has died. As was the practice, he is provided with a small cottage and croft, a salary paid largely *in natura*, and a new—soldiering—name, Rasken (meaning "the brisk one"). The new soldier soon requires a wife to share his life and marries Ida who works on a neighboring farm. Together the couple face good times and bad: Rasken is often in dispute with the parish authorities and the family experiences great poverty. Ida bears Rasken nine sons and only loses two, and she endures with Christian fortitude his drinking bouts and, later in life, his relationship with another woman. Ida is his stalwart helpmate, hardworking, thrifty, and God-fearing. Despite his personal shortcomings Rasken makes a fine soldier and is promoted corporal and given a medal for thirty years' service with good conduct. He is also an efficient husbandman, reviving a run-down smallholding and in so doing earning the admiration and respect of his neighbors. The couple grow old and look forward to being able to buy their croft and thereby assure themselves of a secure future in their declining years. But then Fate takes a hand and Rasken's untimely death leaves Ida to face old age alone as a pauper.

The couple's marriage and their relationship with other characters form the main focus of the story. These relationships are based on contrasts, and there is little development in the characters themselves. Moberg is concerned with providing a largely static picture. Neither does the narrator involve himself to any great extent with the inner life of his characters; their concerns are largely those of active, practical people. Rasken himself is a giant of a man. His stature and well-developed physique make him attractive to women, and he allows himself to be led astray. His size and strength often get him into trouble: in the first two chapters of the book he becomes involved in a savage brawl over a girl, knocks his employer unconscious, and breaks an opponent's leg in a wrestling match. But his size gains him employment as a soldier, and he is much sought after as a farm laborer. His abilities are put to good use when he is given his own plot to till. There are constant reminders of Rasken's ability to work hard, and he is capable of thinking beyond his own brief tenancy of the land, trying to improve it by breaking new fields and slowly clearing the rocks from his acres: "It would be some time before he was rewarded for his labors. It would take many years before a decent crop grew on a new clearing like this, before it was fertile and prepared. Whoever had the croft after him would one day derive the greatest benefit from it" (211). The image is archetypal: the dogged peasant struggles to wrest a living from an unyielding environment.

The opening sequence of the novel displays all of Rasken's moral weaknesses, of which he himself is fully aware: "He knew of old what normally went together: brandy—dancing—women—brawling; they usually came in that order" (24); in these scenes he drinks too much and fights with a rival for the attentions of the beautiful Anna. Over the years he does become less belligerent although brandy always lowers his moral resolve and, years later when he meets Anna again, she can entice him into her cottage and her bed with the offer of a dram. Ida, however, is a girl of a very different kind. Rasken first meets her when he has run away from his master and is hiding out in the woods. She is mowing hay and is not panicked by the approach of an unkempt ruffian: "She looked quizzically at him again with her calm eyes. . . . She wondered of course whether he had any intentions he was concealing, but the expression in her eyes said that she knew how to keep herself to herself, and that she would not allow

herself to be taken in in any way" (39). Even at this first encounter
Rasken respects Ida's obvious strength of will and yet feels himself
attracted to her: "She was a reliable and sensible lass, you could see
that about her. She also looked to be determined. . . . He had seen
prettier girls than her of course—like Nergårds-Anna, for example—
but he had a feeling that in a different way she was superior to them.
She was certainly a girl of a completely different kind to Nergårds-
Anna—he only needed to look into her eyes to understand that" (40).
Two contrasting images of Woman are represented here: the plain,
industrious and chaste wife and the beautiful and sensuous mistress,
and throughout his life Rasken is helplessly torn between the two.[4]

Unlike Anna, Ida brings no dowry with her when she marries
Rasken—her widowed mother has had a struggle to bring up her
children and get them over to America—but Ida makes an incomparable housekeeper and mother and is a full partner in the marriage. In
one chapter Moberg itemizes the tasks that Ida has to perform while
Rasken is away at camp. In an advanced state of pregnancy and
helped only by the children she gathers in the barley and oats, pulls
potatoes, spreads manure on the fields, and threshes the grain. She
chases off a thief and trudges twelve long miles to fetch medicine for a
sick cow. Finally, when suspended on top of a ladder mending the
cowshed roof, she feels her labor beginning and may at last lie down
to give birth to another son.

Ida is also a pious woman who tries to practice her Christian beliefs
in her everyday life. She bears no malice even when people are
malicious toward her, and she possesses true humility of spirit. Her
reaction to the news of her husband's promotion to corporal is indicative of this: "She was not one to set much store by worldly elevation
and folk's praise: she would remain what she was even if Rasken was
so elevated that he stood next to the king and became a chamberlain
or some such" (259). Her simple fatalistic piety contrasts markedly
with Rasken's more material self-reliance. For example, on the untimely death of their first fattening pig—a shattering blow that de-
prives them of much-needed winter meat—Ida remarks calmly: "We
mustn't get upset—if God didn't wish us to have any benefit of the
poor beast. . . . But Rasken thought of the five rix dollars he had
scraped together for the pig and of all the steps he had tramped to and
from the sty for its sake" (153). Ida's strong faith complements Rasken's worldliness, and she is an influence for good upon the head-
strong soldier. He always tries to live up to her example, although he
does not always succeed in keeping all the Commandments—the

seventh in particular. At his deathbed Ida fears for his immortal soul while all Rasken can think of is the croft which will now be lost to him.

Raskens traces a generation. Its subject is the cycle of life, and it chronicles the optimism of youth, the making of a home together, the ups and downs of married life, the rhythm of the seasons and the growing family, the slowing pace of middle age. How the young couple themselves see their life stretching out ahead of them is represented by a picture which hangs on the cottage wall:

It was called "The Ages of Man" and showed a man's journey from the cradle to the grave. Could she [Ida] not see there how a young couple were holding hands; they were their own age and would get married too, of course. . . . And look there, ten years or so later they had several children around them. At fifty they had come to the top of the slope, and then it went downhill. Right at the bottom they sat in rocking chairs, with hair as white as doves, and in front of them a grave was dug into which they could fall at any time. . . . (142)

But nothing in their lives turns out in quite the way they imagine it at this time. Life is harsh, brutish, and short, and Moberg frequently emphasizes its physical rather than its spiritual side. His people sweat, his men get drunk and fight, and his women gossip. He often goes out of his way to erase any potentially tragic or sentimental element from his story: childbirth, for example, is treated in a very matter-of-fact fashion, and the narrator makes more fuss about the death of a pig than about the death of the couple's infant son Martin. The family exists on the borderline of starvation, and when the harvest fails and then the life-giving bread runs out they feel the humiliation of poverty: the proud Rasken is reduced to begging a neighbor for crusts to feed his children. One might have expected a little sentiment in the depiction of, for example, the couple's wedding, but the scene is kept in a very low key. Because Ida cannot afford a proper wedding dress, she and Rasken steal secretly across the fields to the church. The vicar enters to marry them still belching after a good lunch and will not accept payment from a soldier of the crown, at which: "Rasken breathed a sigh of relief. He could keep his rix dollar, which he had gone two long days at work for, and that was a joy" (145).

The narrative incorporates a multitude of concrete details of the rural way of life. Moberg was fascinated by exactly how various rural tasks were performed. When Rasken is first recruited, the precise terms of the contract between soldier and parish are set down:

The soldier would receive four rix dollars signing fee and an annual salary of three rix dollars, which could be lifted half-yearly, in March and September. Then he would receive—apart from the produce of the croft—annually in seed and grain three foot and three quarters of a gallon of rye and three foot and one gallon of barley and Yuletide fare each Christmas, and six pounds of wool and as much flax annually. In fuel he would have twenty loads of three-foot kindling per annum, which he himself must chop and transport, while the parish would provide draught animals both for this and for use on the croft. He would also have the use of a wagon for four visits to the mill each year. (53)

We follow the new soldier on his first tour of inspection of the croft and share in his expert assessment of its drawbacks, the small size of the timber cottage and its lack of light, the weeds among the rye, barley, and potatoes, the waterlogged meadow, as well as his plans to remedy these. Later we discover how an official inspection of the property is conducted when Rasken asks the parish to make some improvements. When Rasken and Ida are to be married, the thorough preparations they make for their wedding are listed: they give each other betrothal gifts of a shirt and a Bible, buy a cow with Ida's savings and a runt piglet; Rasken paints the cottage while Ida sits up at night to finish weaving her linen and must then coach her husband-to-be in the catechism in readiness for the parson's questions.

Work is an important part of the realism of many of Moberg's novels, and he reveals a rare quality in being able to make his characters' labors, the farming tasks, both interesting in themselves and relevant to the story line. The heaping up of physical detail helps in great measure to support the strong illusion of reality, and the inventory at times becomes a stylistic device in itself, as, for example, when all the traditional foods are being prepared for Christmas in Ida's kitchen. The realism of fact is transferred to the fictional elements of the work which in this way are made entirely credible. One method of stimulating the reader's interest in the ethnography of a bygone age is to include its more colorful features. Thus Rasken receives an offer of marriage from an unknown woman through a marriage broker, and Ida has an encounter with an itinerant cloth pedlar, both of which are now long-vanished occupations. In one scene Rasken catches an abundance of crayfish in the stream which flows by his cottage, a facility greatly envied by modern Swedes, and serves them up to his soldier friends accompanied by vast quantities of various alcoholic beverages. Folk beliefs and superstitions are also recalled. Ida goes to great lengths to see into the future and discover whom she will marry: picking seven kinds of wild flower to place beneath her pillow so that she will dream of him, and eating a large salted herring tail first. When this does not work, she walks backward round a well seven times on Midsummer's Night.

Raskens depicts the end of an era. Rasken himself represents the last generation of the soldier-crofters as the system is phased out at the turn of the century, and Moberg is conscious of recording a now vanished world. The isolated and self-sufficient peasant community is beginning to change toward the end of the story: the railway, which in later years allows the soldiers to avoid a long march to camp at Hultsfred, also brings with it industries, and Rasken's sons do not work on the land but in glass factories and paper mills.

The "chronicle," the steady progression of life governed by the seasons and the constant struggle to support a growing family, is counterbalanced by a plot based on conflict and by some violent and dramatic action.[5] From an early stage Rasken is involved in a feud with his neighbors the Olssons, which begins when he is chosen to serve for Momåla parish in preference to one of Elias Olsson's sons. The enmity leads to a terrible brawl between Rasken and the Olsson boys, and then one of the sons, Oskar, is given further cause to hate Rasken when the soldier takes Ida away from him. Oskar carries on the feud after his father's death and tries to make life uncomfortable for the young couple. For a long time the violence simmers just beneath the surface, erupting in a number of minor incidents. Rasken's family grows up and his son Axel falls in love with Oskar's daughter Ingrid. But there is no rapprochement between these Småland Montagues and Capulets, for Ingrid bears a stillborn child and goes mad, whereupon her father murders Axel. A major component of the feud is Oskar's proposal to Ida and her sensible decision to marry Rasken instead. This proves disastrous for Oskar, who sacrifices his happiness for the future of his farm, a common Moberg motif, by marrying a girl who is his social and financial equal. He sees his wife become demented and then his daughter also goes mad, and he has to hurt the people he regards as responsible. He says to Ida: "Well, you see, I've had so much misery and pain that there is some left over for you too!" (227). The great sympathy that Moberg displays toward his characters, which leads to an overidealization of Ida, is seen especially in his treatment of Oskar as one of the victims as well as one of the villains of life.

There is a great deal of violence in this novel, not all of which is associated with the main dramatic conflict. There are fights and

deaths by shooting, hanging, and battering and two cases of madness.
But it is the drama of everyday life, the struggle to survive, that
provides the most effective conflict of all—man against nature. It
proves ultimately to be an unequal contest, for Rasken succumbs to
frostbite one freezing winter's night, and dies of gangrene. The feud
is not the only dramatic motif, and its resolution—the death of
Axel—does not mark the end of the story, but neither is it, as at least
one critic has implied, a motif which is loosely appended to the
narrative.[6] It serves as an important structural link in this rather
episodic work.

Another feature not sufficiently recognized in earlier studies of the
novel is the use Moberg makes of a contrasting subplot in order to
emphasize the themes of the main plot. The life stories of Johan
(Klangen) and Anna are held up as a mirror to those of Rasken and Ida,
reflecting what might have befallen them under different circumstances. Klangen and Rasken are friends at the outset and join the
same regiment, but Klangen's drinking leads to his downfall. When
Rasken discovers Anna's promiscuity he refuses to marry her as they
had planned, and Klangen takes her for her dowry, but Klangen is
fated never to have any luck with women. Anna makes him a poor
wife: when the two soldiers march off together to camp, Rasken's
rucksack bulges with food prepared for him by his capable Ida while
Klangen's empty bag is compensated for by a flask of brandy. Klangen
soon divorces Anna and marries again, a candy seller from Hultsfred
who plunders him of all he possesses and deserts him. He resolves to
keep his third wife on a tight rein and beats her cruelly until finally
she hangs herself. He then disappears from the story for a time,
leaves the army, and is rumored to have taken to the open road.

Anna's downward path is contrasted with Ida's virtuous life in the
incident of the cloth pedlar, Skara-Knallen. He calls on Ida and offers
her some dress material if she will sleep with him. Ida refuses and
resists his violent advances, but later sees Anna wearing a new dress
and realizes how the thriftless Anna had obtained such a costly
garment. Anna later moves into the cottage previously occupied by
the parish whore and herself bears several illegitimate children,
including a daughter by Rasken. The story of Klangen and Anna not
only provides a negative counterpart to that of Rasken and Ida but
also helps to provide a structural frame for the narrative as a whole.
The first two chapters provide a neatly rounded introduction and
serve to summarize and anticipate a great deal of the story to follow:
Gustav (Rasken) is to fetch the horses early one Sunday morning to

take soldier Modig to burial, but drinks too much, dances, brawls, and makes love to Anna, as a result of which he oversleeps. When he appears at the farm, he quarrels with his master, knocks him down and runs off, meets Ida, and eventually reappears at the recruitment meeting where he is signed on as the new recruit in Modig's place, and incidentally alienates the Olsson family by so doing. The seeds are sown here out of which Rasken's life develops. In the first chapter Anna is the reason for Rasken's lateness. Without his knowledge Johan (Klangen) has fetched the horses and taken the old soldier to burial thereby placing Rasken in his debt. In the final chapter Rasken is again on his way home, this time from felling timber in the forest, and is once more delayed. Whereas in the first scene the setting is summer, now it is a bitter winter's night. By chance Rasken comes across Klangen whom he has not seen for many years; it is a sentimental encounter, and for the sake of old comradeship Rasken gives his friend his own fine boots and takes Klangen's tattered shoes in return, thereby repaying the long-standing debt. On this occasion too Rasken meets Anna. But, whereas before she had willingly allowed him into her cottage, now she refuses him shelter; in the first scene she had got him into trouble, now she seals his fate. The thin shoes are no protection against the cold, and he gets frostbite in one foot and then stubbornly refuses amputation as this would mean the end of his soldiering. The gangrene spreads and he dies a horrible death. The tying together of the different threads of the narrative is brilliantly achieved, for the beginning and end of the story both deal with the death of a soldier—Rasken's death closes the circle. Its result, the widowing of Ida, is also prefigured earlier when we see her mother's wretched existence as a widow in a squatter's hut in the forest, a lot which will now befall Ida herself.

A number of episodes in *Raskens* originally appeared as stories in local newspapers, and traces of this are still to be found in the internal structure of the narrative. Three chapters in particular (9–10, 13) still have the character of independent episodes, and a number of others have the completeness of the short story. Gunnar Eidevall shows how the stories published earlier end in a harmonious way, while in the novel the corresponding episodes have a more disharmonious outcome but gain in realism.[7] Two epilogues not found in the published text have since come to light. One, entitled "Raskens efterleverska" ("Rasken's Widow"), pictures the death of Ida some thirty years after Rasken's own death.[8] A second tells of a stranger who visits the deserted croft many years later and who turns out to be Karl, Ida's ninth son.[9] But the novel stands in need of no such epilogue; its ending, with Ida entertaining Anna and her little daughter by Rasken, finds just the right note of reconciliation on which to close.

The tradition of the rural novel was well established in Scandinavia before Moberg and his contemporaries, the "Proletarian Writers" of the 1930s, came on the scene, and some of the earlier works stand out. August Strindberg's *Hemsöborna* (*The People of Hemsö*, 1888) is regarded as a likely influence upon the composition of *Raskens*. The two works do possess a number of features in common, such as the narrative chapter titles ("How Rasken goes the wrong way on his wedding anniversary and how he receives both a reward and a punishment on the same day"), the accumulations of detail, changes in pace and mood, the concentration of the setting, and the authenticity of the depiction.[10] A similar reverence for what is instinctive and natural in rural life is found in Knut Hamsun's *Markens grøde* (*Growth of the Soil*, 1917), but Moberg's compassionate treatment of his Smålanders is closest to the relationship of Ernst Ahlgren (pseudonym of Victoria Benedictsson, 1850–1888) with her Skåne peasants in her short stories from the 1880s. Like Moberg, she often describes the very poor, in contrast to Selma Lagerlöf, the novelist who dominated the first decade of the century: Lagerlöf, in such novels as *Jerusalem* (1901–1902), deals with the wealthier class of freehold farmers.

Raskens is important both for its own intrinsic merits and for the way in which it encompasses so much of the style and technique seen later to be basic to Moberg's writing and often merely varied or further refined. The dualism which underlies the novel has already been hinted at. On the one hand, Moberg aimed to provide an accurate and objective historical record without the romantic shimmer surrounding earlier stories of rural folk. On the other hand, he commemorates a people he felt he belonged to, and the empathy leads to an idealization of some characters and in certain cases a lyrical depiction of scene: examples are the poetic luster associated with Ida's activities on Midsummer's Night, and the love of Axel and Ingrid. The desire for accuracy in the depiction of social conditions leads occasionally to an obsession with the sordidly physical. It can be seen in the simile and metaphor employed, the "organic" imagery which derives from the world of farming, from the characters' own intellectual and social premises, something true of Strindberg's *People of Hemsö*.[11] Images of the farmyard are used to emphasize the instinctive and unreflecting nature of the peasant. When, for example, Rasken and Edvard are about to fight, they "glowered at each other like a pair of young bulls that have lowered their horns and want to butt one another" (20). When he is on the run, Rasken "would not of his own accord creep into a cage like a senseless beast as long as he could avoid it" (36), but "starved like a masterless cur for eight days" (44).

The prose style in the novel is very colloquial: Moberg uses simple syntax, and the result is remarkably direct and concrete, but also very Swedish—he was a great purist. The dialogue involves a degree of Småland dialect imitation and dialect vocabulary which at times necessitates explanatory footnotes, and the author's own narrative is colored by dialect expressions. The dialect is not used, as is often the case, to comic effect, but serves to locate the speakers firmly in one specific environment, thereby strengthening the illusion of reality.

Letters and tales are inserted in a number of Moberg's novels. The letters between Rasken and Ida are fine examples of pastiche which poke gentle fun at the formal biblical style used, but also underline the writers' laconism and understatement. The four tales told by soldier Frejd are no mere digressions. They are all placed in natural storytelling situations: at the party given by the new recruits for their comrades, and on the long march to camp at Hultsfred where they serve to shorten the weary miles. They also form *entr'actes*; the first tale comes just prior to the fatal shooting at the end of the party, and its humor emphasizes the shock of this tragedy.

II   *The Novel about Adolf at Ulvaskog*

Far from the Highway and *The Clenched Hands* chart the course of Adolf Bengtsson's life as a farmer and owner of Ulvaskog. The similarities between *Far from the Highway* and *Raskens* are striking: both stories trace a generation and both are set in Värend in the last quarter of the nineteenth century. *The Clenched Hands* takes up the story in 1913 and pursues it to the mid-1920s. But there is one significant difference: this novel portrays not the least favored class of landless laborers and squatters but the small farmers who own their own land. The two parts of the work each reflect a different underlying intention and show a development in Moberg's conception of the rural novel. In *Far from the Highway* local color and the collective depiction of the old farming community are once again prominent, whereas in *The Clenched Hands* Moberg attempts both a dramatization of the sweeping social changes taking place around the turn of the century and a penetrating psychological portrayal of Adolf himself, a symbol of the unchanging peasant.

Far from the Highway begins with the death of Adolf's father. The farm is made over to Adolf, who has to take out a mortgage in order to pay his brothers and sisters their share of the inheritance. He also takes on the responsibility for brothers Kalle and Hasse, sister Tilda, and mother Lotta, no small burden for a young man to shoulder. Since the seventeenth century Ulvaskog has been handed down from father to eldest son, and it now falls to Adolf to carry on the family line. He is merely "a link in the long chain of farmers at Ulvaskog. He was only an intermediary, he lived only for the next link" (292). Adolf falls in love with Emma, the daughter of a wealthy neighbor and magistrate, Otto at Grimhult. Emma soon becomes pregnant but is too frightened to inform her parents. In the time-honored fashion Adolf confidently sends his marriage broker to Otto to ask for her hand, but Otto is proud as well as rich, and Adolf is warned by his mother that his offer is likely to be refused: "It was the case that every farmer married according to the size of his holding. When farmers' children were paired off, the value of the parents' farms was first taken into account. Someone who owned half a homestead did not marry the daughter of a quarter homestead man" (90). Adolf's suit is rejected, and this social convention militates against the eventual happiness of Adolf and Emma, whose relationship is based not on money but on love and affection. When Emma's parents learn of her condition, they send her away to relatives to avoid a scandal, planning to have the baby adopted. Any hope Adolf may have entertained of marrying Emma is dashed when his brother Hasse is involved in a bout of vandalism at Grimhult for which the master of Ulvaskog is obliged to pay compensation. Emma returns and tells Adolf that she has borne him a son, christened Per-Adolf, and that the child has been sent up-country to foster parents.

After some years, Otto, who can see impending financial ruin ahead, suddenly relents and agrees to his daughter's marriage to Adolf. But, just as the couple's first lovemaking had brought problems in its wake, so now does their marriage. Adolf's mother, Lotta, does not get on with Emma, who replaces her as mistress of Ulvaskog, and there are also quarrels with Adolf's sister Tilda whose illegitimate child is a source of friction. When it is discovered that Otto has lost his money, and that Emma consequently brings no dowry with her to Ulvaskog, the enmity turns into open conflict. This is never resolved, for Lotta demands her rights under the deed of sale and moves into a separate part of the house. For some years life passes relatively quietly and Adolf lives for the work on the land. The couple have four more children and Adolf works for them, to pay off the mortgage on the farm as his father had done. He feels it is his duty to pass on the farm to his heir without any debts encumbering it. But all the time he thinks of his first-born son, Per-Adolf, who will come home and one day take over the farm from him. He finds special consolation in this thought as his second son, Emil, is rather slow-witted and could never become master of Ulvaskog.

Hasse marries, Kalle dies, and so does Lotta who even on her deathbed refuses to be reconciled with her daughter-in-law. Emma and Adolf gradually drift apart, and she is caught up in the religious fervor of a revival which sweeps through the district. When, years later, Adolf finally prepares to travel north to bring back the son he has never seen, Emma is forced to confess to him the awful truth about their child: she drowned the baby when he was only a few days old rather than part with him, and has lied to Adolf ever since. The same evening that she confesses, Emma hangs herself. The year is 1899.

The Clenched Hands takes up the story fourteen years later, on the occasion of Adolf's youngest daughter Mari's confirmation. Adolf has had to manage without a wife but he still has all his children around him helping to run the farm. A new age has dawned, the age of the motor car and the tractor, of electricity and agricultural machinery. Adolf's dogged refusal to come to terms with the twentieth century is a central motif in the novel, and it is his inflexibility that leads to the breakup of his family and inexorably to the final tragedy.

First to succumb to the temptations of a life outside Ulvaskog is the eldest daughter, Signe. She is tired of slaving on the farm for nothing, and when her father refuses to buy her a bicycle from a traveling salesman she leaves home and later marries a railway employee. Erik is next to go. He works first in a store in town and then, during World War I, makes his fortune as a black marketeer. The children want Adolf to sell Ulvaskog so that they may receive their maternal inheritance, but instead Adolf mortgages the farm a second time, pays them off, and starts all over again. When the war ends, Erik loses everything and has to turn to his father for help to pay his debts. Emil leaves Ulvaskog and finds work in a factory. Finally only young Mari remains, and together she and her aged father wage an uneven battle to keep the farm going. Tilda's daughter Gärda is now making a living as a prostitute in Stockholm, and Adolf learns of this while Mari remains in ignorance. She plans to leave too, to stay with Gärda, and, rather than lose his last remaining child, Adolf kills his daughter.

A basic difference between the two parts of the work lies in the number and use of the characters: in *Far from the Highway* Moberg displays a large gallery of rounded secondary characters whose background is sketched in and viewpoint indicated. In Kalle, Moberg introduces a stock figure in his work, the lad destined to die young. Lotta is unforgettable: the down-to-earth matriarch struggling to hold on to Ulvaskog and to her son's affection. Others include Sven Kardmakarn, a crofter at Ulvaskog, and his wife Lina, who are employed to inject a little earthy humor. Sven is one of Moberg's tellers of tall tales, and his fantastic adventures at the hospital provide much-needed light relief, retarding the final catastrophe. Sven believes that the nurses are starving him, and shortly after his operation makes his escape, returning to his wife for a decent meal. In *The Clenched Hands* Adolf's children come to the fore, as does his nephew Alfred, the archetypal agricultural improver, but the emphasis of the novel is placed firmly upon the psychological development of Adolf himself, who steps out from the collective to attain the stature of a Job or a Lear.[12]

The farm at Ulvaskog dominates the story throughout. The name Ulvaskog ("Wolf Forest") itself speaks of the untamed wilderness, and the farm is isolated from others in the parish, so much so that it is given the nickname "World's End," and the villagers say "that the isolation of the farm from the rest of the district left its mark on those who lived there so that they could not be like other folk" (*Far from the Highway*, 39). Much of the action is confined to the farm, and this concentration, especially in *The Clenched Hands*, produces an intentionally claustrophobic effect. After Emma's death Adolf rarely strays beyond his own bounds and eventually becomes a recluse. He is very closely identified with the farm. The two merge into a symbol of a way of life which is doomed to go under, and changes in one are reflected in the other. This is particularly marked toward the end of *The Clenched Hands*, for, as a result of Adolf's physical and mental deterioration Ulvaskog also degenerates: the roofs leak, the fences fall down, and weeds invade the crops. The decay in the once well-run farmstead provides an image of the decline of its owner.

The setting is significant not only for the structure of the novel, however, but also thematically. The main theme concerns the conflict of interests between Adolf's ownership of the farm and his personal freedom and happiness. Most of his problems stem from the lack of freedom that the ownership of the land entails. He is unable to marry Emma until Otto considers him a financial equal, which results in the death of his son Per-Adolf and the split in the family. He has to mortgage the farm twice over to pay off the inheritances just to retain possession, and his commitment to the place seems never-ending. He is enslaved by his possessions, a motif that runs through several Moberg novels and has already been seen in the story of Oskar in *Raskens*.

The stereotype of the erotic novel, with the lovers kept apart by a tyrannical father, is revitalized in *Far from the Highway*. The forces holding them apart are social forces, and their final coming together is, realistically, not the end of their troubles but only the beginning. The plot is basically simple, relying on the traditional devices of selectivity, suspense, and surprise: the narrator tells us only part of the story and withholds the fate of Per-Adolf so as to produce a shock later. The most effective surprise is, upon reflection, motivated by the preceding action, and in both novels this kind of prepared surprise is employed as a climax and resolution of the plot. In *Far from the Highway* the narrator uses foreshadowing to indicate obliquely the true situation: Emma is unwilling to bring Per-Adolf home, becomes pensive whenever his name is mentioned, and grows very devout in order to expiate the feeling of guilt that oppresses her. These clues also serve to heighten the suspense. The initial shock of Emma's revelation of her infanticide is followed by a sense of its inevitability. The second shock, of her suicide, is also prepared for both by her obvious remorse and guilt and by two earlier scenes. When Emma's mother is preparing herself to tell Otto about Emma's pregnancy she unthinkingly sends Emma to fetch some rope, but Otto realizes the danger and finds his daughter before she can harm herself. When she later chooses to die, it is by hanging. Further, the dying Kalle tells Emma of a dream in which he learns that all those who take their own lives on Good Friday will find salvation, and it is on this day that Emma ends her life.

Premonitions based on folk beliefs are also used to prefigure later action. For example, Mari is born on an unlucky day, and Lotta foretells a woeful future for her. Many superstitions concern death and reflect a fatalism which is surprising today: when Lotta is about to die, she claims to have seen her dead husband in the yard at night calling to her to join him. The most successful element of this kind is embodied in the figure of Lump-Fransen, the wandering ragman who calls at Ulvaskog. Although his occupation is much despised,

Franse thinks it a vital task: "He considered that he attended to
something very important in this life. Was he not the person who
eventually accounted for the world's corruptible things? How much
was not destined to become rags? All the gewgaws, all the baubles
and glitter were destined for his sacks—everything in time would be
handed over to him" (114). Franse represents the transience of all
worldly things, the idea of *vanitas mundi*, the futility of all human
endeavor. But bad luck for the family also attends his visits, which
coincide with news of deaths and other calamities, and Lotta regards
him as a messenger of Fate. When Tilda's fiancé dies, Lotta thinks:
"Didn't I have a feeling that there would be bad news? The ragman
was just here on the farm—he always brings evil with him, it never
fails!" (153). The folkloristic element is seldom a thing in itself, and
Moberg here makes it a part of the composition.

Both the obsession with the material world and some harsh detail
reveal the realist at work in these novels. As Bengt is taken to burial
the driver complains of the smell of the corpse, and Lotta does not
attend her husband's funeral—she has to remain at home in order to
look after a sick cow. The set-piece rural festivals, largely lacking in
Raskens, and in particular the hay harvest and wedding, clearly owe
much to Strindberg's *The People of Hemsö*, and Moberg even
attempts to outstrip his master in the realism and observation involved in these depictions.[13] But the extensive depictions of farm
work demonstrate Moberg's greater familiarity with this world, and
he provides an informed account of sowing, harvesting rye and potatoes, threshing and slaughtering animals. He has a keen eye for
detail, showing, for example, how the distinctive rhythm reveals the
number of flails threshing in the barn and therefore the size of the
harvest and the holding. The colorful details of folk life again include
food, especially the richer fare for Christmas and festivals, the activities of the matchmaker, and a wedding, here a very splendid affair.
The exuberance and color of the early scenes in *Far from the Highway* gradually give way to a more introspective tone as the narrative
concentrates on the internal strife in the family and on their contem-
plation of death.

In *The Clenched Hands* Moberg does not, of course, attempt an
objective or factual presentation of the changes which were trans-
forming Swedish society—industrialization, urbanization, migration,
rural depopulation, and the revolution in agriculture—but he does
show how certain individuals react to the forces involved. The
breakup of Adolf's family comes to represent the disintegration of the

old order, and Moberg concentrates into a brief and simple dramatic sequence of events some complex social changes which stretched over decades. The reasons for the flight of Adolf's children from the land are typical of the young people who left farming areas. The regular hours of work, cash wages, and leisure time offered by work in towns contrasted favorably with the toil of working all hours for only pocket money and a share in an inheritance in the future. The social life and entertainments available in town compared favorably with the isolation of life in the countryside, and the nature of the work was often more pleasant.[14] Yet despite the representative function of Adolf's children in the story, Moberg manages to create rounded characters from them and avoids the pitfalls of the stereotype.

Adolf's personal qualities—his determination and inflexibility—coincide with his role as defender of the old social order of self-sufficiency and independence, and he turns Ulvaskog into a last bastion against the forces which threaten that order. Adolf's character and his reaction to change is embodied in the use throughout of a realistic detail, his large hands, the clenched hands of the title, as an adaptable symbol to penetrate and expose some of the basic ideas of the novel. At the outset Adolf's hands emphasize his firm parental discipline. When Signe answers her father back "All the children now had the same thought: Father had such unusually large hands; they were real wooden slabs, big and kind of swollen, rough and hard as bark. The children had never seen anyone with hands as large as father's" (20). The administration of discipline by these hands is a recurrent idea: the hands figure whenever the children begin to challenge Adolf's decisions, in each decisive confrontation between parent and child. Violence erupts on several occasions: Adolf strikes Emil and later fights with Lump-Fransen. Associated with discipline is Adolf's desire to retain the things that are his—his family, his farm, and his money. He wants to protect the children from the pleasures and temptations of the world outside Ulvaskog and from the need for cash which this entails: "Adolf at Ulvaskog had a saying: he clenched his hands hard around what was his, so hard that nothing could escape from them. He repeated this often, and no one doubted that he was quite serious about it" (53).

But his strictness and caution with money turn into autocratic harshness and unyielding meanness; his virtues turn into vices. Adolf's nephew, Alfred, wants him to join with other farmers in a scheme to canalize the stream which runs through their land and turn water meadows into good arable fields, but he cannot persuade Adolf to sign the papers, and on leaving thinks "Yes, Adolf at Ulvaskog clenched his hands right enough. But if he did not let anything out of them, then he would not get anything in either" (83). Because Adolf refuses to modernize his farm it starts to decline. Alfred's thoughts also apply to the children: it is because Adolf fails to slacken his grip on them that they decide to leave.

When, under the combined pressure of his family, Adolf is forced to mortgage Ulvaskog a second time, it seems to Erik that his father's hands are not as terrifyingly large as they were. His power is waning. Money has also run out of Adolf's hands for a different purpose, to pay Erik's debts and save him from prison: "He clenched his hands even tighter—but what good would that do now? Something had poured into Ulvaskog during the war, but Erik had smashed a hole so that much more had leaked out" (180). The idea of money pouring away like water foreshadows the use of the stream and dam as symbols. When the improvers, led by Alfred, begin their work on the stream, Adolf decides to rebuild the old mill dam to flood the meadows once more, and from working in the cold water he falls ill and has a feverish dream in which he is back at the dam trying in vain to hold back the water which runs through his fingers. He is alone except for Alfred who stands on the bank laughing, and then finally the dam gives way, and he wakes up. It is possible to see in the dam and the dream of the dam a conflation of two ideas associated with the clenched hands. It presents in concrete terms Adolf's attempts to shore up his finances— the incident occurs shortly after Erik's embezzlement—but it also embodies his conservatism, his resistance to a progress which threatens his secure world. Alfred is the improver and the canal the irreversible flow of progress, while the eventual removal of the dam is the inevitable outcome of Adolf's stand. Alfred is again employed as the author's mouthpiece in order to analyze Adolf's tragic situation: "what he wanted to protect would instead be destroyed in his hard peasant's hands. Adolf's self-protection was turning into sheer self-destruction" (229–30). This comment foreshadows the climax of the drama in which Adolf kills the very thing he loves and wishes to protect, his daughter Mari. But before this happens, Adolf himself has come to realize the futility of his life, and sees it in these terms: "He had lived a life which had not lasted, which ran away like a stream through his fingers and did not return. He had hung onto a patch of earth—it floated away and sank, it was nothing to hold onto. . . . Now he opened his hands to see what remained in them. He saw they were empty. He no longer held anything any more" (294).

The Clenched Hands is a taut dramatic work in which Moberg has been strict with his material. Its classical unity centers largely on the tragic flaw in the main character. Adolf's downfall is predetermined and fatalism pervades the novel, but the development of Adolf's virtues into vices under changing circumstances is skillfully traced through the symbolic pattern. Moberg paints a bleak picture of a man out of step with his time, failing to understand the new world and desperately trying to hold on to the old. Few novels illustrate the generation gap with such frightening clarity, and what is remarkable about this dramatization of the problems of old age is that the insight is shown by such a young writer. Moberg's attitude to Adolf is strangely ambivalent: he shows great compassion for his tragic hero, admires his courage in trying to take on the whole world single-handedly and standing up for what he believes in, yet is critical of his stubborn refusal to see the social benefits of change. As a Socialist Moberg must reject Adolf's individualistic views and side with the collective, which offers the only hope for the future of the rural community.

The determinist tone in Moberg's early novels is always strong, and it is perhaps no surprise to discover that he admired the works of Thomas Hardy: "In my youth," he writes, "I placed him above all other novelists I had read."[15] In the female characters, in Ida and Lotta especially, a sense of the inexorability of Fate is always ready at hand to provide an explanation for setbacks, but Adolf is unusual in his consciousness of Fate as a power over which the individual has no dominion:

Like the turning of a wagon wheel in its rut, that is man's life. The wheel rolls, and he who sees it and nothing more may be firmly convinced that the wheel chooses the rut in which it runs. But above sits the coachman steering, and he has draught animals in front of him. Forces pull and steer—the wheel follows, continues rolling. It comes to a crossroads, jumps out of one rut and into another. . . . Fear grips him in the face of this unknown power which disposes over people's lives. He is exposed, defenseless before this cruel power which is never visible but only felt. (*Far from the Highway*, 345)

CHAPTER 3

Migrations

I A Pillar of Society

THE central figure in the novel *A. P. Rosell, Bank Director* is director of the savings bank, the brickworks, and the iron foundry, and many more undertakings on which the economy of the small town of Allmänninge is based. Rosell is a founding father of the town and its most prominent citizen. He has seen it grow over twenty-five years from a tiny village with a hundred inhabitants, one store, and a dirt road, into a municipal community with straight paved streets, a hundred stores, and twenty factories, a model community inhabited by three thousand people. The story follows a few hectic days in Rosell's life, and in the process provides a panoramic view of a small town which parallels the pictures of the rural community in Moberg's earlier works.

Rosell is, however, not all that he seems. The urbane and farsighted architect of Allmänninge is, like most of his fellow citizens, only a first generation city-dweller. He was born Anders Petter Fransson in Skallaboda, although even in his youth it was clear that he was destined for higher things. The village schoolmaster once compared A. P. with his friend Johan Magnusson in terms of types of cloth: "You Anders Petter are like cheviot—while you Johan are like moleskin!" (38), and the nickname has stuck, though A. P. himself feels that it is used by the envious to imply that he is an upstart. A different image of A. P. is provided by his antique furniture, renovated of course and with the dates clearly painted which "gave an impression of inherited peasant honor and old fashioned stability" (83). But the dates have been falsified and, like the furniture, Rosell's outward appearance is merely a guise.

Rosell has to confess to Johan Magnusson, his business associate, that he has "borrowed" 120,000 crowns from the savings bank funds: he had lost money in a stock-market crash and had to save himself

from bankruptcy. The audit is imminent and the new auditor one of
his bitterest enemies. If the fictitious assets in the bank's funds are
discovered, he will immediately be exposed and will probably go to
prison. Magnusson calls a meeting of the directors of the bank to deal
with this very sensitive matter, and Rosell appeals to these business
colleagues for their financial support to replace the missing funds in
time for the audit. The bank must be protected at all costs, for any
breath of scandal could cause irreparable harm. It is best for everyone
in Allmänninge that confidence in A. P. Rosell be maintained, but the
effects of the associates' financial support action are far-reaching and
the consequences unforeseen by those who are involved. The result
is a chain reaction which spreads through the community, and the
worst affected are those least able to take care of themselves.

The other important figure in the story is Valfrid Sterner, local
correspondent in Allmänninge for a provincial newspaper. Sterner is
an idealist who lost his job as editor of a paper because he refused to
suppress a news item to which the paper's owner took exception.
Then he believed in the duty of the press to tell the truth fearlessly
but now he has become a cynic, bitterly disillusioned with life, "The
Inhuman Comedy" which he intends to expose in a book with this
title. Sterner's work revolves around the hundred lines of copy he
must find every day in Allmänninge and which leads him into a
desperate search for news. He is the reader's guide to the town and its
inhabitants, and he reveals what goes on behind the scenes. Both
Sterner and Rosell have marital problems. Sterner feels he has failed
his wife; his work brings in barely enough to support her and their five
children, and not wishing to create any more problems he has become a voluntary celibate. His worries drive him to drink. While
Sigrid and Valfrid Sterner have too large a family, Doris and A. P.
Rosell are childless, and Doris, who longs for children, suspects that
her husband is the cause.

Sterner is entrusted with making a collection for a presentation to
Rosell on the great man's fiftieth birthday. He collects eleven hundred crowns but then on impulse attempts a futile revolt against his
life and appropriates the money. He gives some to his wife and plans
to use the rest to abscond with an actress he has met. His plans fail
disastrously when the actress runs off with the money, and he con-
templates suicide, but eventually goes to Rosell himself to confess his
crime. The irony of the situation is for once lost on Sterner as Rosell
proceeds to lecture him: "He had in the most shocking way abused
the trust of those who had signed the list. Didn't he understand that?

54   VILHELM MOBERG

In an irresponsible manner he had taken advantage of the contribu-
tors, large and small. He had taken their money, intended for a
different purpose—and many of them probably needed it more than
he did. . . . Did he not understand that honor was the fundamental
basis for a community and the incentive to a decent communal life?"
(282–83). Rosell nevertheless agrees to lend Sterner the money to
cover up his crime. Rosell too is able to weather the storm which
threatens to sweep him away, and on his birthday receives the
congratulations of the whole community.

The effects of the action to shore up Rosell's position soon make
themselves felt, or, in the imagery of the novel, when the predatory
fish are about, the small fry are likely to be swallowed up. Early in the
story Sterner encounters an unmarried mother, Vendla Danielsson,
who has taken a factory worker, Axel Ljungkvist, to court in order to
obtain maintenance for her child. Because of the financial help to
Rosell, Ljungkvist's employer has to cut down on his work force and
Ljungkvist loses his job. At the same time Vendla's landlord, another
of Rosell's backers, has to press her for the rent she owes. She cannot
support herself and her child, and when Rosell is being fêted by the
entire town, Vendla drowns herself and her baby in the lake. Rosell's
life is one full of duplicity and deceit, yet the ultimate irony is still to
come. The novel ends with the announcement of the birth of a son to
Doris Rosell, but her husband is unaware that he has been cuckolded
by Sterner, and the journalist thus wins a secret victory over his
adversary.

In Moberg's earlier novels the town is seen as very much a corrupt-
ing influence upon young people from the countryside: in the Adolf
novels Gärda becomes a prostitute in Stockholm while Erik is a black
marketeer in Malmö. In *The Clenched Hands* the town was a constant
threat to Adolf's world but never came into the foreground of the
story. Now it appears in close-up, and the typicality of the setting is
underlined (the Swedish word "allmänning" means "common land");
it becomes a microcosm of small town life in the 1930s, complete with
all its corruption. In the debate on the town council concerning the
building of a new schoolhouse, "The struggle between wood and
stone," the opposing councillors' business interests (timber yard and
brickworks) are clearly discernible behind the impassioned rhetoric.
Apart from the venality it is the heartlessness of town life that Moberg
condemns. The victim of the modern capitalist system, the young
Vendla, would it seems have fared much better if she had stayed
home in the country rather than fleeing to the anonymity of this alien

world. The bitterness of the criticism must stem from a deep personal unease with modern "civilized" urban living. Moberg had personal experience of various small provincial towns, and used the town of Alvesta in particular as a model for Allmänninge.[1] Like Sterner he was a small-town journalist for some years, and he too left his job as editor rather than excise a news item, ending up as a local correspondent who wrote fiction in his spare time. Sterner is, wrote Moberg later, a vision of his own fate as it might have been had he failed to get on. But Sterner's cynicism derives from a journalist colleague of Moberg's in Alvesta, who, like Sterner, drank his way into society and then became an alcoholic.[2] In this novel we gain an insight into Moberg's views on the society of the day: the problems he takes up and the features of small-town life which he portrays here would have been only too familiar to many of his readers. The world economic crisis of the early 1930s had serious repercussions in Sweden: some workers were seriously underpaid and the specter of mass unemployment loomed large. By the end of 1931 there were 89,000 unemployed in Sweden, an increase of 180 percent on the 1930 figure, and by December, 1932, this had reached 161,000.[3] In his interview with Sterner, Rosell asserts that "unemployment was no abnormal condition in a modern society, of which it had gradually become an organic part" (54).

In the year the novel was published, Sweden was shaken by the suicide of Ivar Kreuger, "The Match King," and the collapse of his financial empire, and although Moberg agreed that there were certain similarities between Kreuger and Rosell, he denied that the novel was intended as a pamphlet to exploit the case.[4] He had in fact been working on the idea for some years and had treated it in a more humorous way in the play *Embezzlement* in 1925. The narrator's intention of revealing the true and ugly face of society behind the facade is reminiscent of the 1880s. Ibsen had treated this theme in *Samfundets støtter* (*Pillars of Society*, 1877), and the parallels with Strindberg's satirical novel *Röda rummet* (*The Red Room*, 1879) have also been drawn.[5] Corrupt business methods are found in Strindberg's novel, as are scenes of theatrical life which depict the fatal charms of young actresses. Sterner has the pragmatic nature of his fellow journalist Struwe, perhaps the cynicism of the medical student Borg and inherits the function of guide from the young hero Arvid Falk. Moberg seems to have attempted a small-town version of Strindberg's exposé of the institutions of the capital.[6]

Speculation and corrupt business practices were also prominent

themes in Swedish post–World War I writing, and there are parallels
to the plot of *A. P. Rosell, Bank Director* in two works by Hjalmar
Bergman, a major exponent of the bourgeois novel. H. H. Markurell,
in Bergman's novel *Markurells i Wadköping* (*God's Orchid*, 1919), is
also a parvenu who rises to economic prominence and whose personal
career is linked to the livelihood of the whole town. The paternity
motif is also important in this work, which deals with a catastrophe
which never happens. Bergman's comic play *Swedenhielms* (1925)
describes the honoring of a great man—by the award of a Nobel
Prize—and a scandal that threatens to mar the occasion.

Valfrid Sterner is a guide to the characters and institutions of
Allmänninge, and initially he seems to represent the author's own
views; we naturally identify with him because he is the underdog who
has already suffered for fearlessly telling the truth. But our hero turns
out to have feet of clay, and only utter cynicism and disillusion
remain, weakening the effect of the novel. An unusual and discon-
certing feature here is the way that Moberg distances himself from his
characters, although as is often the case in his work, it is the plight of
the women that is portrayed with the greatest understanding and
compassion.

A. P. Rosell, Bank Director possesses several new features for
Moberg: a biting satirical tone and marked pessimism; an involvement with the contemporary world; a new and for his readership
unfamiliar setting. In many ways it points forward to the political
satires and polemical essays, which, however, were aimed at a more
restricted target.

II *An Outsider*

Moberg's most important work from the 1930s is the massive
trilogy about Knut Toring, comprising *Memory of Youth* (1935),
Sleepless Nights (1937) and *The Earth is Ours!* (1939). The story
opens in an apartment in Stockholm in 1934, where Knut lies dreaming of his childhood in Småland, when he ran barefoot through the
grass in summer and went fishing for pike in the local streams. Knut is
thirty-five years old and has been successful since coming to the city:
he has an attractive and intelligent wife, Aina, two children, Rune
and Kajsa, and a well-paid job as editor of a weekly magazine. But
despite this he is not satisfied with life. He is increasingly repelled by
his work, which involves sifting through piles of badly written stories.

His marriage has also lost its freshness, and he begins to seek happiness elsewhere.

Knut is one of an army of country-born people who have exchanged the soil of the countryside for the asphalt of Stockholm:

Through these first-generation city-dwellers Stockholm had trebled its population in half a century. The capital had become a great metropolis by means of the migration from the countryside. A peaceful and tranquil migration—but with repercussions that were too great to be foreseen. They came here from the earth to conquer the town and in it to create their dreamworld. But it was the town that instead conquered them and created them in its own image. These hundred thousand went about treading the hard asphalt like changed beings. And one of those who had been changed was Knut Toring from the village of Lidalycke. (43–44)

Knut feels that he has sold his soul to the city and prostituted his talents, a crime worse than selling one's body like the young country girls who cannot support themselves any other way in the big city. Sometimes the life of Stockholm, symbolized by its main street of Kungsgatan, becomes too much for Knut, and he is overwhelmed by "the unbearable," a terrifying attack of *Angst* which makes him want to scream out his hatred of the city, to shout to everyone he meets that he must get out, must go anywhere as long as it is far away from this place.

In the introduction to *Memory of Youth*, entitled "The Man," Knut's thoughts stray constantly to his childhood home in Småland. The fine summer weather makes him wonder whether his parents have finished getting in the hay. Hearing a woman on a tram speaking with a Småland accent sets him thinking of home, as do the letters he receives from his mother. One of these tells of the death of Bruns Ebba, the first woman he ever loved, and he begins to wonder about his early life and the people of the soil he left behind. Why is he in the city? Why does he not return to the countryside?: "Deep down in the past lay the roots of the present. Before the man was first the child and the youth" (85). In the second part of the novel, "The Child," Knut's search for his identity leads him to retrace his steps through childhood in a recapitulation of his formative years.

The story begins with Knut's earliest memory, when he dreams of a very different city, the golden city of heaven. In the idyllic description that follows, Moberg paints the world of nature of which Knut is then a part, the animals and birds, fruit and berries, the fish playing in the stream, that make up a child's memory of summer in the country-side. Knut climbs into the branches of the cherry tree and can see the whole of Lidalycke village spread out beneath him, but beyond this the world ends. Above him sits God on his rocking-chair throne, and "if he did not obey God and Jesus, then he would not get to the heavenly city, but instead come to The Dangerous One" (101).

As a youngster Knut is constantly irritated at having to take his sickly brother Sture along on his expeditions: Sture is a crybaby. But one afternoon when Knut returns alone after having caught his first pike, he finds that Sture is quiet and very still. His mother tells him that Sture has gone to the heavenly city because Jesus loved him so much. The child's introduction to death is a frequent motif in Moberg's novels, and here it is most effectively conveyed by adopting the child's own viewpoint:

Knut went with his father to the carpenter's and fetched a little box for Sture. It would be his resting place. It was like a casket. Knut wanted to help his father carry the box, but his father said that it was not heavy; Sture was so small, you see. He had been lying in the attic since he became so still. Knut wondered about many things and had a lot to ask his father about. How would they go about getting Sture up to the city of heaven? Would they winch him up in the box? Would no one go with him? Will you go to heaven with Sture, father? (111)

At the funeral Knut cannot understand why, if Sture is to go to heaven, he is lowered into a dark hole in the ground, into the darkness which he has been told is the habitation of the Devil. He weeps from fear of the unknown and disturbs the service. Johan and Hilda Toring consider Knut to be a difficult child, and he soon acquires an extra problem, a speech impediment. When it comes time to kill an old horse, curiosity compels the lad to watch and he is horrified to see the dying horse, half-skinned, rise to its feet. The shock leads him to stammer, which has fateful consequences for his childhood.

On Knut's first day at school the rough old soldier who is the village schoolmaster asks him to demonstrate his reading skills, but Knut is so afraid that he stammers and cannot get a word out. After this inauspicious start he settles down and at school encounters two children who are later to play an important part in his life, Lill-Alfreds Helgo and Bruns Ebba, the first girl he loves. Schoolmaster Mård is only concerned with the children's moral education and teaches them their catechism and biblical history but little else. His successor, fröken Hjärtkvist is very different. She upsets her charges on the very first day by burning the boys' snuffboxes and playing cards. But Knut comes to idolize her, for she lends him books. His parents cannot understand the lad's extraordinary desire for reading material: "They had been happy as long as the boy read the Bible and other books that benefited his soul and which he derived useful learning from. But then he began to want worldly and unwholesome reading. Everything that men themselves thought up and put into print was sinful, and if it was not sinful then it was certainly unnecessary" (190). Everywhere Knut turns the country people show the same unhelpful attitude to his requests for worldly books.

By the time that Knut climbs once more into the cherry tree his outlook has changed. From its branches he sees Ebba, for whom he is beginning to experience new feelings, and he is acutely aware now of his lack of personal freedom which in his mind is associated with his hunger for books: "His parents rule over him as if he were a slave. He has to work for his food and clothes and will grow up to be their farmhand. But why can't he do what he enjoys? To be free, to be one's own master! . . . To have something to read. He has nothing to read. No one lends him books any more. He starves and yearns and feels as if he will die sometimes" (229). Knut steals and lies and cheats in order to obtain books. They become a drug, a craving that he must satisfy. Now, as he sits atop the tree, he knows that there is no heavenly city, but beyond his narrow horizon there are many cities with houses filled with books. From here he can also see the railway which one day will take him away to a free life in the city.

The end of Knut's compulsory schooling proves to be just as traumatic for him as was its beginning, and for the same reason. An insignificant occurrence takes on a very much inflated importance. The children are on their way to school a few weeks before they are to finish their schooling for good, and some are worried about their final grades. It is common practice for the parents to try to soften the heart of the teacher by sending gifts in secret, and Knut discovers his friend Helgo concealing a pancake intended for the new schoolmistress, fröken Kamp. Without thinking, he lets slip a comment he comes to regret, asking Helgo: "Do you want pancake-grades?" (276). Soon his words are on every child's lips and come to the attention of the teacher. Samuel Brun, Ebba's father and a member of the school board, is summoned to confront Knut with his "crime," and the boy is ordered to beg the teacher's forgiveness. But Knut grows so tense that he cannot get the words out, and knows that if he tries he will only stammer. The lad's tortured silence is taken by his accusers to signify defiance, and the teacher gives him a bad conduct mark (the Swedish title of the novel means "Lowered Conduct Mark"). Knut leaves school with a final report on which is written: "Behavior— Unsatisfactory," an epitaph on his childhood.

In the third part of the novel, "The Youth," Knut makes a number of important discoveries about life. He borrows books from an old stonemason, among them one by Robert Ingersoll from which he gains a different view of the Christian religion:

He had been deceived throughout his childhood. Neither God nor the Devil existed, and Jesus had lived as a normal human being and been executed as a revolutionary. The Kingdom of Heaven did not exist either; the heavenly city had earlier begun to crumble for him, but now it collapsed entirely in ruins. . . . He saw a new heaven and a new earth. No God peered down at him from behind the cloud banks, observing whatever he did. No Devil lay down in the underworld laughing and revelling in blissful expectation when he sinned up here. And he could not sin, for sin did not exist. . . . Neither original sin nor sins of commission existed, and he had nothing to beg forgiveness for. Throughout his childhood he had had to beg for forgiveness for nothing. Throughout his childhood he had been afraid of God and the Devil. . . . Knut's childhood had been a cage, built with the iron bars of fear and prohibition. Now he broke out. (297–98)

Knut loses his faith, his terror of Hell, and his feelings of guilt, but he still feels uneasy with this new explanation of the Universe. He is left with a vacuum: God and the Devil provided an order and method in existence; if God did not exist, then how would the evildoer be punished and the virtuous man be rewarded? Yet despite this initial reaction Knut feels reborn into Lidalycke and begins to view the world in a new light.

He has now developed into a tall, strapping fellow, and he discovers a new self-confidence. He learns to dance, and soon falls in love with Ebba, but cannot think of marrying her. He has seen how unhappy his own parents have been, although they had married not for love but for the sake of a farm. Knut realizes that the farming people of Lidalycke cannot appreciate the beauty of the land; they can only see it in terms of money. Their real god is the homestead. They do not own the land; instead it is the god of the homestead that keeps them in slavery. Knut loves his village but hates to live among these narrow, land-hungry souls. He vows to break free and make a life for himself elsewhere. Knut's craving for books is satisfied for a while when he sends for a circulating library of a hundred volumes from Stockholm, and he sees Stockholm as his savior: he has asked for its support and this has been freely given, and now the city looms larger than ever in his thoughts as a heaven on earth where he will find freedom to develop.

Knut's final steps toward manhood are associated with work and with his first sexual experiences. He astonishes his father one day when at long last he is able to carry a full sack of rye up into the barn loft, the test of a grown man in the village. He has at last become his father's equal. On the following day his father sends him to mow the oats for Samuel Brun at Lyckemålen. In an unforgettable scene he works together with Ebba: he cuts the oats with his scythe and she gathers up the bundles for him. He feels his full strength being employed and finishes the whole of the field in a single day, a feat not accomplished by any mower before him. The shared task draws the couple together; at the edge of the field at dusk, surrounded by nature, they experience the joy of sex for the first time.

When Ebba's father can no longer look after his farm, Ebba has to find a husband for the sake of the farm. Her life will be different from Knut's, and she marries Helgo, Knut's school friend. Knut decides then that he must leave Lidalycke for the city. On the night before Ebba's marriage the lovers meet for the last time and Knut, wandering homeward, looks out across the village again and takes leave of his childhood: "And the young man felt a reverence for the village and in this a premonition of what was to come passed through his soul. A perception of the fact that he was divided—divided·between the strength of the soil and his own life that seemed to lie before him. And out of this his destiny would be shaped" (441).

In 1929 Vilhelm Moberg and his wife Margareta had moved from Alvesta to Stockholm, where Vilhelm embarked upon the unfettered but precarious existence of the professional writer. But after some years of this city living he began to have second thoughts about the wisdom of the move. In later life he described his situation in the early 1930s in this way:

At that time my transplanting into an urban environment had long since been completed and for every day that passed I became more deeply unhappy with the town. I had begun to yearn for the countryside of my childhood. A decade and a half had passed since I left it, and life in my home village seemed more beautiful with the passing of time. The mechanical and industrial urban culture, the concentration of people, the careerism, the pressures, the

rush—all of this made me ill at ease. I wanted to escape from all of it; I
considered returning to the life-style of the farmer. I felt torn between town
and country. Where did I belong? The problems which a writer struggles
with in his private life he attempts to solve in his works. A man's dualism
between town and country is the main theme in my trilogy about Knut
Toring.[7]

At this time Moberg did buy a small holding at Börsnäs in Sörmland to
work off the stresses of writing. *Memory of Youth* can, therefore, at
least in broad terms, be regarded as an autobiographical novel.
Knut's search for identity reflects Moberg's own search. The novel
also includes a number of other themes, episodes, and incidents that
derive directly from Moberg's life. In 1931 he had started a weekly
newspaper called *Veckans Bästa* which had folded after only a few
months, and this unsuccessful venture appears in the novel as Knut
Toring's paper *Blosset*.[8] As we have seen, Moberg had considerable
experience of the provincial press, and from 1925 to 1935 wrote a
weekly column for *Familjetidningen Smålänningen*.[9] The depiction
of Knut's schooldays and of his teachers also has parallels in Moberg's
own experiences. The old soldier turned schoolmaster, Mård, is
based on a similar figure, one Elias Stark, who features in *Raskens*
under his own name, but who never actually taught Moberg.[10] He
was in fact taught by only one schoolmistress, a fröken Maja Johans-
son, whereas Knut has two, the mild and friendly fröken Hjärtkvist
and the stern fröken Kamp. In the portrayal of fröken Hjärtkvist
Moberg intended to right a wrong he felt he had done his old teacher:
for a long time he was unable to forgive the bad conduct mark she had
given him. But she also lent him books and he could now repay her
kindness to him in this way.[11] "One predominant sensation from my
childhood is still clear in my memory," writes Moberg, "a never
satisfied hunger: a hunger for reading matter. It survives as the
memory of something that was always aching, always tormenting
me."[12] The mature writer attaches great importance to this particular
conflict with his youthful environment as the impetus to his final
breaking out from this world.[13]
    The important motifs in the novel, religious development, the
experience of death, puberty, and first sexual experiences, are
documented in *Tales from My Life* (1968) in terms very similar to
those used in *Memory of Youth*. But it must be remembered that
much of Moberg's early life took a rather different course from
Knut's. Moberg's family situation, for example, was quite different:

Knut's parents are better off than were Moberg's, and Knut is the eldest child whereas Moberg was the fourth of seven. Moberg's involvement in politics, membership of the Good Templar movement, and experiences of work in local industry do not figure in the novel, nor do his periods of study at Grimslöv and Katrineholm. Whereas Knut goes straight from home to Stockholm, Moberg worked as a journalist in Småland for a number of years and wrote local stories. All of these aspects of his life are dealt with in his second novel of development, *Soldier With a Broken Rifle* (1944), in which greater emphasis is placed upon the early manhood of his other alter ego, Valter Sträng.

The autobiographical novel of development was a flourishing form among the "Proletarian Writers" of the 1930s, although its progress can be traced from Strindberg's *Tjänstekvinnans son* (*The Son of a Servant*, 1886–1909) through Hjalmar Söderberg's *Martin Bircks ungdom* (*Martin Birck's Youth*, 1901) and Pär Lagerkvist's *Gäst hos verkligheten* (*Guest of Reality*, 1925). For the first time in his career Moberg now followed the main stream of Swedish writing among writers of very similar backgrounds and experiences. Other major works in this form are: Harry Martinson's *Nässlorna blomma* (*Flowering Nettle*) which came out in the same year as *Memory of Youth*, that is 1935, and its sequel, *Vägen ut* (*The Way Out*, 1936), which tell the story of Martin Tomasson; Eyvind Johnson's tetralogy *Romanen om Olof* (*The Novel about Olof*, 1934–1937); and Ivar Lo-Johansson's *Godnatt, jord!* (*Good Night, Earth!* 1933), the story of Mikael Bister. Each of these works is set in the first years of the century among the peasantry in the rural provinces, in Blekinge, Norrbotten, and Södermanland respectively, and in each the mature writer undertakes a kind of spiritual stocktaking, standing back from his childhood persona.

Common to all of these works is the central character's spiritual isolation as well as his dream of a freedom outside the narrow confines of his particular collective, a dream of the city for Mikael Bister or of the sea for Martin Tomasson. Unlike the earlier generation of proletarian writers in Sweden, these writers place the individual at the center of the narrative, although Johnson and Lo-Johansson do attempt to broaden the scope of the autobiographical form by giving nearly as much prominence to the class background as to the development of the central character. Moberg emphasizes Knut's dilemma and tones down the detailed cultural picture, whereas in *Soldier With a Broken Rifle* the social history and politics are given much greater prominence. Another feature of these works by 1930s writers is the way in which they tackle sexual matters in particular with a new honesty and frankness. While it was unusual for most of these writers to deal in their autobiographical novels with contemporary society, the story of Knut Toring takes as its starting point the present day, employing as a basis the tension between past and present, and in the following two parts of the trilogy, to which we now turn, the action is firmly located in the world of the late 1930s, revealed by Knut's continued search for his identity.

III   Stockholm, Lidalycke, and Europe

In *Sleepless Nights* and *The Earth is Ours!* there is a double shift of focus: first, from exposing the ills of urban civilization represented by Stockholm, Moberg turns to examine the problems of the agrarian community of Lidalycke, and second, he turns from the future of Lidalycke to the awful prospect for all European culture of another great war.

At the beginning of *Sleepless Nights* the story returns to the present and to Knut's situation in Stockholm. The recapitulation he has undertaken of his early life does not help him accept his present situation, and the narrative repeats in greater detail the reasons for his growing alienation from his surroundings. The civilized life of the city-dweller is ridiculed in a series of interiors: Knut and Aina Toring's visit to her brother's home demonstrates the materialism of the modern world and its paucity of spirit, and Knut's visit to a night club is used to stress the shallowness of urban pleasures. Knut questions the artificiality of modern life: Why have piped water and then indulge in physical exercise when you could take a healthy walk to the well? In this respect Moberg's views closely correspond to those of his contemporary Harry Martinson, who in *Verklighet till döds* (*Reality Unto Death*, 1940) attacks the dubious benefits of our materialist times, the radio used for propaganda and the airplane used to bomb civilians, and who also sees salvation in a return to the simplicity and authenticity of country living.

Knut feels that three contracts bind him to his life in Stockholm: his contract of employment, his marriage vows, and his duty to his two children; and gradually these bonds are loosened one by one. Aina makes it clear that she will not return with him to the countryside, and for a while Knut stays only for the sake of the children. The strain of his unhappy marriage and growing disillusion with his work lead to

insomnia, and he takes refuge from his worries in drink and brief
sexual encounters with other women. But it is the commercial pressures that he feels are lowering the standard of his newspaper that
finally cause him to throw up his life in Stockholm entirely and return
to his roots.

He goes back to Lidalycke, but cannot return to the village of his
childhood. The second part of the novel begins with a panoramic view
of life in the village which emphasizes the changes that have taken
place since Knut left some fifteen years before. A new motor road and
regular bus service now bring the place nearer to the outside world,
and there is even an airplane flight which passes overhead on its way
from Stockholm to Berlin. Knut's old schoolhouse in the forest has
been replaced by a fine new building in the village itself, but a
number of the desks are empty for the population has declined
drastically. Lidalycke is fast becoming a village of old people. The old
Lidalycke is dead and buried. Knut visits the graves of two people
who represented this world, fröken Kamp and Bruns Ebba, and then
wanders about as if searching for something. It is only when he comes
to Lyckemålen, to the deserted croft where he first made love to
Ebba, that he feels he has come home, and he rents the remote croft
with its thirty acres and tiny cottage. Knut's adaptation to a life of hard
physical work is not easy, and the attempt to farm at Lyckemålen fails,
but the year spent in isolation allows him time to think, to adjust.

The most interesting secondary character in *Sleepless Nights* is
Betty Eskilsson, a farmer's daughter who is the counterpart of Alfred
from Grönäng, the agricultural improver in *The Clenched Hands*.
Betty has progressive views on farming and puts them into practice
on her father's farm which she runs practically single-handed. She
represents change and the new order in Lidalycke, yet Knut sees her
independence as typifying generations of Värend womenfolk and in
her finds an ally. Betty wishes to encourage young people to stay on
the land, and believes that the village should provide more facilities
for the young. She herself has founded a lending library, which is of
course applauded by Knut, and she convinces him that it is his duty to
stay and make the village a fit place to live in. She argues that it was
his success in Stockholm that convinced many others that they too
should leave: "Stay here and make amends now! See to it that those
who are left do remain here!" (465). Betty and Knut maintain a
Platonic friendship, and Knut breaks his celibacy only for a few brief
affairs. At the end of a year Aina and he agree to a divorce, and the
novel ends with the arrival on a visit of his daughter Kajsa.

The action of *The Earth is Ours!* takes place during a few weeks of 1938, from July 29 to the fateful September 24, and the machinations of European power politics form the backdrop to the continued story of Knut Toring and Lidalycke. Throughout the international crises of that summer and autumn, Knut keeps in touch with the outside world via the radio, and he follows closely the way that Europe prepares for war. The story is interrupted at intervals by news summaries reporting important events that have taken place in Lidalycke and outside on the continent of Europe, for example:

On August 28 the British Government recalled its ambassador from Berlin. On August 30 it was reported that England and France had several times explained to Germany that the two countries were quite determined to take up arms should an attack be mounted against Czechoslovakia. On August 26 Helgo Alfredsson in Lidalycke bought for 19,500 crowns Oskar Nilsson's homestead in the northern village. . . . On August 28 the Village Youth Association met to approve plans for the construction of a parish center but the matter was postponed as a plot for the building still had not been obtained. (163–64)

Much of the novel is devoted to the future, to the young people who are the next generation in Lidalycke, but Knut's attitude to them proves ambivalent when put to the test. He does not discourage Helgo's son Harald when he intends to leave the village to become an airline pilot, as he believes that everyone should be given freedom of choice, and that only those who can find full employment for their talents should stay on the land. Nevertheless, Knut helps Betty in her efforts to establish a community center, and past and present come together when building begins at Blotekullen, on the same site where their ancestors sacrificed to the gods. A new character whose appearance enlivens this novel is Knut's daughter Kajsa. She is a city-bred child, and at first reacts against the coarseness of her new surroundings and wishes to return to her mother, who has now remarried. But under the guidance of Betty, Kajsa comes to terms with life on the farm and eventually decides to stay with her father. She is not the only representative of the continuation of the Toring line. Knut's brother Gösta and his wife, who have long been childless, await the birth of a child in September, 1938.

One thread that links all three Knut Toring novels is Knut's relationship with his parents. When he was young this was fraught with conflict and misunderstanding, and things are not always easy after his return to the village: they cannot understand either his decision to separate from Aina or the way in which he gives up a well-paid job. Hilda Toring has always been a tender mother and frequently worries about Knut and his problems. Now it is discovered that she is suffering from cancer and has only two months to live. Hilda takes the news with typical fatalism: "I'm old and finished. It's time I was gone from here" (151). Moberg employs the relationship between mother and son over these last weeks of Hilda's life in order to explore the antithesis of belief and disbelief: "Knut believed in Man and his earthly kingdom. His mother believed in God and His heavenly kingdom. He had no belief about anything after this life; as far as his brain could grasp it, this 'afterward' was . . . a nothingness, an unconsciousness. . . . But his mother was done with this earthly life and was secure in her expectation of eternal life. And it was good for her that she could die calm and in full confidence in her beliefs. In this way she would be relieved of the distress of dying" (196–97). Hilda Toring's last weeks are nevertheless filled with suffering. She has led a blameless Christian life yet she has to endure this senseless pain, which reinforces Knut in his disbelief: "She should be spared now, and yet the good Lord continues to torture her, which by human reason must prove that the Christians' good Lord cannot exist" (250).

As he sits in lonely vigil at his mother's bedside, Knut works on his book, *The Kingdom of the Earth Is Ours*, and in a chapter entitled "A Dream to Die For" he attempts to express his own reactions to what is happening in the world and especially to the threat to Sweden. Soon he may be called upon to defend Sweden with his life: "One does not sacrifice the higher for the lower. What I die for in battle must be something of higher value than my own life—something I cannot do without should I wish to lead an existence worthy of a human being. Something which is great enough to die for, and to kill for" (288–89). That "something" is the peaceful Swedish society based on the rule of law, and Knut is determined now to resist the forces of evil and violence: "No one can be a pacifist in the sense that he considers the violence used to apprehend a gang of criminals as something insupportable and repudiates it" (294). Sweden is a country that has lived in peace with its neighbors for one hundred and twenty-four years, and the individual has a measure of freedom in which to develop, to hold his own beliefs: "If now the inhabitants of a foreign land make an armed invasion of our country, they become for me criminal elements. . . . And I have a right of self-defense. . . . Here I must resist evil, I am given no choice" (299). Knut decides which principles he is willing to defend: "It is the right to dispose over myself, over mind

and body. It is the right of my children to a free life in the land where
they were born. . . . It is the free spiritual life on our earth, it is belief
in the sovereignty and inviolability of the spirit—it is everything that
I summarize in the beautiful dream of the earthly kingdom that will
one day be Man's" (301).

Past, present, and future are drawn together at the end of the
trilogy: On September 24, 1938, the British prime minister and the
German chancellor meet at Godesberg to discuss Czechoslovakia. In
Lidalycke, Hilda Toring dies and her daughter-in-law bears a baby
son while Knut Toring lays the foundations of a parish center at
Blotekullen, the ancient sacrificial mound.

Novels which treat of specific social problems tend to date as
quickly as these problems are overcome, and novels used as vehicles
for strongly held views easily turn into tracts. This is particularly true
of the second and third volumes of the Knut Toring trilogy in which
the documents, Betty's plans for a model rural community, and
Knut's patriotic declaration especially, are only loosely linked to the
narrative. Also, the original didactic aim of *The Earth is Ours!* had to
be modified as international politics loomed larger in the author's
thoughts, and he seems here, unlike the later novel about Valter
Sträng, unable to blend in the political events and social background
with the intimate personal story.

Perhaps the most serious criticisms have been made of *Sleepless
Nights*, undoubtedly one of Moberg's weakest novels.[14] The first part
of the novel merely repeats and develops the reasons for Knut's
alienation, but the one-sided and simplistic view of life in the capital
is also to blame as is the mistake of repeating the incomparable love
story of Knut and Ebba in the shabby interlude with Jenny.

In concentrating upon his message, Moberg has sadly neglected
artistry and composition, but the work does reveal a great deal about
its author, not only his childhood difficulties but also the feeling of
rootlessness and alienation which were to follow him throughout his
life. He later wrote of the trilogy: "But these three books do not
provide a final answer to the question: Where did the man really
belong? Neither in life nor in art could the problem be solved. The
explanation is that the writer was in reality not torn between town and
country, not between environments and cultures, which is why a
return to an earlier way of life was not possible for him. The duality
was a spiritual condition; it was to be found within himself."[15]

The works also reveal the difficult choices posed by the threat of
war. From his youth Moberg had been a pacifist and antimilitarist,

yet now he advocates armed resistance, and declares himself willing to die in order to defend certain inalienable rights. "A Dream to Die For" is the first indication in Moberg's fiction of his conviction that Sweden must react promptly to the threat implied to its sovereignty by Nazi Germany. Throughout the 1930s Moberg was deeply involved in the antitotalitarian cause, and this involvement was to take up much of his time in the early years of the war. In this he was not alone, for many of his fellow writers spoke and wrote in defense of democratic values in terms that closely parallel his.[16] In Eyvind Johnson's novel *Nattövning* (*Night Manoeuvres*, 1938), for example, the two friends Tomas Gyllem and Mårten Torpare each decide to resist tyranny in his own way: Tomas goes off to Spain to fight fascism by military means, while Mårten, who intends to use literary means, "has the mounting, bitter conviction that force might have to be met with force, that life is so fantastic that grenades must tear apart human bodies in order for mankind to achieve the possibility of happiness."[17] Like Knut, Mårten is prepared to sacrifice his life to preserve the values of a society which he passionately believes in. In *Reality unto Death*, Harry Martinson also analyzes what it is that is worth defending in Sweden: not the Sweden of the new materialism, the "crayfish-eating classes" as he calls them, but the poor unspoiled rural Sweden of folktale, atmosphere, and unreality. As war came to Scandinavia from both east and south, all three writers, and many more, were quick to mobilize in their various ways in defense of what they saw as their culture's inherent values.

CHAPTER 4

Song of the Earth

I Man's Woman

AFTER his excursion into small-town life in *A. P. Rosell, Bank Director*, in his next novel, *Man's Woman* (1933), Moberg returns to the countryside of Värend and to a historical setting, the 1790s. The action is set in the small, remote village of Hägerbäck, which comprises twelve crofts huddled together for protection against the thieves and wild beasts that lurk in the surrounding forest wilderness. A number of the farmers of Hägerbäck play important parts in the story but it is a young farmer's wife, Märit, who is its central character. A year before the story begins she has come from neighboring Ljuder to marry Påvel Gertsson, a capable and hard-working farmer whom she respects but does not love. When Håkan Ingelsson, the couple's nearest neighbor, becomes infatuated with Märit, she is at first terrified by the force of his passion and by thoughts of the moral and social consequences of answering his love. Eventually she does respond and finds a joy she only dreamed of in her relationship with her husband. Märit and Håkan meet and make love in secret places, usually in the fields and copses, but as spring turns to summer and then autumn, so their initial untroubled joy, a total abandonment to the senses, gives way to darker forebodings about the future. Märit cannot continue to belong to both men, and Håkan refuses to share her. The deceit involved troubles him, for Påvel is his good and generous neighbor during some hard times. Märit becomes pregnant and decides to bring about a miscarriage as she cannot be sure which of the men is the father of her child. The climax of the story sees the lovers betrayed by Håkan's jealous maid, and surprised together by an angry Påvel. Håkan is a failure as a farmer, and he has already decided to leave Hägerbäck to pursue a life of freedom in the forest. Now he makes ready to go, and Märit decides to leave Påvel and go with him.

70

This is a straightforward tale of passion, depicting the irresistible attraction the two hold for each other, and it is largely freed from the wider social concerns that characterize Moberg's other novels from the 1930s. In fact, this work marks a deliberate departure from these and an attempt at thematic renewal. The cultural detail is consequently pared down to bare essentials, a process begun in *The Clenched Hands*, thus allowing concentration upon Märit's moral dilemma.

In *Man's Woman* the erotic motif is more strongly underlined than in the Adolf novels, and is conveyed with considerable lyricism. Märit is a beautiful young girl who feels unfulfilled in the sexual and emotional relationship with her husband. As a maid she dreamed of the miracle that would occur on her wedding night, but:

What she experienced did not fulfill her expectations. She became Påvel's bride and they did what man and wife do at night. But afterward she felt disappointed. This could not be considered a miracle. Her longing reached out for something quite different. She wanted to be snatched away from what tied and pained her—she wanted to go off on a giddy flight with all her senses numbed. But she could not let go completely. Påvel took her, but he did not lift her. She only traveled a very short way and then sank down again. (19)

Märit's first year of marriage is seen both realistically and symbolically in terms of her work preparing the flax, whose field of blue flowers greets her as a blossoming promise when she first comes to Hägerbäck as Påvel's bride. After four months of marriage she begins to spin the yarn and after six months she is ready to weave. And all the time she wonders about her life with Påvel, for they will rest on these linen sheets for thousands of nights to come. Eventually Märit ceases to believe in miracles until one night when she is disturbed by a noise outside the cottage. She believes that a thief is stealing her sheets, which are spread out to bleach, but discovers her neighbor Håkan caressing the material: "And before she realized it, she lay laughing; silent deep joyful laughter was released inside her" (48).

Håkan comes to Märit when she is milking in the copse and kisses her, but she is afraid and implores him to spare her. She tries to resist temptation but when her husband is away from the village Håkan comes to the cottage at dusk. She spreads her new sheets on the bed, the sheets that are linked to her dreams, and now she finds sexual bliss: "From her flax field, which blossomed out there with a blue glow last summer, she had finally made her bridal bed. Now she was a man's woman" (99). The flax field and the sheets also occupy Håkan's thoughts, and in a dream he takes her away from Påvel by force: "And Märit follows him willingly, glad to be free. She tears the sheets from the bed and takes them with her, for they are her bridal sheets. They are as green as grass and as blue as flax flowers; when she comes out of the house she spreads them on the ground. Here is a great bed for them" (146–47). The poetic nature of the love scenes is heightened by the way in which the world of nature is integrated into the depiction. In perhaps the finest scene, their lovemaking takes place beneath a cloudless sky, exactly as in Håkan's dream, and they become an indivisible part of nature:

Now in June the evenings were quite warm, and Håkan and she hid in among the dense bushes and embraced. There, on the ground, they felt the intoxication of their blood. The new leaves concealed them beneath their foliage; they could smell the fragrant grass beneath them. A scent of earth and sweet birch. And in the dusk birds began to sing one after the other in the bushes. They rested there after the union of their bodies, stretched out on the ground. They were close to the earth, in a world of procreation which was untroubled by thoughts of life and death. A natural freedom from care prevailed. Birth and extinction belonged together and caused no anguish. Above them glistened the fresh leaves of spring, beneath them decayed the fallen leaves of the previous year. One depended on the other. And they themselves were two newly opened leaves suspended from their twig, from the firmament of life, while the summer passed. And they were small and trembling in the eternal wind—in the wind that would one day tear them from their firmament. (152–53)

The ecstasy that obliterates all worries is, however, only short-lived, for the couple both realize that their relationship cannot continue in the same way for long. Initially, Märit's scruples are of a religious and moral nature: she regards Håkan's desire and her own weakness as the work of the Devil which will make her into an adulteress, and she seeks strength to resist by going to church. Yet even when warning Håkan that he is leading them both to perdition, she is irresistibly drawn to him.

The moral dilemma is intensified after they have made love, for Håkan refuses to share Märit, and she is forced to make excuses to her husband. This only succeeds for a short while, however, and Märit soon becomes two men's woman. She is horrified by the ease with which she can lie to Påvel, but deceit is more difficult for Håkan who wishes to take her openly from her husband. Märit is Håkan's but remains with Påvel. The situation is complicated by Håkan's innate honesty and his feeling of indebtedness to his generous neighbor.

Håkan and Påvel are contrasted in a number of ways. Påvel comes from a long line of respectable farmers, is successful and content with his life in the community. He boasts of his possessions, his good farm, and his beautiful wife. Påvel is steady and calm while Håkan is fiery and hot-blooded, a vagabond and rebel at heart whose forebears include Stark-Ingel, a defiant heathen who took the woman of his choice from her parents and ran off to live with her in the forest, beyond the law. Defiant to the last, Ingel died by sinking into a bog within calling distance of help. He was free, and in comparison Håkan considers himself a thrall, enslaved by the rent he pays to a rich merchant in Kalmar and the tax he pays to the sheriff. For Håkan the forest represents freedom from all of these constraints of society, and it tempts him even before his love for Märit brings matters to a head. The antithesis of village and forest is underlined, the one representing security but pressure to conform, the other freedom but isolation and danger.

Märit's character may be seen as an amalgam of those of the two men in her life. Like Påvel she comes from a more populous, less forested area, and this has determined her personality: when Håkan presses her to follow him into the wilderness and leave her good home and possessions, she first thinks of the practical difficulties: "She hasn't the strength to free herself from everything she owns as Påvel's wife. She cannot be without the security. She is not able to tear herself away like a blade of grass out of the ground and leave the life she has been used to since childhood" (214). It is only after the final dramatic confrontation between husband and lover, when Håkan declares that he will leave the village never to return, that Märit seriously begins to consider what kind of relationship she has with her husband: "She is like one of his animals" (245). She also realizes just how much Håkan means to her: "To her he is dizziness and anguish, joy and agony, restlessness and quiet calm, he is everything that feels good and everything that feels painful" (247). She cannot live without him, and she at last discovers that she possesses free will. The trappings of her life in Hägerbäck fall away and, without waking her husband, she steals out into the night to join Håkan.

The enslavement of an individual to the farm and the continuation of the family line, with a consequent sacrifice of personal happiness, is a theme found in most of the early novels, but here the idea of personal freedom encompasses more: primarily the concept of sexual freedom and sexual equality. Both men wish to own Märit, but ultimately it is she who chooses between them, realizing that she has a greater opportunity of asserting her true self with Håkan. The freedom of the individual from the constraints of society becomes a major concern of Moberg for the first time here, and is developed in various ways in most of the works to follow. The traditional place of sanctuary in earlier times was the forest, and in *Ride This Night!* the main character also becomes a "skoggångare" ("forest-goer," "out-law"), a common practice in Sweden which Moberg has described elsewhere.[1] The desire for freedom frequently involves Moberg's characters in a flight from civilization into the wilderness, or merely an attempted flight as in *A. P. Rosell, Bank Director,* where the urbane Rosell must return from his self-imposed exile because he misses his home comforts.[2]

In order to develop the freedom theme in *Man's Woman,* Moberg employs the character of old Herman, one of the parish paupers who spend the summer at different farms in the district. Herman's arrival in the village at the beginning of spring marks the opening of the novel, and he serves as a guide, moving between the farms and providing a perspective on the action from within. In Herman, Moberg has combined the two roles of observer and philosophical commentator: initially he is merely a pair of watchful eyes, noting Märit's growing love for Håkan. But soon he comes to represent the author's view of the action. Moberg provides him with a past that directly reflects upon this latter role: Herman once owned a farm, but gambled it away and contemplated killing himself. As a result of this cathartic experience, he now feels free of the trappings of this earthly existence; he has broken the fetters of materialism that he sees binding others around him.

In Herman's commentary is found the familiar *carpe diem* motif: "Life, like intoxication, has the great drawback that it soon ends. Life has no other fault. Now all that remains for man is to enjoy himself as long as it lasts" (31). But Herman also realizes the problems and dangers faced by the lovers in following their desires rather than their reason: "If life has its way with them the consequences may be hard to bear. Strength and courage are needed, then their core will be revealed in them—if there is a core" (67). Herman is especially suited to understand Märit's dilemma, the sacrifices she must make in order to find peace of mind: "Now they are bound by the things around them, and they let themselves be owned by houses and fields and animals. When will they become free? When will men possess the earth with all the glory to be found in it?" (203).

A frequent feature of Moberg's narrative method is the use of an inserted narrative. In *Man's Woman* the story of Stark-Ingel, the forest dweller, prefigures at an early stage the climax of the story, while a more substantial story is that of Frans-Gottfrid, the farmer who as a young man shot and wounded a thief, and has since gone in fear of retribution from one-armed strangers. The two parts of this story—the exposition and the resolution in which Frans-Gottfrid falls dead from sheer terror—form *entr'actes* which appear to be digressions from the intensive relationship that forms the main plot. They retard the climax in order to heighten the suspense. But this story also demonstrates some of the same themes as the main story. Frans-Gottfrid is fettered by his own possessions, and, unlike Märit, is unable to confront his own fears and conquer them.

The historical detail of the novel is subtle and unobtrusive, for the erotic theme is a timeless one. Of the period setting Moberg wrote: "I placed *Man's Woman* in a historical setting in the 1790s in order to achieve an intensification and a deeply serious dramatic conflict: adultery could in certain cases mean the death penalty for a woman at that time. And Märit's fear of hell is a vital constituent of the piece. . . . It would not be conceivable in our day. . . . If a married woman in present-day Sweden hesitates before going to bed with the man she loves outside marriage, it is not out of fear of eternal damnation!"[3]

As in *Raskens*, Moberg employs a number of dialectisms and archaisms as coloring in both dialogue and narrative, although the language is generally remarkably modern. Unlike in later works, it is not used here to suggest a specific historical period. Apart from the lyricism, it is the unity and concentration of *Mans kvinna* that is so striking. Moberg has in part explained the unity of tone by the fact that he wrote the novel in only five weeks when he himself was isolated from the world in a fishing hut in the Stockholm archipelago. Certainly the work is provided with a firm dramatic structure; the action is concentrated entirely on the small village and on a very few characters. The action follows the changing seasons from spring to autumn of one year, and the change in the seasons both shapes incidents and reflects the changing emotions of the main characters, forming an integral part of the narrative. Spring is a time of rebirth and hope, and it stirs Märit's desires and feelings of disquiet. The

cows are freed from their winter captivity, and Märit milks them in
the aspen grove by the stream, which is where the lovers meet. In
May, Påvel is away, and Märit waits for Håkan to come to her at
home, but because of the light nights she waits, like Juliet for Romeo,
with growing impatience: "Where is God's dusk tonight?" (94). The
lovers become part of the cycle of nature: at midsummer their relationship is at its most natural and instinctive, but as autumn begins
to draw in, so their worries about the future grow; at harvest time the
benefits of a settled life are brought home forcefully to Märit, while
the darkness of autumn is a marked feature of the last part of the
novel.

A number of the 1930s generation of Swedish writers were, at least
for a time, influenced by the writings of Freud and by such literary
works as D. H. Lawrence's *Lady Chatterley's Lover* (1928) and
Sherwood Anderson's *Dark Laughter* (1925), and the style they
developed at the end of the 1920s and beginning of the 1930s has been
called "primitivist" or "vitalist." Artur Lundkvist (b.1906), the
theoretician of the Swedish primitivists, defines the term in this way:
"Primitivism comprises nothing more than a spontaneous—but also
ideologically fully motivated—revolt against a civilization which
threatens to lead to sterility through a restriction of the instincts, and
a striving by means of a new and more adaptable culture to make
contact with the strong, primitive instincts and the basically human
qualities."[4] Although in the works of the poets Artur Lundkvist and
Harry Martinson this worship of life is more universal, encompassing
more than its merely primitive aspects, and consitutes almost a
literary programme, in the works of many other writers, including
Moberg, primitivism was influential only in a more restricted sense.
It can be seen in the greater stress placed upon the instinctive and
natural aspects of human existence. The prevalent symbolism found
is that of running water, of seed and ripe cornfields, and lovemaking
in the open air. In *Memory of Youth* the rye forms a leitmotiv,
culminating in the union of Knut and Ebba at the edge of the newly
mowed field, and a similar use of the seed motif is found in *Raskens*
and *Far from the Highway*. The lyrical eroticism of *Man's Woman* is
also found in the earlier works and is most marked in *The Brides'
Spring*. Artur Lundkvist stresses that the sexual-romantic movement
must have contributed to the composition of *Man's Woman*, and that
"The accentuation of eroticism as a life-enhancing force has acted to
liberate him [Moberg] artistically, has renewed his stylistic re-

sources, strengthened the rhythmical suggestion, and heightened the realism to often brilliant symbolism."[5]

Thus for a few years in the 1930s Moberg found that some of his basic themes and motifs coincided with those of the group of writers most deeply affected by primitivism, and produced what one critic has called "Without doubt the best work artistically that sexual romanticism produced in Sweden."[6] However, these points of contact form only a starting point for Moberg's depiction of a moral dilemma, and the continuing discussion of the conflict between individual freedom and happiness and the constraints imposed on the individual by society, a conflict that in this novel remains unresolved. For Håkan and Märit escape is not the end, but only the beginning of their problems.

II *Love and Death*

In *Man's Woman* setting is of great significance both for establishing mood and for emphasizing the theme of the novel. The same is true of *The Brides' Spring* (1946), in which setting is as important as character. The novel consists of four stories from four different periods in history, told by four musicians. They are connected by the setting: the action of each story takes place at midsummer on Ekekullen, a meadow overshadowed by a grove of oak trees, beside a spring. Love and death are closely linked in the book. Midsummer is traditionally a fertility festival, a time of lovemaking, but for the four musicians it is also the day of their death. The spring of the title is both the origin of all things and their end, a mother who gives birth to men and then gathers her children to her again.

The first of the stories is set in the twentieth century and is narrated by Anders Eriksson, an old man who has played his fiddle at the midsummer dance at Ekekullen for forty years. Now at his last Midsummer Eve, he thinks back over his life and in particular of the midsummer when he first lay with Ellen, taking her maidenhood. Their love involved a kind of death, for he associated the drops of her blood in the clover with a biblical sacrifice: "Now I thought of sacrificial blood. The sacrifice was made to me" (32). Afterward, Ellen has performed a cleansing rite in the spring. Anders reviews his wasted life. His trouble has been his hot temper: in his youth he killed a man, spent three years in prison, and has suffered public disapproval ever since. Anders knows that the midsummer dance is taking place in a cemetery, that the couples dance over the graves of victims of an eighteenth-century plague, and increasingly his thoughts turn to his predecessors in the musician's seat in the oak tree, and to his own death. A new musician, a young accordion player, waits to replace him in the seat of honor. In a last feeble attempt to assert his vitality, Anders molests a young girl (Ellen's daughter) and is dragged from his place and beaten by the young men. He crawls to the spring to wash away the blood: "Spring, take now my blood in your waters and flow away with it so that I may be pure again!" (67). But the blood continues to flow, and his life ebbs away from him.

The second musician is a young man, Anders Eriks Son, who sits among the freshly dug graves of his family at midsummer in the plague year of 1711. He is the last person still alive in the village, but is himself smitten with the plague and has dug his own grave. He thinks back over the course of the tragedy he has lived through: the first dreadful portents, the coming of a beggar with the disease, and the inexorable progress of the plague, which carries off the entire household except for his son Erik who he sends away to a safe place. But he has other, happier, memories—of Kerstin, the "midsummer bride" whose maidenhood he took by the spring, and who washed there afterward because she had heard of an old legend that the spring could restore virginity: "It was a blessed spring that welled up in the meadow, a healing spring. It received all the evil we brought to it with us, it took it in its course and carried it away. . . . And it helped the girls and wiped away the traces of their weddings on Midsummer Eve. They washed in its running water and it made them chaste and honest again: the spring gave them back their maidenhood" (110).

The third musician is Anders Pipare, and the time of his story is the 1540s. Anders has a great appetite for life, but also a keen sense of sin and fear of hell fire. He has a weakness for drinking, gambling, and whoring, and afterward suffers bitter pangs of remorse—but not for long. Anders steals from the spring the treasures that grateful maidens have cast into it. As a Christian Anders disapproves of heathen practices, and believes God will reward him for taking the gifts from the pagan spring and giving the money to his church. But on his way to see the priest he is sidetracked at the inn, drinks, gambles, and finally, on Midsummer Eve, seduces the girl he fancies with the gift of a silver necklace from the spring. When the sun rises, the girl is horrified to discover where Anders had obtained the necklace. The treasure is cursed, and she dare not keep the necklace, and thus has no further interest in Anders. Anders, full of repentance for his sins and distressed to find that his sweetheart was interested only in the necklace and not in him, resolves to go at once to the priest. He gets drunk on the way and, in his befuddled state, tumbles into the spring, which thus claims back its own.

The fourth musician, Bockhorn, tells his story in prehistoric times. Failure of the crops and infertility among the tribe call for the appeasement of the god of fertility with the sacrifice of a young maiden. Bockhorn is in love with the girl Toa, who is chosen as the sacrificial victim: at midsummer she is drowned in the spring, and then hung in an oak tree to propitiate the god. Bockhorn rebels against the deity that has taken his beloved, but he dies beneath the knives of his fellow tribesmen when he tries to attack the giant phallic image.

The theme of the novel is the interdependence between procreation and death. Life must be sacrificed in order that new life can be created. This is strictly true in the case of Toa, who is drowned to increase fertility. In other stories the girls' sacrifice necessary for procreation is of a less drastic nature. The structure of the novel is intriguing. Since the stories are told in reverse chronological order, half-remembered tales and obscure symbols gradually become explained as the reader moves backward in time. Anders Eriksson in the twentieth century is unaware of the significance of his bride's washing in the spring; Anders Eriks Son in the eighteenth century knows that it is supposed to restore a girl's virginity; the origin of the belief is only revealed in the final story of Bockhorn and Toa. However, the strength of the novel lies not so much in the linking of the somewhat disparate elements of the four stories as in the rhetorical and rhythmical style, which frequently lifts the narrative to the level of a prose poem.

CHAPTER 5

The Novelist at War

I Värend 1650

RIDE THIS NIGHT! is Moberg's second historical novel and possesses a number of features in common with the earlier *Man's Woman*. Both are set in small villages in Värend, and despite the difference of one hundred and fifty years in time, in both the social scene is much the same. *Man's Woman* examines the problem of lack of freedom within the community, and only ends with the idea of "forest going," a life beyond the law, whereas *Ride This Night!* develops this idea and pictures the life of a man forced to take to the forest. Both Håkan and Ragnar Svedje have forebears who lived in the wilderness and who serve as models for their own actions, proud and fearless individualists who refuse to be limited by the petty restrictions imposed by society. But the freedom motif in *Ride This Night!* is writ large as freedom from oppression, and is relevant not merely to the Värend of 1650 but also to the situation in which Sweden found itself at the time Moberg wrote the novel, and indeed to the relations between individuals and states in all ages.

The novel contains an allegory of Sweden's predicament in the early years of World War II, and was written in the dark days of 1941. Many critics have, however, tended to overemphasize and oversimplify this aspect of the work. Also, when Moberg first published the book, he became embroiled in an extended debate with academic historians over the accuracy of his account of social and judicial conditions in the seventeenth century, a debate reviewed briefly in chapter 8 below. But *Ride This Night!* is a work of narrative art which possesses intrinsic merits and weaknesses on the basis of which its reputation ultimately will rest, and it is as such that we will approach it.

The action develops along fairly simple lines, and is set in the village of Brändebol during the reign of Queen Christina. In order to replenish an exchequer depleted by the Thirty Years' War (1618–1648) and to reward those who fought on Sweden's side, Christina allowed the nobility, including foreign noblemen, to purchase the tax rights of farmers who formerly paid tax to the crown. Brändebol thus finds itself paying tax to Lieutenant-Colonel Bartold Klewen of Ubbetorp, a German nobleman.

After two disastrous harvests the men of Brändebol are unable to pay their *in natura* dues and receive a summons to present themselves for work on the lord's estate. The men come together at the village meeting to consider their response, and are predictably angry: "No lord can buy us from the crown like so many beasts. We are not running like dogs when a master calls!" (20). One villager, Mats Elling, wonders what they would do if Klewen used force against them, and suggests that they go some way toward meeting his demands—perhaps every third man should go to Ubbetorp? But the young Ragnar Svedje leaps to his feet at this and reminds the meeting:

Justice is on our side! If we should submit and go to the manor then we are accepting an injustice! . . . Klewen is appropriating one homestead after another under his domain. That lord is therefore our enemy. . . . The more we give way the more he will demand. If we provide four men's work tomorrow we will have to give eight the day after. But we are not bound to provide any. We have a legal right to our farms. . . . The crown cannot sell us like crofters. According to the law we are in the right. (23)

Svedje's impassioned speech strengthens the men's resolve and they swear as one man to defend each other against anyone who by any means may try to force them to work on the lord's estate.

Svedje is convinced that Klewen intends to turn them all into serfs: "It was known that he had come from Germany. This German nobleman moved here bringing his customs from his native land. In the southern and eastern lands they had heard that the people were kept like thralls" (28–29). But the village's unity is soon tested. Early one morning Klewen's sheriff, Lars Borre, arrives with armed men and calls first at the cottage of the village alderman, Jon Stånge. By describing the horrific violence meted out to recalcitrant peasants on other estates, Borre induces Stånge to accompany him to each cottage in turn to persuade the men to go peaceably to work at the manor. Unprepared, the men are unable to resist and are shepherded away—all, that is, except Svedje, who has been away and returns to find the village deserted. Borre and his men return for Svedje but meet violent resistance, and Svedje is able to make his escape to the freedom of the forest. The narrative then develops along two parallel lines, tracing both Svedje's free but hunted existence in the woods and the life of the remaining villagers under the new regime.

Svedje is convinced that justice will prevail, and his mother tries unsuccessfully to pursue his case through a local priest attending the meeting of the Estates at Queen Christina's coronation. But Christina plays off the nobility against the other estates and will not accede to demands for a recall of peasant lands granted to the nobles, and the priest finds the time inopportune to plead the case of a dispossessed peasant. After much hardship Svedje falls in with Ygge, a notorious thief, and lives with him in his secret hideout in the middle of a large marsh.

The men of the village are now obliged to spend much of their time laboring for the lord of the manor and are deprived not only of their physical freedom but also of their freedom of speech. Mats Elling betrays his fellow villagers and willingly aids Lars Borre, and in reward for his help Borre persuades alderman Stånge to betrothe his daughter Botilla, actually Svedje's betrothed, to Mats. Thus Svedje loses not only his farm but also his wife-to-be, and Stånge comes to regard him increasingly as a threat to the status quo. Another threat is the "budkavle," or fiery cross, the age-old token sent round to the men of Värend with its message to rebel against the tyranny of their masters and to rise up in bloody revolt. When the token reaches him, Stånge swears an oath that he will pass it on in his turn, but actually buries it secretly. However, under the leadership of Klas Bock some of the men of Brändebol meet in secret to plan for the restoration of their rights and freedoms. Bock regales them in these words: "In all other countries the common people are held in thraldom. Only in our land do we still seek to defend ourselves against the foreign yoke; only our land remains. Now the nobles want to enslave us too. Shall we now submit meekly to the will of these nobles as we have been counseled to do by our own village alderman?" (253).

The men ostracize Stånge, and one morning Mats Elling is found on his own dunghill with both legs broken. Klewen then induces the local assize to sentence his wayward serf, Ragnar Svedje, to outlawry and death for injury to his servant and for theft (of Svedje's own property, confiscated by Klewen). A posse led by the public hangman, Hans i Lenhovda, finally traps Svedje, who is buried alive in the same way as the message of freedom. Yet even as his life is ending

Svedje remains convinced that one day justice will prevail and the rule of law inevitably return to his land. A new "budkavle" is now sent out from Bråndebol "through nights and days, through years and centuries, on its vital errand carrying from age to age the urgent message, the most important of all: the 'budkavle' goes! Ride this night, this night!" (358).

In *Ride This Night!* characterization is very much subordinated to the message, and several of the main characters are essentially only the physical embodiments of abstract principles: Svedje, for example, personifies the spirit of resistance to the oppression embodied by Klewen. The danger in this use of a representative character as a major tragic figure has been outlined by E. M. Forster: "A serious or tragic flat character is apt to be a bore. Each time he enters crying 'Revenge!' or 'My heart bleeds for humanity!' or whatever his formula is, our hearts sink."[1] Svedje is a "flat" character in Forster's sense: he does not develop and never surprises. He is frequently absent from the action, and achieves nothing by his defiance except to provide a symbol to the others in his village: "The man in the forest is here invisibly with them. He eggs them on and gives them confidence and faith: if we were even fewer, right would still be on our side! The man in the forest is the one who followed the course of the sun and showed them: justice will remain justice!" (252). Other protagonists also express only a single idea: Botilla is the innocent maiden, Lars Borre the brutal henchman, Mats Elling the collaborator, Klas Bock the unbending patriot. The function of these figures is to dramatize the message; they are puppets in the hands of the narrator and scarcely aspire to any independent life.

There are, however, several characters in the novel who do attain a credible individuality. Jon Stånge is in some ways the most important figure in the book, the village alderman whose cowardice allows Klewen to dominate Bråndebol. Stånge is split between his desire for peace at any price and his loyalty to the other villagers, and he has a bad conscience which is pricked by Svedje's continuing defiance. Two of the minor characters are among the most colorful: Hans and Ygge. Hans once accidentally killed a man, and was saved from execution to become the public executioner. As a mark of his dishonor he lost his ears and wears a skin cap to hide his disfigurement. Ygge is a Robin Hood figure who shares his spoils with the poor. Hans detests Ygge because so many love him while he himself is despised and feared. Hans also hates Svedje, a man who unlike him has maintained his honor intact, and the executioner eventually takes a terrible revenge by killing both men. Hans is a terrifying figure, regarded with superstitious awe by the villagers, and yet Moberg reveals understanding for him and even compassion. The comparison readily presents itself with Pär Lagerkvist's novella *Bödeln* (*The Hangman*, 1933) in which the central character, a symbol of timeless evil, is also a victim and a scapegoat.

In establishing the historical atmosphere Moberg has learned his lesson from his earlier works, and he strives to integrate the carefully researched and documented historical detail into the overall pattern of the narrative. The novel is rich in omen and portent: in the first pages the raven sits on the weathervane at the Svedje farm boding ill, and the peasants believe in the supernatural power of other birds: the hoopoe brings news between the lovers while the black woodpecker foretells disaster for them. Early in the tale Svedje and Botilla dally unwittingly beneath the gallows oak, and Botilla saves a nail from the hanging tree which she uses to summon up her lover in the forest. Svedje is tempted by the Forest Woman, a beautiful spirit without a face, and a similar specter disturbs Stånge's repose, while the only important subplot concerns the charge of witchcraft—here inter-course with the Devil—leveled at Botilla by a rival for Svedje's affections. Tragedy ensues for Botilla, who drowns during a self-imposed ordeal by water.

Ride This Night! is a novel about the great forest wildernesses of Värend whose enveloping darkness pervades the story and helps evoke the oppressive mood of impending doom. Moberg depicts nature in meticulous detail—wild flowers, berries, trees, and wildlife are found in profusion—but he also explores the more practical concerns of a man forced to rely on the meager resources of nature and equipped only with the essentials of black powder, shot, and salt. This motif, the struggle for survival in a hostile environment, recurs in the emigrant novels in a greatly extended sequence, and demon-strates Moberg's fascination with the tangible, with basic skills no longer possessed by civilized man. Research into conditions in the Värend of the past takes on a new importance in this novel. For example, the idea of Ygge's den, concealed beneath a great fallen oak, is taken from the lair of one Åke from Dufwemåla mentioned in court records from 1620,[2] and a telling detail is the description of how the peasants had to resort to "bark bread" in times when the rye harvest failed (236), a feature to which Moberg later devotes a whole chapter of his history.[3] Customs long since extinct such as those associated with the love story—the betrothed couple lying side by side "in all honor and trust," and the present of an embroidered shirt to the bridegroom—find a natural place in the novel, and the sense of period is strong in the atmospheric interiors at the wayside inn and the cottage of the parish whore.

Vital in establishing the atmosphere of the seventeenth century is the use of archaic and dialectal language, and Moberg not only employs terms for household objects and cultural features long since extinct but also word forms and syntax no longer in use. The effect of the archaic style is a complex one, both supporting the historical realism and the rhetorical pathos of the novel, but it provoked widely differing responses from critics.[4]

The dominating image of the novel, the "budkavle" or fiery cross, shows Moberg's genius in applying a telling detail. This wooden token was used legally throughout the Middle Ages to call men to the "thing" (or meeting) and illegally to raise a peasant army in revolt against their masters, but in the novel it becomes a symbol of the common people's ability through the ages to join together to resist oppression, and this is underlined when the token is handed to Stånge: "This token was carved by the hands of his fellow men; it has been carried through night and day, journeyed mile upon mile and passed from hand to hand. . . . It has passed along a chain of heavy peasant hands which by themselves are not capable of achieving freedom but which now reach out for support from each other" (116–17).

An important motif complex is that of deformity and illness. Moberg employs physical signs to concretize the concepts of honor and dishonor. Mats Elling, who has betrayed his fellowmen, suffers broken legs as a mark of his loss of honor while Jon Stånge's cowardice when confronted by Borre and his men is explained as a morning chill. In a key scene Svedje, the man of honor, confronts Stånge:

"You betrayed your solemn promise."
"I betrayed no more than the rest."
"You went first and counseled the others."
"Should we have brought destruction upon ourselves?"
"You had each other's help, but forfeited it."
"We were forced to save our lives. A man only has one life."
"You all live, but without honor!" (160)

Stånge's betrayal plagues him in the same way as the worms that gnaw at his vitals, and as the posse finally traps Svedje the alderman lies abed wondering what ails him: "It was a miserable fate to live and toil and work to feed the worms. Why had this affliction beset him? He was not guilty of anything as far as he knew. He who did harm suffered harm. But what harm had he done?" (339–40). Both Klas Bock and Ragnar Svedje, on the other hand, bear honorable marks, Bock a scar he received when resisting another attempt at foreign oppression, by the Danes, and Svedje a scar from a close encounter with Hans i Lenhovda. Both men resisted evil and oppression, and Bock received a sword wound when he refused to go with Borre to Ubbetorp: "But it is not a shameful wound that must be hidden away. The gash in his arm is an honorable wound which he can openly display. It is a sign of a man's honor, and so he can squeeze at the others' aching secret festering sores" (107). Stånge also believes that Svedje bears "open wounds himself and this is why he wants to bring the old hidden wounds of others to light" (166).

A leitmotiv which can be traced throughout the novel and which impinges on several different themes is the movement of the sun across the sky. Svedje's farm stands "with the sun" (i.e., east-west). His family own legal title to it, and the link is stressed between its position and the legality of its ownership. Even before the men of Brändebol are enslaved, the sun becomes associated with natural justice: "The orb of light begins its course in the heavens from east to west, and reveals in its motion what justice is for man in the circle of the earth" (46). When Svedje is forced into flight and his farm confiscated, the sun comes to signify for him the inevitability of a return to the rule of law: "He knows that the day will dawn when he will regain his rights. He knows it as surely as his eyes now see the sun: there will come a day when that which is unjust shall again be just, when injustice will once again be turned into justice" (86). But Svedje is alone among the villagers in not succumbing to the perversion of the course of justice, and unlike the other eleven he "followed the path of the sun and went into the woods" (86). The others have also lived according to the sun, risen at sunrise, gone to rest at sunset, and followed its movement in their everyday tasks, working sunwise, but now: "The sun still follows its ancient path across the heavens, but for them things are distorted and happen counterclockwise. What was done right yesterday is done wrongly today" (105). When the men trudge to the manor to do their new master's bidding they thus feel out of step with the world. The "budkavle" also follows the sun: "A 'budkavle' is sent out through Värend, it travels through night and day. It travels as so many that have gone before it among the peasants of Värend, sunwise from farm to farm, from county to county" (111). The symbol of the oppressed peasantry in revolt to regain their lost freedom is therefore associated with the symbol of the justice and freedom which they seek. In the chapter entitled "But the sun follows its course" Svedje is pictured in the forest awaiting the return of justice so that he may regain his farm, and here the motif of the sun is repeated and varied a number of times. The immutability of justice is likened to the irreversibility of the sun's path across the sky: "The sun could never move from right to left, from far to near. Just as little could his rights be taken away" (344). The sun motif makes a final appearance as Svedje is about to be put to death: "The farm stood east and west with the sun. . . . I shall lose my life. But the farm still stands in the same quarter. Right will remain right, and cannot be wrong. I shall lose my life but justice will remain on the earth" (350).

In *Ride This Night!* Moberg provides a richer historical canvas than in *Man's Woman*, and the features of setting are more varied. Not only does the story shift constantly between the tight-knit village community and the man in the forest, but events in Värend are also placed in a wider national context by means of the letters written to the parish priest by a fellow cleric attending the meeting of the Estates in Stockholm. Against this absorbing and vivid background is placed an exciting adventure story in which the interest lies in the fate of the hero, but into this is woven the story of the lovers incorporating some of the lyrical elements of medieval ballad and folktale. Nevertheless, the immediate impact of the work was as a political statement and must be viewed against a different background—that of the troubled world of 1941.

II *Sweden in World War II*

The fall of the Spanish Republic marked a turning point in Moberg's view of world affairs: "The kingdom of violence had been resurrected: each people now had only itself to rely upon; and the right of a people to live in freedom was only respected to the extent that it could be defended by means of force."[5] Moberg tried for a long time to retain his faith in the essential goodness of man, but with the fall of Austria and Czechoslovakia he was forced to reevaluate his long held pacifist principles: "I could only come to the conclusion that insofar as I was able, I must resist evil. Under the pressure of events out in Europe I was forced to abandon beliefs I had held unswervingly for more than a quarter of a century."[6]

In October, 1939, with the threat to Scandinavia growing from
both south and east, a group of Swedish writers including Moberg
published *Uppbåd för dessa* (*Mobilization for Them*) in which they
argued that "the Swedish desire for peace must be asserted by a
mobilization to the utmost of all the forces of the nation,"[7] and the
government was urged to strengthen the country's defense immediately. But, ironically, on the day that this pamphlet was published the
Soviet Union attacked Finland. During the winter of 1939–1940
Moberg visited Finland and spoke at meetings to raise support for
this David battling against the Soviet Goliath. In the spring of 1940 he
volunteered for military service and during the summer served in a
home guard unit. When Denmark and Norway fell he found morale
among his fellow soldiers strong: then there was no doubting their
will to resist an invasion, but gradually this changed. Sweden
appeared to be making concessions to the Germans and troop trains
began crossing Swedish territory on their way to Norway. The result
was a fall in morale: Hitler seemed indomitable and Sweden's ability
to defend herself apparently nonexistent.[8] Moberg was horrified at
the widespread spirit of defeatism he encountered, and his growing
anger and defiance found expression in a great outburst of activity
both on the political and literary fronts, in protest meetings, newspaper articles, and pamphlets as well as in *Ride This Night!*, a work
regarded by Erik Hj. Linder as "the literary contribution to the
wartime political discussion which attracted the most attention. . . .
It can be described as an expression of unqualified defiance; in its
allusions it challenges the oppression that Sweden and Europe saw
threatening from Hitler's Germany, and ridicules those Swedish
politicians who for one reason or another—by diplomatic concessions
or the politics of obstruction—seemed to be doing the oppressor's
bidding."[9] In 1941 Moberg brought out a propaganda pamphlet for
the Swedish armed forces, entitled *The Swedish Struggle*, which in
many ways parallels *Ride This Night!* and in which he outlines the
situation in Sweden in 1650:

Only our land was still a bastion of popular freedom. . . . Now the ground was
prepared for the feudal conception of justice by countless foreign noblemen
who during and after the Thirty Years' War streamed into the country. It was
in particular the German nobility who upheld those ideas of popular liberty
which were alien to the common people of Sweden: a peasant farmer could
neither possess the right of ownership of land nor the right of determination
in parliament, he was the subject of the nobleman and nothing else. A large

number of the Swedish nobles naturally lent willing ears to this tempting message. Serious attempts were made to place the peasants in the position of serfs, and violence was undoubtedly employed in many cases against the recalcitrant. (11–12)

Moberg leaves his readers in no doubt as to where the threat to Sweden's sovereignty lay then and now, in 1941, and there are many references in *Ride This Night!* to Klewen's German origins and the feudal ideas of his homeland. As in Europe in the 1930s, the threat to Brändebol goes largely unnoticed until it is too late. The men of the village swear at their meeting to defend one another against outside aggression in much the same way as the heads of state of the Nordic countries at a meeting in Stockholm in 1939. But soon the villagers are picked off one by one: unprepared to defend themselves and unable to unite together, they are forced into servitude. The parallel with the fall of the states of Europe and especially of Norway and Denmark is evident. Hitler's tactics in his takeover of, for example, Austria, are even reflected in the early morning confrontation between sheriff Borre and alderman Stånge, threatened with violence if he does not willingly give his people into bondage, and the warning to Sweden is clear.

The men of Brändebol have been sold into slavery by their young queen and betrayed by their village alderman, Moberg's way of launching a veiled but bitter attack on the Swedish wartime administration for its apparent cooperation with the Nazis. In Moberg's eyes the greatest compromise to Swedish neutrality and a major concession to Hitler was the opening of Swedish railways to German troop trains, a decision taken at a secret meeting of the Parliament on June 21, 1940, and not fully revealed to the public until April, 1943, when the extent of the traffic came as a shock to many Swedes. Public knowledge in 1940 was the "permittenttraffik" ("furlough traffic") along the west coast, but there was also the "horse-shoe" traffic from July, 1940, onward from Trondheim to Narvik on the inland line, used to strengthen German forces in northern Norway. This brought strong protests from the Norwegian government in exile. There was no check made that the soldiers "on leave" ever returned from leave, and in fact regular troop transports crossed Swedish territory until August, 1943. The local people rechristened them "permanenttraffik." Parliament was not told of this "horse-shoe" traffic.[10] Moberg did not regard this or other concessions as likely to appease Hitler in the long term: "Every new concession to the Nazi regime was de-

scribed as an 'isolated concession,' "[11] and in the pamphlet *The Truth
Emerges* (1943), published after censorship was lifted, he revealed for
the first time the extent of the concessions the government had been
forced to make.

The stifling of the press was regarded by Moberg and many others
as almost as great a threat to the democratic values that Sweden
represented. Moberg describes a free press as "the weapon which
must not be surrendered."[12] The national government in Sweden
employed censorship of books, pamphlets, newspapers, and magazines from 1939 to 1943, confiscating all offending material. Bengt
Landgren provides a detailed account of how censorship operated.
The government eventually amended Sweden's press law on June 18,
1941, to allow confiscation of any printed matter containing "views or
opinions abusive to, injurious of, or aimed at creating discord with,
foreign powers, relating to views and statements about contemporary
nations or states with which the realm has friendly relations."[13]
Paragraph 6, the "Censorship Law" decreed prior scrutiny of all
publications so as to prevent publication of "statements intended to
weaken the security of the realm or to disturb the relationship of the
realm with foreign powers or . . . seriously to disrupt public order."[14]
This furnished the authorities with draconian powers to suppress any
adverse comments on the activities of foreign states or their own
actions, and the power was used extensively, in particular against
newspapers and magazines, and especially against material that criti-
cized the Axis powers.[15] Even plays were censored: when *Ride This
Night!* was performed at Dramaten in Stockholm in September,
1942, the text was amended and the word "German" replaced by
"foreign."[16]

One of the newspapers that suffered repeated confiscations was
Göteborgs Handels-och Sjöfartstidning whose editor, Torgny Segerstedt, was a focal point for opposition to the government. With a
number of politically active writers Moberg would later be able to
declare that "*Handelstidningen* became my breathing-hole during
the period of the fettered word . . . a sanctuary of press freedom."[17]
In September, 1940, for example, Segerstedt attempted unsuccessfully to publish the truth about the rail transports, and in March,
1942, about the harsh treatment meted out in occupied Norway. In
fact, smuggled copies of the paper provided a vital source of news in
Norway during the early years of the war. But the paper was repeatedly seized by the police, and Segerstedt himself subjected to
much vilification and great pressure from different groups to cease his

criticisms. Even King Gustav V summoned him to a personal audience.[18]

In *Ride This Night!* the reactions of the men of Brändebol to Klewen come to typify Swedish attitudes to Hitler as Moberg saw them. At the village meeting Mats Elling's is the voice of appeasement, arguing that concessions should be made in the face of possible violence, and when Brändebol has fallen into Klewen's hands Mats becomes a quisling, collaborating openly with the enemy and betraying his friends, for which he is rewarded by the occupying power. Elling even volunteers for the posse sent out to hunt down Svedje in the forest. More interesting is Jon Stånge's role in the novel. Stånge is the democratically elected village leader who, when confronted with the forces of evil, not only sells out his fellow villagers, choosing appeasement to violent resistance, but is then gradually induced into a passive collaboration. Stånge comes to favor the new status quo, and regards Svedje's resistance as a threat to a quiet life. Stånge betrays the trust of the village meeting which has expressed its collective will, and by his action allows the rule of the sheriff to replace democracy. But his greatest treachery, born of cowardice, lies in concealing the message of revolt and resistance, the "budkavle," an allusion to the censorship of news in Sweden introduced by Prime Minister Per Albin Hansson. It is likely that the highly critical picture of Stånge is intended as a reference to Hansson, whom Moberg attacks elsewhere in his writing.

Life under Klewen is harsh. Not only does he demand more and more work of the villagers, and becomes master of their bodies, but he also tries to enslave their minds:

They had also been given a master over the tongues in their mouths. To say that they were forced to work beyond their due, this was to show defiance toward their lawful lord and master. To say that no free peasant could be coerced by force, this was insubordination and disobedience. To say that the day would dawn when they would again become free peasants, this was to incite rebellion and civil war. To say that Svedje was right to defend himself, this was to praise rebels and incur their punishment. God had not placed a tongue in their mouths so that they could criticize their superiors and masters who had dominion over them. (175)

The men of Brändebol use indirect methods to cirumvent this suppression of the free word, and when they go aside to carry out their natural functions, they call out: "Now I am off to give our sheriff a ride!" (176). Similarly, the censorship situation in 1940–1943 influ-

enced the writing of fiction in Sweden. Writers were forced to avoid
direct criticism, to use allegory, myth, and historical guises to em-
body their political message. But, as Bengt Landgren points out, the
great interest in historical motifs in these years is probably not only
the result of censorship. It may also have been a response to the
demand for escapist writing, and Landgren cites as an example the
success of Frans G. Bengtsson's tale of the vikings, *Röde Orm* (*The
Long Ships*, 1941).

A problem with novels like Eyvind Johnson's *Krilon* trilogy and
Moberg's *Ride This Night!* is whether the indirect criticisms made
did not "presuppose both knowledge and sensitivity to nuance on the
part of the general public. There was the risk that the effect of the
political propaganda was diluted."[19] Landgren also wonders whether
the reception of Moberg's novel was quite what the author intended,
whether some critics did not choose to "stress the indeterminately
national and traditionally patriotic aspects of *Ride This Night!* at the
expense of the criticism of the government's policy of appeasement
which can be interpreted from the novel and which Moberg intended
to make in it."[20] This is certainly true of some reviewers. Örjan
Lindberger considered the novel to be merely "a critique in principal
of those conditions which now obtain in several occupied countries."[21] But not all critics were deaf to the broadside Moberg leveled
at his country's policies: Stig Ahlgren wrote: "*Ride This Night!* is in
fact a bitterly disillusioned book despite generally being regarded as
the glad tidings. It is about the 'budkavle' that does not arrive in time,
about the man who is thirsting for freedom and finds his mouth filled
with soil."[22]

The reception of the work as an uncomplicated and chauvinistic call
to arms in defense of the motherland is only one example of how the
ideas of the novel have been oversimplified. Sven Delblanc indicates
another difficulty regarding the message of the novel. Svedje is forced
to leave the community and become an outlaw in order to save his
honor and independence, but this has a strange implication: "As an
outlaw in the forest, Svedje is morally compromised and forced into
the company of the thief Ygge. This complication may seem unnec-
cessary, interfering with the highly topical anti-Nazi pathos of the
book."[23] Delblanc shows that this flight into nature has occurred
before—in *A. P. Rosell, Bank Director* and in *Man's Woman*—and
that "although flight from society is the only politically and morally
acceptable action,"[24] it is this very action that is doomed to failure.
The flight motif in *Ride This Night!* has no direct analogue in the

contemporary situation but may be seen as a deep underlying ambiguity recurring in several works. The complication of Ygge is simpler to explain, however, in that the historical detail of Åke from Dufwemåla simply proved too tempting to the author, who included it even at the cost of complicating his message.

Ride This Night! has a dual origin: the basic idea was the product of several years of historical research before the war,[25] which Moberg came to see as highly relevant to the immediate situation in 1940, whereupon he quickly completed the work. This is also the case with his second wartime novel, which is examined in the next chapter.

CHAPTER 6

Memoirs of an Idealist

I *The* Bildungsroman

MOBERG'S intention in the massive, 800-page novel *Soldier With a Broken Rifle* (1944) is to portray an idealistic young man from the first decades of this century against a backdrop of the institutions and events that shape his life. But the novel of development and the historical novel have here been conflated with the author's more immediate and urgent reactions to the wartime political scene in Sweden as he saw it.[1] Moberg intended to hold up a mirror to the Social Democrats, to reveal just how far they had deviated from the high ideals they had espoused some twenty-five years before. The novel is thus a result of differing aims, and may be thought to have suffered somewhat as a work of art from the stridency of its political message, even in this indirect form. This is Moberg's most political work, and also until very recently one of his least known, for many years neglected by both critics and reading public alike. In the 1970s the book was reissued and a television series made from it.

First, *Soldier With a Broken Rifle* is a *Bildungsroman*. It is the story of Valter Sträng from his birth in 1897 through a variety of trials and discoveries up to the point in 1921 when he feels that he has found his calling in life: to describe the people he comes from. Valter is born the seventh child of a soldier-crofter in Småland, and his earliest impressions are of the deprivation suffered by his neighbors and relatives, the "wooden-shoe people"—crofters and squatters— whose poverty is symbolized for him by the clogs they wear. A more affluent world is represented in the soldier's cottage by the portraits of relatives who have emigrated to America, and by their letters, newspapers, and gifts. One by one Valter's brothers and his sister Dagmar also emigrate, and Valter makes an early discovery: "Here in

Sweden you are born and grow up. You go to America when you're big" (28).

Valter's development is spurred on by his insatiable curiosity and guided by a series of mentors. His first teacher is his father, and the first part of the novel is called "The Soldier's Valter (1897–1909)." Valter takes his first unsteady steps out beyond the confines of the cottage clutching his father's hand. When he is a little older, he accompanies his father into the forest and proudly becomes his workmate. The idea of comradeship that he learns from his father becomes basic to his development: "*Comrade* is the greatest word!" he bursts out in later years (714). And Valter soon has to demonstrate the qualities of comradeship, as his father develops diabetes, becomes blind, and dies.

With his father's death the period in Valter's life as "The Soldier's Valter" comes to an end. The family loses the tied croft and moves to a squatter's hut. In other ways, however, Valter has already ceased to be "The Soldier's Valter," becoming "Valter" in his own right. Valter's meditations on his identity and role in life begin when he sees a mystical bird, a woodcock, fly over the house at dusk. Valter discovers from the local carpenter, the village's religious advisor, that man consists of a soul that belongs to God and a body that will return to dust. But Valter is not satisfied: "He would never be content with that. He strove beyond that. There must be something that was his own, that he disposed over—something that was himself. When he stood in the evenings outside the cottage, watching the mysterious bird of twilight or woodcock that flew by so strangely fast beneath the firmament, stretching out and disappearing in its infinite freedom, then it felt as if there should be something more" (59). A little later Valter realizes that God does not exist and that he is his own master. Yet if he is answerable to himself for his soul, he must still surrender his body to the earth, and his struggle "beyond the brief and inadequate life of the body" (the book's motto) is the basic theme of the work.

While Valter separates himself from his father as an individual, he also rejects his father's trade. He is born under his father's rifle, and in his early years he can think of nothing better than following in his footsteps and becoming a soldier. However, in 1908 he goes off to work at the local glassworks and comes under the influence of a new mentor, Elmer Sandin, a member of the revolutionary Young Socialists. Sandin notices Valter's enquiring mind and opens his eyes to a society founded on class oppression and exploitation, through "the throne, the sword, the altar, and the moneybag." Valter is an eager pupil, easily seeing through the humbug of the rich from his own position among the poor. After a dramatic political meeting in the glassworks in protest at death sentences passed on two comrades, Valter's mission in life is revealed to him: he will become a class fighter. But he is a pacifist fighter, opposed to "the sword," and becomes "a soldier with a broken rifle."

There is one further side to Valter's childhood, which is not developed until much later: his imagination. Valter's fantasy world is as real to him as the physical world, as is shown in the incident when he terrifies his brothers with a report of an old man on the porch with a sackful of children's heads. For Valter the old man actually becomes real.

The title of the second part of the novel is "It must be by his own efforts (1910–1915)." Valter has broken out of his family environment, but he still has to break out of the spiritual and material poverty of rural Småland, and he must do it on his own. During this part of the novel he passes through a number of experiences that lead him to doubt his worth as a class fighter, to doubt even that the world can be saved through socialism. He comes to feel that he must leave Sweden altogether and follow the rest of the family to America.

Valter has lost his father, but a fellow worker at the glassworks, Joel Nattstoppare, becomes a new father and mentor to him. He persuades Valter to join the local temperance lodge, which soon becomes a second home to him. There he finds companionship, entertainment, books, and a cause, and he soon becomes one of the leading members. Even his storytelling proves useful when he writes a prize-winning tale, "The Drunkard's Dog," warning of the dangers of drink. After some years, however, he feels that his pledge of teetotalism restricts him and he deliberately gets drunk. The lodge has been a home and a school for him, but by 1915 he has developed beyond it.

If Valter is suspicious of wine, he is equally so of woman. To begin with he regards women as a dangerous diversion from his calling, and in the notebook where he jots down his discoveries—"Containing Truths"—he writes: "A class fighter shall live alone and steel himself against women" (179). However, Valter's thoughts become increasingly occupied with a girl at the lodge called Agda, and he worships her from afar. Unfortunately, sister Agda becomes pregnant, and what is worse, is not even sure who is responsible. Valter is deeply shocked: "But then at the same time he had seen through female baseness and depravity right down to its depths, and by doing so had been further steeled against temptation" (238). The next sister to cross Valter's path is Karin, whom he meets at an idyllically portrayed midsummer picnic which the lodge has organized. Valter and Karin while away a chaste and romantic summer (1914), cycling down the country lanes.

Because of Karin, Valter tears out a page of "Containing Truths" which now seems childish, and makes a new entry: "One can easily wither and shrivel up in loneliness and self-denial. A leader and fighter needs a woman to egg him on to great achievements" (270). Karin's family moves to another village, her letters become less frequent and less passionate, and one day Valter sees in the newspaper an announcement of her engagement. He burns "Containing Truths" and starts a new exercise book with the words "He who wishes to achieve anything in this world needs peace and harmony in his soul. He should not tie himself to any woman. Women only cause worry and disharmony" (285). Valter's changing attitudes to women show clearly the dynamics of the *Bildungsroman*: "And life went on, with discoveries of false discoveries. His whole life was one continuous discovery" (285).

The cause of teetotalism is not one that deeply seizes Valter's imagination, but the ideals of socialism become something very like religious principles for him. Valter is introduced by a glassblower called Sjölin, a veteran Social Democrat, to a pamphlet by a young party member called Per Albin Hansson, who writes: "Socialists must hold fast to their principles and always, *always* pursue the politics of idealism" (215). Captivated by P. A. Hansson's idealism, Valter joins the Social Democratic Youth League, a more moderate group than the Young Socialists. For Valter socialism is a clear extension of the comradeship he learned from his father.

A vivid illustration of comradeship is in Valter's work among the wagoners at a peat bog. Pushing their wagons as a team, they are totally interdependent: if one is delayed, they are all delayed. But, although this little group holds together, and Valter proves himself worthy of it, in other ways his socialism is tested. When war is declared in 1914, Valter is consoled by the Second International's resolution ordering workers' leaders to prevent mobilization. Valter takes the wording of the resolution to work to show his comrades, only to find that they are talking of the fighting: "About other comrades' betrayal of one another, about the great inconceivable treachery. About betrayal of the great idea, the idea of comradeship"

(273). Valter's faith in workers' leaders is shaken, and later his faith in his own calling is upset. He and his comrades strike for higher wages. The management call in strikebreakers, and Valter, as a picket, goes to deal with them. He finds himself confronting an aged and toothless couple, his own people. After an argument Valter raises his fist to the old man, but cannot strike him, feeling physically sick and over-whelmed by the wretchedness of life: "And the doubt grew: was he good enough to be a class fighter?" (318).

By 1915 Valter has suffered a series of blows to his self-confidence. He is trapped in despair and in dead-end jobs. He realizes that if he is to break out, then it must be through his own efforts: no one is going to help him. He decides to emigrate and saves up for his ticket, but recalls the last wish of his father, that one of the children should stay to look after their widowed mother. Faithful to his old comrade, Valter stays.

Valter now seeks other ways to escape his restricting milieu. In the third part of the novel, "The Knowledge of Truth (1915–1918)," he tries to advance through education. He has been stung by the remark of one of the peat directors: "You are ignorant, Sträng" (330). He is determined to give this the lie and become "an educated class fighter" (361). He spends the "America money" on a course at a Folk High School during the winter of 1915–1916, but feels only more ignorant at the end of it. He returns to physical labor in the forest, and here he is led into temptation: "To become a forester, live in a little red cottage by a lake, and go about with a shotgun looking after the game and the timber-felling" (419), but he rejects this escapism. In 1917 the political struggle in Sweden is approaching its climax, with bread riots and threats of revolution. Valter enters into the 1917 election campaign with enthusiasm, and is rewarded with the first appearance of Social Democrats in a Swedish cabinet. Still thirsting for knowledge, Valter decides he must take *studentexamen*, the university matriculation exam, and prepares to spend several terms at Hedvigsholms praktiska skola, a crammer.

One of the teachers at Hedvigsholm lends Valter Schopenhauer's *Die Welt als Wille und Vorstellung (The World as Will and Idea)*, and he is captivated by Schopenhauer's vision of life as evil and death as a release: "Dying is easy, the easiest thing of all, ceasing to exist is sweet and good. The secret is to overcome the desire to live. Life is something that should not be. Its meaning is to deny and overcome it, to sink into the bliss of nothingness" (475). For Valter, who has seen his father die young and his brother younger, whose whole energy has been directed against death, "a striving beyond the brief and inadequate life of the body," Schopenhauer's theories are tempting. For some days he is entranced, until the consequences sink in: that the class struggle is pointless, that the joys of life are deceptive. He cannot accept this. He has experienced moments of intense joy in his life and he has faith in socialism: "Schopenhauer had not lived his life, he could not know what a working lad had experienced" (476). Yet Valter's vitality is already sapped by inadequate food and overwork, and when he accompanies his roommate, a virile militarist, in search of prostitutes, he discovers to his humiliation that he is impotent. He suffers new attacks of Schopenhauer, but resists: "And if existence itself had no meaning, then one was driven to provide it with a meaning oneself by striving beyond this poor inadequate life. This thought helped him resist the attacks of Schopenhauer" (497). Valter's physical and psychical collapse is completed in November, 1918, in the Spanish flu epidemic. He overcomes the first attack of flu and lies recuperating under the care of his landlady, the young wife of a policeman. Ingrid and he become increasingly attached to one another. Valter suffers a relapse and is carried off to hospital for an operation, and manages to survive the disease.

In the fourth part of the novel, "Servant of the Free Word (1919–1921)," Valter tries to pursue his socialist mission as a journalist. After convalescing at home, he returns to Hedvigsholm full of life and energy, and joins *Hedvigsholms-Posten* as unpaid apprentice to its eccentric editor, Olle Setterblad. Setterblad has strong views on a journalist's responsibilities, and impresses on Valter: "A newspaperman is a servant of the free word" (559). Valter finds to his surprise how much he enjoys writing, and recalls his creative imagination from childhood in writing tales for the paper. Through Setterblad Valter begins to realize his artistic talents.

In Hedvigsholm he also makes up for his previous disappointments in love. Walking to and from work he keeps meeting his former landlady and nurse, Ingrid, and it eventually dawns on him that she is seeking him. Emboldened, he asks her out and she accepts. After some struggles with her conscience she invites Valter home when her husband is at work and then takes the initiative: "She took his hand and walked before him. In the bedroom it was even darker; she led him by the hand through the darkness as a thoughtful sister leads her younger brother through the great wild, dark forest" (591).

The majority shareholder of the newspaper company removes a news item unflattering to his son-in-law, and Valter resigns from the

paper in a blaze of idealism. He finds a job on a new Social Democrat
newspaper in the venerable and conservative county town of Helgestad. The editor of the newspaper, Viktor Fläderbaum, is an intellectual socialist from a bourgeois background, and Valter finds it difficult
to get on with him. Nevertheless, he starts off full of hope, writing at
last for his own people. Soon Valter can inform his readers that
Sweden has acquired its first Social Democrat prime minister, Hjalmar Branting, and that he now writes for the government press.

Valter's move to Helgestad means a break in his relationship with
Ingrid: "He didn't need a big sister any more, he had grown" (721).
Valter's affair with journalism is also nearing its end: "He wanted
some time to write something of his own, to open himself up to all
ideas, to write wholly from within himself, to allow his imagination to
roam free, to narrate the experiences of his imagination. It was what
was called creative writing" (722).

Valter's relationship with Fläderbaum reaches a breaking point
when Valter attempts to insert in the newspaper a report of a political
speech he has just delivered. Valter has expounded the party manifesto in his speech, and Fläderbaum is horrified when he reads
Valter's enthusiastic account of the party's policy on nationalization,
an election-losing issue that is better suppressed. Fläderbaum points
out the need for tactical compromise and evasion, but for Valter the
claim of the idea is paramount: "Always to be faithful to the Idea"
(752). When Fläderbaum refuses to print the speech, Valter leaves
his party's newspaper.

He wanders out into the night, into "the wilderness of anarchistic
individualism" (758) and looks up to the stars for consolation. In the
epilogue, "The flower of the cottage slope," speaking to what he calls
"The President of the Universe," Valter summarizes his hopes and
ideals:

We beings on this dark star of earth all share the common fate of death, the
sentence of extinction, but we also share throughout our lives a longing which
impels us to annul extinction and to transcend it. I believe, you see—and I
have believed it for several years—that if our existence seems meaningless to
us, then we can find a meaning for it by striving beyond this poor, inadequate
life. In my own case this striving has been associated with a search for justice,
with the class struggle. (760)

He can no longer pursue his class struggle through the press or among
party tacticians like Fläderbaum. But he sees another possibility:
recreating his childhood and the people he was brought up among,

giving them a voice: "So it occurred to me that this could be my true calling—*that this henceforth could be my class struggle*" (762). He has come like "the flower of the cottage slope"—the cowslip—from unpromising and poor soil in an ungenerous motherland, but he has made the most of his opportunities and won through by his own efforts. All his faculties and aspirations can now be realized in the writing of a novel about his childhood, "The Soldier's Croft." And in this task he can conquer his main enemy: "And by this means I would now fulfill my striving beyond the brief and inadequate life of the body. By this means I would be able to conquer death, which in my life so far I had never fully been able to accept. . . . It is in this that I now see the ultimate meaning of my life" (763).

II   *The Historical Novel*

Vilhelm Moberg has an extraordinary talent for bringing history to life by the application of imagination to material that is always solidly based on fact. In his earlier works, such as *Raskens* and the Adolf novels, he convincingly recreates his native environment through an account of its customs and labors. In the later emigrant novels he conveys the historical background as much by using documents as by action, and this use of contemporary documents—which may be real or fictitious—is noticeable in *Soldier With a Broken Rifle*. These "documents" include songs, newspapers, books, pamphlets, letters, minutes of meetings, even a political banner. They provide a strong sense of historical accuracy.

In *Soldier With a Broken Rifle* contemporary history is seen from the point of view of a poor boy struggling for advancement, and Valter's position is representative of many of his generation. The possibilities open to him are few: emigration and the byways of the education system, particularly through the popular movements.

Emigration to America plays an important role in Valter's early life, where the America portraits stand on the writing desk and are gradually complemented by those of his only sister and all his brothers. The basic reason for emigrating is to seek better job opportunities, though there are individual embroideries on this theme. Valter's eldest brother, Albin, has dreams of finding gold in Alaska, sister Dagmar emigrates to escape being a servant—in America all are equal she tells her astonished and disapproving mother. Brother Fredrik emigrates to evade the new, longer military service. The studies of the causes of emigration in the novel can be seen as a sketch for the much more detailed analyses found in *The Emigrants* which is set some fifty years earlier, although in *Soldier With a Broken Rifle* it is individual emigration rather than family emigration that is prevalent.

When Valter gives up the idea of advancement through emigration, he turns to the educational system. Valter's primary schooling has only been part-time. His next school is a Folk High School, an establishment intended to provide additional schooling in the form of short courses for those with only elementary education. The prevailing spirit at Valter's school is right wing, and when he attempts to introduce socialist arguments into the debate on "What a young man should consider in his choice of a wife," he is sternly told by the conservative headmaster that politics are not discussed in the school. Valter's final school at Hedvigsholm is for those who need paper qualifications to improve their careers, thus only for the materially minded and not for idealists like himself. On the whole the novel gives a disenchanted view of educational establishments—perhaps unrepresentatively so in the case of the Folk High School. Valter's real education takes place through the popular organizations that are such an interesting feature of the development of modern Sweden, and the novel provides a detailed picture of the ceremonies and activities of a temperance lodge: the initiation rites, the songs, the debates and study circles, the picnics and dances.

Soldier With a Broken Rifle also provides a fascinating picture of the Social Democrats' rise to power, and of the arguments and schisms within the party, all seen through the eyes of a participant. For Valter is deeply involved. He demonstrates, distributes leaflets and newspapers, despatches telegrams, collects money, disrupts political meetings. Through Elmer Sandin at the glassworks Valter first becomes a Young Socialist, a group on the extreme left wing of the Social Democrats and known as "Unghinkar" after their leader Hinke Bergegren (1861–1936). Valter reads their newspaper *Nya Folkviljan*, admires the illegal banner they carried at Kosta glassworks on May 1, 1908 ("Down with the throne, the sword, the altar and the moneybag") and distributes a seditious leaflet by one Leo Tolstoy. An early event described in considerable detail is the Amalthea incident. In July, 1908, some Young Socialists threw a bomb at English strikebreakers on board the ship *Amalthea* in Malmö harbor. One man was killed, and two of the bombers were sentenced to death. The episode is presented through Valter's parents' conservative newspaper, through Valter's socialist newspaper, through Val-

ter's intense involvement in his comrades' fate, and through the
brilliantly painted meeting in the glassworks when Valter's mission in
life is revealed to him. As a result of the Amalthea incident Hinke
Bergegren is expelled from the Social Democrat Party. The Social
Democrats' leader, Hjalmar Branting, is the idol of another employee
at the glassworks, Mäster Sjölin. The quarrels between Sjölin and
Sandin reflect the split in the Socialist movement; when Hinke
Bergegren is expelled, Sjölin celebrates with beer all round. Sjölin
and Branting believe in revolution through the ballot box, not
through bombs. After the electoral reform of 1909, greatly extending
the franchise, Valter begins to wonder if Sjölin is not right, and the
elections of 1911 lead to a Social Democrat landslide, taking one of his
comrades in the glassworks of Småland, Anders Nyström, into parliament. Elmer Sandin disappears from the novel and his place is taken
by Sjölin, who persuades Valter to join the Social Democrat Youth
League. An event that echoes in a less violent way the Amalthea
incident and also leads to a split in the party is the "Treason Trial" of
1917, arising from the call in Z. Höglund's newspaper *Stormklockan*
for a general strike to hinder possible mobilization of the Swedish
army. Höglund and his colleagues are accused of high treason, and
Valter again takes an active interest in the case as secretary of the local
Social Democrat Youth Club. He signs a telegram to his arrested
comrades, he collects money for their defense, and he attends a big
protest meeting. Here he meets Sjölin and Anders Nyström, and
their conversation is full of information about attitudes in the party
and the approaching split that leads to Höglund's expulsion. Sjölin's
last appearance in the novel is in the newspaper office in Helgestad,
when he is dying from diabetes, a reminder of Valter's father. Sjölin is
worried about the party's future; so few of its members of parliament
are workers, so many are professional people whom he suspects of
opportunism and lack of idealism. Sjölin is a symbol of the old
party—Fläderbaum of the new.

Most important events both in Sweden and abroad are mentioned
in one way or another, starting with the Russo-Japanese War of 1904.
Many of these events impinge on Valter's life in curious ways. After
the peaceful resolution of the 1905 crisis between Sweden and Norway, Valter's soldier-father celebrates by returning from camp with a
sugarloaf; the excitement of the Russian Revolution (under Kerensky)
leads to the burning of Valter's dinner; the civil war in Finland causes
Valter to move lodgings in Hedvigsholm when he discovers that his
roommate supports the Whites. As a journalist Valter is more directly

in contact with events: he stops the presses to report the signing of the Treaty of Versailles; he writes biographical notes on the members of Sweden's first Social Democrat government. In these, and many similar cases, Valter's life is momentarily touched by public happenings, but there are other events that are symbolically interwoven with his own fate. For example, the outbreak of World War I is linked with both Valter's girl friend Karin and his brother Gunnar.

Gunnar, sent to America to be safe from militarism, dies there on August 15, 1914: "Several thousand workers had perished in the war that day. But none of them had been his brother. There was a difference when it was your brother" (297). If Gunnar is a reminder of the carnage of war, Karin is a reminder of those who did nothing to prevent it. In Karin's engagement Valter sees "a betrayal of the same kind as that which the workers' leaders in the warring countries had been guilty of" (278). The end of the war coincides with Valter's recovery from his first bout of Spanish flu: "The war is over, and he never took part. But where he is lying he feels like one of the wounded" (511). Another very important event is also presented in this indirect way: the crucial struggle for electoral reform at the end of 1918. The undemocratic "40-degree" scale that favors the bourgeois parties is confused in Valter's feverish mind with his temperature (in degrees centigrade); the final fall in his temperature and his recovery in December, 1918, occur simultaneously with the political parties' agreement to abolish the 40-degree scale. It is the abolition of the scale that finally ensures the Social Democrats' succession to power, a power that, the novel proclaims, ultimately corrupts.

III   The Political Novel

Soldier With a Broken Rifle bears at the end the dates 1939–1944. During this period the prime minister of Sweden was the Social Democrat Per Albin Hansson, who had been prime minister almost without interruption since 1932. It might seem, then, that Valter's goals would have been achieved by 1944. Clearly they had not. Moberg's novel is an attack and accusation born out of disillusion, out of the observation that the throne had not been overturned, the sword not broken, the church not disestablished and the moneybag not nationalized. In his pamphlet The Truth Emerges Moberg noted that P. A. Hansson has shown during World War II that he cares as little for democracy or freedom as those who had attempted to suppress the Social Democrats a generation earlier. Many of the arguments of this pamphlet are reflected in *Soldier With a Broken Rifle*.

Moberg's method of dealing with P. A. Hansson and his colleagues in the novel is that of dramatic irony, since events have to be presented through the young Valter Sträng's eyes. Valter is unaware of what the future holds, but the reader sees another dimension in the promises of the 1910s and 1920s, for he knows how they were fulfilled. For example, when the left-wing weekly *Stormklockan* is impounded in 1916, Valter declares: "But when the workers gain a majority in parliament and power in the country, then the cops' grubby hands will not touch THE FREE WORD" (409). In 1917 *Stormklockan* is again seized, and again Valter reflects: "Stupid bourgeois who thought that the truth could be confiscated. One extenuating circumstance for those in power was their stupidity. Luckily the workers' leaders were more intelligent. They would never have been guilty of such idiocies during a critical period" (434). Valter cannot forsee, of course, that the man he so idolizes, P. A. Hansson, will introduce strict censorship of the press and confiscation of newspapers only twenty-three years later.[2]

Soldier With a Broken Rifle also provides a more general attack on the Social Democrats' betrayal of their original ideals. This attack is launched principally through Valter's election speech at the very end of the novel, a speech called "When our party programme is implemented" (738–45). The first point in the party manifesto is "Freedom of expression and of the press": "No one in our party will tolerate any, even the least, restriction of this right" (738). Valter's next item is "Republic." He reminds his listeners of King Gustav V's interference in politics with his support for the right-wing "Bondetåget" ("Farmers' March") and his "Palace Yard Speech": "There may come another frenzied, tumultuous and dangerous year, another 1914, when the monarch may again assault representative government" (740)—as in fact the king did during World War II, explaining his actions in a speech known as "the Second Palace Yard Speech" in 1943. Valter, however, sees the approaching end of the monarchy: "The day we have a majority in parliament, the demand for a republic will naturally be implemented, a fact that goes without saying" (740). (Sweden is still a monarchy.)

Valter's next target is "the state church," when he reminds his audience of the party's pledge to disestablish the church: "A Social Democrat minister for the church will consider it a release to be free of the priests' affairs" (742). He quotes with approval the words of the

Social Democrat Arthur Engberg about the church: "It is a bastion of
reaction, the stronghold of liars and the men of darkness in the
struggle between light and darkness, truth and lies among the children of men" (741). It is almost as if Valter could foresee that Engberg
would become the cabinet minister responsible for the church and
education from 1932 to 1939. (The Swedish church is still established.) Having demolished the throne and the altar, Valter comes to
the moneybag and presents the party's nationalization programme:
"Private ownership of capital will in the near future cease to exist in
our country" (742). (Ninety percent of Swedish industry remains in
private hands.)

A forewarning of what will happen to Valter's party's program is
provided by the reception his speech is given by Fläderbaum, the
up-and-coming bourgeois-socialist, with his motto: "One must do
what is most prudent in every situation. It is the situation that
determines the measure" (716). Valter clings to the absolute idealism
that for him is associated with Per Albin Hansson's words: "Never
throw your principles overboard. Never tussle with the bourgeois
horse swindlers in the political cattle market; always pursue idealistic
politics!" (690). It is not surprising that when Moberg discusses press
censorship in *The Truth Emerges*, he says of P. A. Hansson: "His fall
is for me the most tragic experience in this context" (11). In the same
article he continues: "It seems to me that the history of the Social
Democratic party's struggle would be salutory reading for a number
of prominent men in that party which is now the largest and most
powerful in the land" (12). *Soldier With a Broken Rifle* is among other
things an attempt to set the idealism and sacrifice of the early Social
Democratic party under Branting and other "prisoners of a free
press" against the cynicism or cowardice of its leaders in the 1940s.

IV The Autobiographical Novel

There are obvious correspondences between the lives of Karl Artur
Valter Sträng and Karl Artur Vilhelm Moberg.[3] Vilhelm was born in
1898, Valter in 1897. Both are the sons of soldier-crofters, work at
glassworks, consider emigrating, are influenced by socialism and the
Temperance movement. Both attend Folk High School and work on
local newspapers. Both write stories of peasant life and a great novel
about their origins. As the outlines of their lives are so similar, some
interesting glimpses of Moberg's intentions in the novel are provided

by studying where and why he has departed from his own experiences in depicting Valter Sträng.

The first difference between Valter and Moberg lies in their family backgrounds. Moberg has made Valter's background poorer than his own: after the death of his father, Valter and his mother are removed to a squatter's hut, whereas Moberg's mother was the daughter of crofters, and in 1907 his parents bought their smallholding and moved there—Moberg's father did not die until 1950. It is even doubtful whether squatters' huts of the kind Moberg depicts still existed at this time. Valter's poverty and lowly status no doubt add greater weight and urgency to his class struggle for "the wooden-shoe people." In the untimely death of Valter's father Moberg combines the death of his own grandfather from diabetes with the death of his brother in 1909—the latter being reflected in Gunnar's death in *Soldier With a Broken Rifle* and, on a much larger scale, in the death of the hero's brother in the novel *A Time on Earth* (1963). Another important difference between the Sträng and Moberg families is the emphasis placed on the theme of emigration in the novel. Valter is the youngest of seven children, and all except him emigrate. Moberg was the fourth of seven children, of whom two died in infancy, two died in youth, and of the surviving three only one emigrated.

Some differences between Valter and Moberg may be ascribed to Moberg's unwillingness to repeat himself. He had already used a number of autobiographical motifs in the description of Knut Toring's childhood in *Memory of Youth*. This might explain the brief treatment of work on the farm or lessons at primary school in *Soldier With a Broken Rifle*, and, more seriously, of Valter's reading. One of Valter's reasons for joining the temperance lodge is its collection of books, but little is said about his reading them. In sex and religion, too, Knut Toring is closer to Moberg than Valter is. Moberg's initiation into sex is described in Knut's ecstatic experiences with Ebba, while Valter is given through Anny a different, embittering introduction that is only much later exorcised through Ingrid. Religion does not seem so important in Valter's life, and he loses his faith on becoming a Young Socialist. Moberg, on the other hand, has described his childhood terror of hell fire and eternal damnation in both *Tales from My Life* and through Knut Toring. For these reasons it is dangerous to treat *Soldier With a Broken Rifle* as a faithful record of Moberg's spiritual development.

Valter's stay at Hedvigsholm has recently been shown to be very different from Moberg's period in Katrineholm,[4] and the last section of the novel reveals important differences between Valter and Moberg in their journalistic careers: Valter's experience with Olle Setterblad and *Hedvigsholms-Posten* seems to be a fair reflection of Moberg's with Pälle Segerborg and *Vadstena Läns Tidning*, but the episodes in Helgestad with Fläderbaum and the Social Democrat *Läns-Demokraten* have no foundation in Moberg's life. Although Moberg was in "Helgestad" (Växjö) in 1921, he was there as a conscript. When he later worked for a Växjö newspaper, it was as local correspondent in Alvesta for *Nya Växjöbladet*. Fläderbaum is introduced as a way of driving home the message of the Social Democrats' later betrayal of their earlier ideals. Valter's literary development is also more politically defined than Moberg's was, and one aspect of Moberg's writing—drama—finds no expression through Valter. By the age of twenty-four Moberg was the author of a successful peasant comedy, while Valter shows no interest in drama, not even as theater critic in Helgestad. Magnus von Platen has recently pointed out other discrepancies in line with this tendency: Moberg's portrayal of Patron Lundewall at the Ljungdala glassworks as an archetypal cognac-swilling capitalist accords ill with his model, patron Tengvall, a teetotaller who sacrificed a fortune to keep Modala going. There was apparently no strike at the peat diggings while Moberg worked there.[5]

The conclusion must be that the novel is not an accurate autobiographical novel—neither in fatual, spiritual, intellectual, nor literary respects. Moberg has taken the outlines of his own life but has changed, omitted, or inserted events, both to emphasize the political and social themes of the work and to avoid repeating earlier works.

V *Conclusion*

The personal elements and the political and historical elements of *Soldier With a Broken Rifle* are intimately interwoven, in that the political and historical material is presented through Valter's perceptions and its influence on his life. Moberg has, however, avoided the danger of presenting Valter purely as an observer or mouthpiece by emphasizing his individual life alternately with his social life. For example, Valter's intense involvement in politics with the Young Socialists is offset by the moving scenes between the boy and his dying father, just as Valter's close involvement in the outside world as a journalist is relieved by the intensely personal affair with Ingrid.

Not only the historical background but also the other characters are seen from Valter's point of view. In a sense, they lack dimension, since they are only presented through Valter and through their own actions and words; their unspoken thoughts are missing. The characters of a *Bildungsroman* are important, however, not so much in themselves as in their relationship to the central character. Personal relationships are one of the strengths of this novel: Valter and his father, Valter and Joel Nattstoppare, Valter and Gunnar, Valter and Ingrid, Valter and Sjölin. These relationships are particularly expressive of the comradeship that is such an important feature of the novel and is brought out especially in the fine scenes of work—in the forest, at the peat bog, at school, in the newspaper office, even in the hospital ward. In showing the world through Valter's eyes Moberg is almost identical with his character—but achieves distance from him by gentle mockery. Examples of Moberg's slightly irreverent attitude toward Valter occur in Valter's changing ideas about Woman or when Valter and Karin visit Kalmar Castle and Valter resolutely ignores the grandeur that captures Karin's attention and thinks only of the underpaid workers who built it all. In his treatment of Valter, Moberg displays a playful, ironic style that is far removed from the mannered rhythms and repetitions of some of his other novels. At other times, reminding us that he is a dramatist as well as a novelist, and especially at moments of great emotion, he makes use of dramatic dialogue. This occurs, for example, when Valter's father dies, and when Valter argues with Fläderbaum.

Several of Moberg's novels depict a deprived childhood. In this work it initially provides the impetus for an ideal, a class struggle that is "a striving beyond the brief and inadequate life of the body," that conquers death by giving life a meaning. At the end of the novel Valter returns in imagination to his childhood and recreates it to fulfill his ideal. *Soldier With a Broken Rifle*, subtitled "A human being from the past, questioned as to the circumstances of his life," is the memoirs of an idealist, Valter Sträng, and through its autobiographical elements and its oblique attack on men who have forsaken their ideals, the memoirs of another idealist—Vilhelm Moberg.

CHAPTER 7

The Emigrant Novels

I The Background

BETWEEN the years 1851 and 1930 about one million two hundred thousand Swedes emigrated to the United States. Of these some two hundred thousand later returned to Sweden, but altogether Sweden lost a million inhabitants to the New World over this period, and this from a country whose total population in 1870 was a mere four million.[1] Emigration had no single economic or social cause, but initially at least the great impetus was local overpopulation and the attraction was the offer of plentiful cheap land held out by the American Homestead Act of 1862. The flow of emigrants began slowly in the 1840s and built up to peaks during the famine years in Sweden of 1868–1873, the economic recession of 1879–1893 and the extension of compulsory military service after 1901, before subsiding in the 1920s. One identifiable trend over the decades is a gradual shift from family emigration to individual emigration, from a desire to "take land" to a desire to "take work."[2] Many of the early emigrants traveled together as families and households whereas later young unmarried men and women formed the bulk of the emigrants. It was often the youngest and most able people who left their homeland.

The parts of Sweden hardest hit by emigration form a belt running through western and south-central areas and include the provinces of Värmland, Dalsland, Bohuslän, Halland, and Småland.[3] Across the Atlantic most Swedish emigrants settled in Minnesota and Illinois.[4] Moberg's native province was one of those most severely affected: the scale of emigration and migration here may be judged by the fact that the total population of Kronoberg county (an area the size of Connecticut) did not increase at all between the years 1870 and 1960.[5] Some sixty-two thousand persons, almost half the present population, left during the period 1850 to 1910.[6] In human terms this meant that frequently most of the inhabitants of a parish would depart in only a few years, leaving behind only the old and a countryside dotted with deserted farmsteads.

America was from his earliest childhood always a part of Moberg's world, and he writes of his inspiration for the emigrant novels:

I did not sit down to write the series because I felt it was a job that someone ought to do. I was simply fascinated by the life stories of people who were near to me; I was compelled by purely personal feelings. My father had four brothers and sisters; *all* of them emigrated to North America. Father and mother were both the only remnants of their families who were left in Sweden. . . . The result of this family emigration of the nineteenth century has been that today I have over a hundred relatives in the United States. . . . It is natural that I have always taken a great interest in the country where practically all of my relatives live.[7]

What emigration must have meant to his forebears is illustrated by Moberg's account of the tragic life of his grandmother, Johanna Johansdotter: "In 1870, at the age of thirty-seven, she became a widow with seven children. . . . America took six of her children from her. She saw one of her sons again, when he spent a few weeks visiting the home country. She never saw the other five children in this life. Add to this the fact that grandmother was not able to read or write. . . . She could, therefore, neither write letters to her children in America nor read their letters to her."[8] Moberg's own generation was also infected with emigration fever: his sister emigrated and he himself planned to join a group of young men America-bound in 1916; he even bought his ticket, deciding only at the last minute to stay at home.

The theme of emigration appears in several of the earlier novels. In *Raskens* it figures only briefly in the story of Ida's mother, Inga-Lena, whose fate closely resembles that of Moberg's grandmother Johanna, but in *Soldier With a Broken Rifle* it forms a major theme in the story of Valter's early years, and his brothers and sisters are given typical motivations for the emigrants of the pre–World War I period: the search for work and the avoidance of military service. Like his creator, Valter considers abandoning Sweden but changes his mind. Moberg probably first began to plan a major literary treatment of the emigration theme as early as the mid-1930s, and in 1939 was due to leave for America to gather material, but then much occurred, and it was only in 1945 that he took up his plans again, and not until 1948 that he was able to pursue his researches in the Swedish areas of the United States.[9] When he began this work he writes that he was surprised to find that Swedish historians and writers seemed largely to have ignored this, "the greatest event in the modern history of Sweden,"[10] although Helmer Lång has indicated that Moberg is too critical of the historians and that emigration is given adequate treatment in several early textbooks on Swedish history. Moberg himself mentions Helge Nelson's pioneer work *The Swedes and the Swedish Settlements in North America* (1943).[11]

In Swedish literary writing the subject is certainly only rarely found, notably in Fredrika Bremer's travelogue, *Hemmen i den nya världen* (*The Homes in the New World*, 1853–1854), and in Henning Berger's stories of emigrant life in the American city in *Där ute* (*Out There*, 1901). For an epic treatment of the theme in Scandinavia we must look to the tetralogy by the Norwegian emigrant Ole Edvart Rølvaag, *I de dage* and *Riket grunnlaegges* (translated together as *Giants in the Earth*, 1924–1925), *Peder Seier* (*Peder Victorious*, 1928), and *Den signede dag* (*Their Father's God*, 1931) which depict a pioneering family's experiences of the desolate Dakota prairie in the 1870s and the assimilation of the next generation into the American way of life. Johan Bojer, a contemporary of Rølvaag and fellow Norwegian, wrote of Norwegian settlers in America in *Vor egen stamme* (*The Emigrants*, 1924), part of a trilogy on contemporary Norwegian working people, and both Rølvaag and Bojer follow in the footsteps of Hans E. Kinck, whose *Emigranter* (*The Emigrants*, 1904), set in Norway, attempts to provide a psychological explanation of the causes of emigration. In seeking possible literary influences upon Moberg's work we cannot ignore Selma Lagerlöf's epic novel *Jerusalem* (1901–1902) which portrays a group of peasants from Dalarna in Sweden who are transformed by a religious revival and leave to settle in the Holy Land. Moberg's tetralogy possesses a similar structure and also places great stress upon a religious revival as an impetus to emigration.

Moberg's initial researches were based upon letters from American emigrants and church registers in Sweden, and he also examined the phenomenon of Åkianism, a religious movement in Småland in the 1780s. Subsequently, he investigated conditions on mid-century sailing ships and the Atlantic crossing, as well as every aspect of Swedish settlement in Minnesota and the assimilation of the Swedes into American life. Moberg visited libraries and museums in the United States and studied the diaries of emigrants and local histories, and interviewed Swedish-Americans in the mid-West and California. He spent some time at Carmel, California, where he met Gustaf Lannestock, himself a Swedish emigrant, who became his English translator,[12] and it was here beside the Pacific that he came to love that Moberg completed both *The Emigrants* in 1949 and *Unto a Good Land* in 1952.[13] His work on the series was, however, interrupted on several occasions for long periods by his involvement in controversies in Sweden. He had to seek refuge from these battles abroad, and it was not until 1954, at Laguna Beach on the Pacific Coast, that he could begin writing the third part of *The Novel about the Emigrants*, entitled *Nybyggarna (The Settlers)*. Parts were also written in Italy, France, and Sweden, and it was completed in 1956; it was originally intended to be the final part of the series, and only at a late stage did the planned trilogy become a tetralogy. The work took another three years and the novel was written in eight countries, evidence of a restlessness caused by problems in completing the series. In 1959 the final part was published as *Sista brevet till Sverige (The Last Letter to Sweden)*. The English translation has a different format. The first two volumes were published unabridged, and in 1954 *Unto a Good Land* was chosen as the Literary Guild's Book of the Month, but the American publisher then radically abridged the translation of the last two volumes into one, entitled *The Last Letter Home*, an action rightly condemned as severely weakening the overall unity of the novel.[14]

In Sweden the literary critics were almost without exception unstinting in their praise of the tetralogy, stressing in particular the interplay: of Sweden and America, the physical and the spiritual, naturalistic earthiness and subtle symbolism, highly personalized characterization and accurate documentation of mass movements. In America, too, critics lauded Moberg's epic achievement. Gerhard Alexis summarizes thus: "The merit of Moberg's work as fiction may be judged first of all by his ability to create living people."[15] Acclaim was not universal, however. A group calling themselves the "Free Band of Light" distributed an appeal in Sweden in 1950 for a "storm of protest against dirty Swedish literature in general and against *The Emigrants* in particular."[16] Moberg was attacked for depicting the forefathers of Swedish-Americans as "perverse individuals," and a second appeal talked of the work's "coarsely sexual composition." The protesters, both in Sweden and the United States, took exception to the coarse language of Ulrika, the reformed parish whore, and the ribald tales of Jonas Petter and "The American." The protest continued for several years and Moberg hit back, calling his detractors "word ferrets" and defending his choice of vocabulary on the grounds

of authenticity: "When an author who is striving for accuracy in his
depiction is to place a sentence in the mouth of a character in his
book, he asks himself: What does this character say in this environment? Which words would this person use in just this situation?"[17]
The reading public as a whole showed their support for Moberg by
buying his books by the million, and the tetralogy soon became a
record-breaking best-seller in Sweden. It was later serialized on radio
and then made into two feature-length films directed by Jan Troell in
the early 1970s and nominated for Oscars.

II   The Course of the Narrative

The Novel about the Emigrants is the story of a group of sixteen
people who in the spring of 1850 leave their homes in Ljuder parish in
Småland. They journey by wagon to the coast, by sailing ship from
Karlshamn to New York, by railway and steamer across the continent,
and eventually, on foot, arrive at Taylor Falls in Minnesota Territory
where they take land in the virgin wilderness and make their homes.
The work goes on to examine the problems the immigrants face in a
strange new land—the alien environment, homesickness, and the
new language—and traces their progress by virtue of hard work to a
position of relative prosperity. A community grows up as more of
their countrymen join them, and the series ends as the second
generation takes up the yoke from the pioneers.

In Moberg's *The Emigrants* the reasons behind the momentous
decision to leave behind their farms, friends, relatives, and the
country of their birth and to travel to an unknown continent are
explored in depth and vividly dramatized in the first section of the
novel, "Gates on the Road to America."[18] Moberg carefully analyzes
the Smålanders' motives, demonstrating the push factors and pull
factors that influence their actions. A major factor is the harsh physical environment of their home parish: working an infertile, rock-
strewn soil in a poor climate, the peasant farmers, crofters, and
squatters of Ljuder are scarcely able to eke out an existence from the
land. Subdivision of farms has resulted in tiny homesteads, barely
able to support a family, and the system of inheritance leaves the
eldest son perpetually in debt while the other sons are fated to
become landless laborers. Religious intolerance is widespread among
the representatives of state and church, and the rigid class system
allows little hope of social advancement. The New World, on the
other hand, holds out the promise of abundant fertile land on which,

with hard work, the Småland farmers should be able to improve their lot. America possesses a democratic system where men are judged not by their birth or inherited wealth but by their ability to work. A haven of religious tolerance where men may worship God as they wish, America thus appears as a Promised Land to the persecuted dissenters of Ljuder, and the possibility of a new start in life appeals to those whose reputation holds them back in the Old Country.

What little the folk from Ljuder know of America, what they have gleaned from books and newspapers, has often been distorted, and when they set out they have in mind no definite destination in the United States. Those who have farms to sell dispose of them, and they all pack their most vital belongings into old clothes chests and bags and board the brig *Charlotta* at Karlshamn in April, 1850, bound for New York. In the second part of this novel, "Peasants at Sea," Moberg depicts the group's experiences on a voyage filled with drama and danger. During the ten-week passage the peasants suffer terribly from seasickness, and scurvy claims the life of one of their number. They have cramped quarters in the hold and find it impossible to keep free from vermin. On this wearying journey they are entertained by two storytellers whose drastic and often ribald tales test their credulity but help the time to pass more quickly. Moberg now presents the thoughts of his characters in a series of inner monologues, exploring in greater depth personalities established earlier, and revealing his characters' secret fears and longings. *The Emigrants* functions both as a novel complete in itself and as an introduction to the series, and one of Moberg's main concerns is to establish his *dramatis personae*. There is little plotting in the usual sense; characters are employed to demonstrate particular aspects of emigration, and these aspects are presented through a series of dramatic scenes. At the same time the characters are developed as individuals interesting in themselves, personalities with whom the reader can easily identify. They incorporate in this way both a representative and an individual element.

The relationship between Karl Oskar and Kristina Nilsson is of central importance to the series. The couple's attitudes to life differ considerably and these differences are defined in the dialectic which they carry on throughout the series, yet their personalities complement each other in a very stable relationship. Karl Oskar is self-willed and obstinate, and an emblem of this is his prominent nose, a Nilsson family trait. His self-assurance is frequently tested, notably when the parish priest attempts to dissuade him from his decision to emigrate: "He was forced to let the minister know that he could cease his dissuasion. If the bishop himself came and helped, still he would not change his mind; if the king himself tried to persuade him he would stand fast" (I, 242).[19] Karl Oskar is ready to take the risks involved in a dangerous journey to a distant land, but his adventurous nature is offset by a great sense of responsibility, especially to his family and his brother Robert. Karl Oskar is a born leader and the obvious choice by the group of emigrants to lead them to the New World. He is a realist and yet he has a dream: having broken his plough on a rock, he catches sight of a photograph in a newspaper of a wheat field in North America; he dreams of what this could mean for his family and is convinced that his dream will be realized.

Kristina is more deeply rooted in the soil of Småland. She prefers the certainty of the little they have to the uncertain possibility of attaining prosperity. She is afraid of leaving her home parish and having to live among strangers in a foreign land; she does not possess the pioneering spirit of her husband and, whereas he comes to represent progress she stands for conservatism. Differences are also evident in their spiritual outlook. Kristina is pious in a fatalistic fashion: "Kristina came from a God-fearing home and she knew that God disposed with man as He wished, according to His unfathomable and omniscient way" (I, 35). She believes in predestination, and her God is a personal deity but as much an avenging Jehovah as a compassionate Savior. An important theme is Kristina's willingness to place her fate in God's hands, a view which contrasts with Karl Oskar's more humanist outlook. Karl Oskar trusts in God but also trusts in his own abilities to change his situation; he carries his fate and that of his family in his own hands. He thinks: "The old folks believe that everything is determined from the beginning, before we are born. Then it doesn't much matter whatever you do. . . . But I don't think like the old folks. I believe that you have to exert yourself as much as you can and try to use your head and do as well as you understand after a deal of thought" (I, 338). In one of the key scenes which form the dialectic between husband and wife, Karl Oskar finds Kristina apparently bleeding to death from scurvy aboard ship. She has already resigned herself to her fate: "Kristina believed that it was predestined that she would die here on the ship, that she would never reach America. But Karl Oskar didn't agree with that. He always thought, nothing is so definite that it cannot be altered. If you try, then you can probably change things. You have to try" (I, 487). Karl Oskar acts and Kristina survives. Throughout the tetralogy Karl Oskar's view is worldly, Kristina's otherwordly. Karl Oskar's vision is of a better life for the next generation, but Kristina sees even further, to an everlasting heavenly paradise.

In the figure of Karl Oskar's brother Robert the freedom motif in the work attains greater depth. Karl Oskar seeks freedom from the physical restrictions of Sweden while Robert seeks freedom from masters. In their Cain and Abel relationship Robert is the adventurer, the landless son. He is brutalized by a tyrannical master, quite legally, for the Servants' Law permits corporal punishment, and he determines to escape all masters. Robert is also a dreamer, but his imagination is so vivid that at times he loses contact with reality. He is the bearer of the dream of America to the others even though his reports of what he has read about the New World are often wildly exaggerated. He is the storyteller, the liar who entertains—and as such one of several projections of his creator in the work—and his friend Arvid is employed as a foil to his excesses. Arvid is Robert's willing audience, his confidant and the butt of his wit, and these two provide much of the situation comedy of the series.

Danjel Andreasson is, next to the Nilssons, the most important figure in *The Emigrants*, a prophet who leads his little flock out of captivity to a Promised Land. Danjel's role is to demonstrate the iniquity of the Swedish church law, which forbids gatherings in private dwellings for religious worship and which is used by the state and church authorities to maintain a rigid orthodoxy. In this mild peasant is reborn the teaching of the eighteenth-century revivalist Åke Svensson—"Åkianism." Danjel's primitive Christianity involves a true love of all his fellow creatures and a communal sharing of all property, but he falls foul of the authorities by distributing the sacraments to his flock. For this he is fined and imprisoned, and he emigrates to avoid further persecution and perhaps the horrible fate of his forebear Åke, who died in the asylum. The proud prophet Danjel is humbled by his apparent lack of faith aboard *Charlotta*, and his ambition to found a community in America comes to naught. Among Danjel's followers is Ulrika, the reformed parish whore, and her illegitimate daughter Elin. Ulrika is the true revolutionary spirit among the emigrants: she has most reason to hate her hypocritical "betters," and when the sheriff and priests disturb Danjel's communion gathering it is she who reacts most violently to the intrusion. In *The Emigrants* a conflict develops between Kristina and Ulrika founded upon the virtuous woman's revulsion for the whore. With uncharacteristic lack of charity Kristina refuses to believe that Ulrika has been reborn in Christ, and Ulrika in turn finds Kristina unbearably self-righteous. But on board ship Ulrika is miraculously spared the plagues of lice, sea sickness, and scurvy. She is also revealed to be a victim of a cruel society.

Jonas Petter leaves Sweden to escape a shrewish wife. Because of his experience of marriage he has become a misogynist and the tales he tells reflect this, often dwelling on woman's inhumanity to man, extending in one case to castration and in another to murder. Violence is often associated with sex in Jonas Petter's tales, while another archetypal target for his burlesque humor is the clergy. Jonas Petter is a fascinating study in psychology: he is a man who compensates for his deep personal unhappiness by entertaining others with stories that themselves reflect his own frustrations.

In "Gates on the Road to America" much of the action derives from an intention to dramatize different causes of emigration, the reasons behind individual decisions to leave. For the Nilssons the key scenes underline their uneven struggle with the elements: Karl Oskar finds rock everywhere beneath his fields; fire destroys his hay crop; he breaks his plough; his little daughter dies horribly as a result of famine. For Danjel important scenes emphasize the struggle to worship freely: his confrontation with the local priest and the forcible invasion of his peaceful communion. For Robert the decisive moment comes when he receives a terrific blow to the head from his master for his laziness.

Unto a Good Land is divided into three parts. In "Seekers of New Homes" Robert and Arvid are seen exploring New York, and the story follows the group's journey from New York to Albany by steamer, by railway—a new experience for them—and steamer to Chicago, by riverboat down the Illinois and up the Mississippi to Stillwater, and finally on foot to Taylor Falls. The journey is not without incident. Kristina and Ulrika are reconciled, Danjel's daughter dies of cholera, and Karl Oskar is attacked by robbers. The Smålanders, who are forest people, are terrified by the unending expanse of the Prairie, but in the Minnesota forests they begin to feel at home. In "The Settlement" we follow them as they go out from Taylor Falls into the wilderness to take land. Karl Oskar typically seeks farthest afield and stakes his claim by the lake with the Indian name Ki-Chi-Saga. His dream of good fertile land is realized, and the story now concentrates upon him and his family. He builds a shanty and is helped by the others to raise a log cabin. Kristina, aided by her new friend Ulrika, gives birth to a son. In "Keeping Alive over the Winter" the Nilssons experience their first mid-West winter with no crops harvested to tide them over. When they run out of bread Karl Oskar trudges some thirty miles to Stillwater for flour, gets lost in the dark, and nearly dies in the snow. In the spring the restless Robert leaves with his faithful Arvid to seek gold in California. Ulrika, now respectable, marries a baptist pastor in Stillwater.

The Settlers takes up the story three years later when other Swedes arrive to settle near to the Nilssons, who have gradually improved their farm, plowed up more land, bought beasts and even a fine ox, Starkodder. Starkodder is detined to become a sacrificial animal: trapped in a blizzard with his young son Johan, Karl Oskar is forced to slaughter the ox, placing Johan inside the still-warm carcass to save him from freezing to death. The Swedish settlers form a Lutheran congregation and build a church. But soon the religious intolerance of the Old Country reappears as the Nilssons' nearest neighbors warn them of associating with the sectarian Ulrika and are as a result thrown out of the house by Karl Oskar. Always improving, Karl Oskar builds a bigger timber-frame house; the immigrants begin to receive their own newspaper, *Hemlandet* (*The Home Country*), decide to build a school, and select a site beside the lake for their new churchyard. Robert returns a sick man from his four years of wanderings and without Arvid, and the central section of the novel, "Gold and Water," describes in a series of flashbacks in the form of inner monologue the awful fate that has befallen the two lads. They first travel down the Mississippi to St. Louis, and having reached St. Joseph set out west for California, tending the mules for a Mexican called Vallejos. But in the desert the two lads lose their way and Arvid dies after drinking water from a poisoned well. Vallejos also dies, of yellow fever, leaving Robert all his money. Robert has now lost his will to live and accompanies the "American," Fred Mattsson, to a ghost town amid the sand dunes where he becomes one of the living dead. Mattsson exchanges Robert's gold for bills, and it is these that Robert brings home to Karl Oskar, but they prove to be worthless. Robert goes off into the forest and dies beside a stream.

The story now concentrates upon Kristina. She finds it difficult to overcome her homesickness for the Old Country and her fears extend to the likelihood of another pregnancy when she has had so many. She even comes to doubt the existence of God when he does not answer her prayers. She becomes pregnant and then miscarries. But eventually she resigns herself to her fate.

National events begin to impinge upon the little community. Minnesota becomes a state and Lincoln becomes president, and *The Last*

Letter to Sweden opens with the outbreak of the Civil War. Karl
Oskar, after debating the morality of war with Kristina, volunteers,
but is rejected because of a leg injury. Kristina is also unfit: her doctor
tells her that another childbed will mean her death, but she places
her life in God's hands and becomes pregnant again. In the middle of
an Indian uprising in which Danjel and many other settlers are
massacred, Kristina dies, and Karl Oskar grows bitter at the Almighty
for taking his beloved wife from him. Ulrika also loses her spouse, and
donates a bridal crown to the church back home in Ljuder. Karl
Oskar's children grow up and take over the running of the farm when
their father is left bedridden after being struck by a falling oak tree. It
is Karl Oskar's sons who come to build the great house that he always
intended to build, while the old emigrant spends his last years
pouring over a map of Ljuder parish given him by his son-in-law,
tracing in his memory the paths he wandered as child and youth and
where he courted Kristina. Karl Oskar dies in 1890, and so the cycle
of emigration is complete with the end of a generation.

III *Narrative Technique*

What makes Moberg's novel cycle not merely a fascinating account
of early Swedish emigration but an important literary work of much
greater relevance is the way in which the themes of the work are
presented and developed by means largely of a subtle use of images.[20] Different aspects of the major theme, emigration from the
Old World to the New, are each presented in this way. The image of
the "King in his Stone Kingdom" expresses the hopelessness of Karl
Oskar's situation while the "Gates on the Road to America" represent
the social restrictions placed upon the Ljuder peasants, and in particular upon Robert, barriers that are removed one by one. The gates,
like most symbols in Moberg's work, also function as elements of the
epic reality: when the emigrants finally set off by wagon, Robert is
actually given the task of opening the gates along the road. When the
group reach North America the sudden unaccustomed freedom
frightens the emigrants. They feel lost. The possibilities before them
are as endless as the great prairie that stretches out as far as the eye
can see. No paths are charted here and they must find their own way.
The Nilssons' daughter does get lost for a while on the journey, and
when Robert and Arvid lose their way, the consequences prove fatal
for Arvid.

The symbols of family emigration are Kristina's bridal cover and the America chest. The blue cover, embroidered for the Nilssons' wedding night, is lent extra significance when it is taken into the fields at harvest time to gather up the precious fallen ears of corn. It accompanies them on *Charlotta* and attains a mystical relevance for them: "things would never go well for them if the bridal cover were not part of their new home in America" (I, 519). Whilst the cover is a sign of the bonds between Karl Oskar and Kristina, the America chest stands for the physical removal of the family from Sweden. The old clothes chest is packed with all the possessions necessary for making a new life. Fetching out the chest is for the Nilssons, as for each of the families who are to emigrate, a physical sign of their irrevocable decision, and this simple act is employed to mark the spread of the idea from household to household. Ultimately the chest comes to represent all Swedes who leave, the collective decision: "Thus dawned a new period of greatness for the old clothes chests in rural areas. After centuries of obscurity in dark corners they were scrubbed clean and made ready for their journey across the ocean" (I, 230). The chest has many uses on the way: as a desk at which Karl Oskar writes his first letter home, as an altar, and as the only piece of furniture in the Nilssons' shanty. Significantly, it changes name to the "Sweden chest" and from it Kristina unpacks Sweden in the New World. The family also use it as a dining table, and it thus stresses family unity and the impermanent life of the emigrant, being replaced at the first Christmas in Minnesota by a great oak table, a symbol of permanence.

The theme of emigration is also emphasized in other ways. Reference is made to several exodus stories in the Old Testament which provide parallels to the flight of Danjel and his disciples. In a dream the Lord appears to Danjel as he did to Abraham, saying "Get thee out of thy country and from thy kindred, and from thy father's house, unto a land that I will show thee" (I, 205; Gen. 12:1). At the burial service for Danjel's wife Inga-Lena, Danjel says: "The Lord said to you as He said to Moses: Thou shalt not go thither" (I, 510; Deut. 32:52), and when the group give thanks beneath a giant oak in the Minnesota forest, Danjel reads the words of the Lord to Joshua at the crossing of the Jordan: "Be strong and of good courage; for unto this people shalt thou divide for an inheritance the land which I sware unto their fathers to give them" (II, 262; Josh. 1:6). A further exodus story alluded to is that of Ruth, and Inga-Lena's reason for emigrating is phrased in Ruth's words to Naomi: "Whither thou goest, I will go. Where thou diest, will I die, and there will I be buried" (I, 258; Ruth

122   VILHELM MOBERG

1:16–17). The voyage across the Atlantic has parallels with the oldest
exodus story of all, that of Noah, when after many weeks without sight
of land a little bird alights on the ship "like a miracle from the Bible"
(I, 478). Danjel, who is likened to Abraham and Moses, is also
depicted as a Småland Job and given some of the features of his
biblical namesake: like his namesake he is persecuted for his beliefs
and like Job he praises the Lord in his adversity. He loses his wife and
young daughter on the journey but his faith remains unshaken.

The dominating image of the novel cycle, a developing symbol of
some subtlety and complexity, is that of the Astrakhan apple. Initially
apples are associated with Kristina's homesickness: when in New
York Karl Oskar brings her a large apple, it leads her thoughts to her
home in Dufwemåla, and during her first spring in Minnesota she
thinks of the Astrakhan apple tree at the corner of her parents' home,
and of its large juicy apples. Soon Karl Oskar writes home to his
parents: "I wonder if you could ask Kristina's parents to send us some
seeds from the Astrakhan apple at Dufwemåla, we want to plant a new
Astrakhan apple tree here in Minnesota so we can have the same sort
of apples, at home they were so fresh to eat as we well remember.
And we would then have moved something over from there. Sweden
has good apple seeds and out here there is good soil to sprout and
grow in, so with the Almighty's help there might some time be a great
tree in bloom out here" (II, 568). Clearly Karl Oskar's words may be
interpreted in a wider sense: America offers a potentially favorable
environment for the growth of sound Swedish stock, be it plants or
humans. The parallel is drawn explicitly on several occasions. The
large apples that the transplanted tree will bear are likened to children; they are as big as a child's head and have a clear transparent
skin. As the apples are like little children, it is natural that the tree
should be associated with Kristina, the mother of the coming generation: "She was closely bound to the tree, which had been moved
across to a new land and which shared her fate" (III, 602). The
parallels between Kristina and the apple tree are drawn clearly
during her last pregnancies. Weakened by her many previous child-
beds, Kristina becomes pregnant again, while at the same time the
apple tree blooms profusely. A few days later a hard frost attacks the
tree and the blossoms die. At the same time Kristina loses the child
she is carrying: "The deadly frost had that spring harried her womb
and her apple blossom" (III, 608). After this Kristina is warned of the
dangers of a further pregnancy but resigns herself and conceives,
whereupon her apple tree blooms again. Having miscarried once

more she lies dying as the apples ripen. Karl Oskar brings her one of the first ripe fruits to taste and she dies with the taste of apple on her lips. The maturing of the fruit and Kristina's death complement one another, for the growth of the apple tree mirrors her spiritual development. She overcomes her homesickness and begins to contemplate not this world but the next: for her, death is the culmination of life, her true religious maturity.

Another major major theme of the cycle, the differing outlook on life of the brothers Karl Oskar and Robert, is highlighted by means of a series of antithetical images. Robert is an adventurer and Karl Oskar a steady tiller of the soil and they have very different reasons for emigrating: for Karl Oskar, America is symbolized by a newspaper picture of a vast wheatfield, and he finds his America soon after arriving, whereas Robert seeks a different goal, a goldfield and the freedom gold can buy. The different paths are represented by the two ships, the emigrant transport *Charlotta* and the *Angelica*, which lies in New York harbor, bound for the California goldfields. Robert thinks: "*Charlotta* sounded like a farmer's wife, like a master issuing orders and like the name of a fat old woman—*Angelica* was like a delicate and beautiful girl, it rang free and tinkled like the twittering of a bird. . . . There was joy and freedom in that name" (II, 63). For Robert, one signifies masters and drudgery, the other a dream of a new life, its passengers seekers of gold and freedom. A further pair of symbols are those of gold and water. The bubbling waters of the mill stream are meaningful to Robert early in the work, representing escape to the young lad on his way to a life of service on a neighboring farm, and beside the stream he fakes his own suicide by drowning; the stream is associated with death. The dream of freedom soon becomes a dream of gold, "the yellow gold that would make him free" (III, 321), but gold is death, the California trail becomes a trail of death, and Arvid dies while Robert is dreaming of the mill stream. When Vallejos also dies, Robert realizes that he has made the wrong choice: "It was *water* that man could not be without" (III, 415). He now inherits gold but it no longer has any meaning for him. Robert dies beside a stream which he confuses with the mill stream of his youth, but the freedom it symbolizes is only attainable in death. True riches on this earth are the fruits of honest toil, of tillers like Karl Oskar, while lust for gold leads only to death. As a permanent result of his beating at the hands of his master, Robert suffers all his life from a rushing noise in his ear, a sound like that of the ocean calling him to freedom from masters. In Minnesota the ear repeats its call: "Come!

Do not stay here" (II, 342), and it eventually becomes his persecutor, perhaps his conscience. Ironically, he realizes that the ear has become a master whose persecution he can never escape, his Fate.

A further image associated with Robert is the Indian Head, a great sandstone rock face standing above the woods near Ki-Chi-Saga, that initially represents the Indians whose presence is seen as a threat by the white settlers. Typically, the two brothers react in different ways to the Indians: Karl Oskar despises them for their laziness while Robert is attracted to them—as he is to the rock—identifying with the freedom inherent in their nomadic life-style. On his return to Minnesota Robert revisits the rock and notices the changes in its appearance: the deeper furrows in its brow, the missing teeth, the dark eyes. His description of the rock puzzles his brother and sister-in-law: "They listened in puzzlement to this talk of the sandstone rock. It sounded almost as though Robert has spoken of himself. He too had furrows in his brow, young as he was, his eyes protruded, and he had lost his front teeth" (III, 352). The Indians are destined to share the same fate as that of Robert and Arvid; they are all victims of the settlement.

A feature of Moberg's presentation of scene is his use of an observer figure whose movements enliven the depiction and whose reactions involve the reader more closely in it. Robert Nilsson is the most skillfully employed observer in the novel: he is inquisitive and possesses a vivid imagination, and he frequently introduces us to new settings, as when he and Arvid inspect the *Charlotta* or explore Broadway. Moberg also on occasion shifts the viewpoint away from his main characters to emphasize by providing an objective view that these are not heroes but wholly ordinary people. This happens, for example, when they arrive at Karlshamn and are seen through the quizzical eyes of two well-dressed gentlemen: "Several genuine grey homespun peasants with their virtuous shawl-clad wives and their pale runny-nosed children, two farm lads in new clothes that were too wide and puffed out in great bags front and back—jacket and trousers carelessly tacked together by some village tailor. And whole loads of old chests, flowery bags, baskets and boxes and bundles—folk from up country off on a long voyage across the sea" (I, 286). The viewpoint is also shifted to similar effect to Captain Lorentz of the *Charlotta* and to Pastor Henry Jackson who witnesses the group's arrival at Stillwater.

The emigrants receive many new impressions on their journey, and Moberg has a gift for seeing these through their own eyes, expressing them in terms of their own limited experience. This feature appears early on, when Robert examines the hatch aboard *Charlotta* and finds it "pierced by a number of small holes, like a milk sieve" (I, 309) or is disappointed at the ship's sails which are "as dirty grey as potato sacks in a muddy field in autumn" (I, 320). Typical are the emigrants' thoughts at their first encounter with a railway locomotive: "On the steam wagon was a tall chimney, wide at the opening and narrowing downward; it sat there like a funnel stuck in the neck of a bottle. In front of the wagon was fastened an object plaited together from iron bars like a great bent scoop or shovel" (II, 91). Kristina associates the paddle-wheel of the river steamer with her household chores, watching "in fascination the spinning drive-wheel which whisked the water down there like the beater in a butter churn full of cream. When you churned butter the cream splashed in your face, and now the wheel threw water up against the side of the vessel, so that drops splashed in her eyes" (II, 138). All of the Ljuder peasants see life in biblical terms, of course, as the Bible is such an important part of their cultural background. Such allusions occur most readily to Danjel, as, for example, when the group encounters some strange trees in the Minnesota forest: "Danjel thought that they were fig trees, which were also found in the land of Caanan and which Jesus often mentioned in his parables. They stood in bloom there now, just as white as Jesus himself when he was clad in his heavenly raiments" (II, 109). This presentation as through the eyes and minds of the characters not only brings the depiction of scene to life but also provides a double perspective by setting off the Old World against the New and deepening the evocation of both.

Two features of the language of the novel, both, unfortunately, impossible to transpose into English, are Moberg's use of the dialect of his native Småland and his registering of the influence of English upon the immigrants' Swedish, the gradual development of a mixed Swedish-American dialect. Not only does he imitate the distinctive pronunciation of Småland Swedish in the dialogues between his peasant characters, but he also employs specific dialect words and forms.[21] Of the forty or so indisputable dialectisms found in *The Emigrants* several occur frequently and are consciously placed in an unmistakable context, Moberg's aim being to reintroduce these long-vanished words into modern Swedish. Of these forty words, half are found not as one might expect in the speech and thoughts of the characters but in author narrative, an indication of the closeness of the author to the world he depicts. Dialectisms serve to locate the characters firmly in one specific region, thus supporting the realism, but they also help to mark a social distinction, for the peasants speak broad dialect while their masters, temporal and spiritual, employ standard Swedish. The admixture of English words in immigrant Swedish is a well documented phenomenon, and is found in the novel first in Ulrika's language—she marries an American—and then in Robert's and Karl Oskar's, where it can be traced as a growing influence in the eight letters to Sweden sent over the years. The accuracy of Moberg's Swedish-American was the subject of a debate in the press following publication of the later novels of the series.[22]

A marked stylistic feature is the rhythm of Moberg's prose, which often has a dignity all of its own. The rhythms are the result of a number of features including phrase-pairs like "cooped up in pens and shut up in stalls" (II, 248), sometimes alliterating as in "untouched and unmarked by edged tool or axe" (II, 250) and various kinds of parallelism involving the repetition and development of the basic idea, as in: "But nowhere did they catch sight of a tilled field, nowhere was seen a furrow dug, nowhere did they see a space cleared for building a house" (II, 253). The constant use of these stylistic features not only imparts a definite rhythm but also slows the tempo of the narrative. It reveals an analytical mood, a striving for clarity and fullness of expression. In the following example the progression from idea to idea is quite clearly seen: "It was the most courageous who left first. It was the enterprising who took the decision. It was the unafraid who first set off on the forbidding voyage across the great ocean. It was the bold and discontented who could not reconcile themselves to their lot at home who became the first emigrants in their district" (I, 6). One critic has counted over two hundred cases of parallelism in *Unto a Good Land* alone, and it seems likely that the Old Testament has provided the major stylistic model, though word-pairs are also common in the medieval Swedish laws, whose style Moberg so admired.[23]

While engaged on his researches on emigration for the novel Moberg wrote: "I have the ambition that in all important respects my depiction shall be accurate. It is not the comments of the literary critics that I am afraid of. . . . It is for my own sake that I want it to be as accurate as possible."[24] Moberg's researches were deep and painstaking, and he drew upon a large number of different sources, not all of which are listed in the bibliography provided at the end of *The Last Letter to Sweden*. A large collection of books, notes, and early drafts was donated to the Emigrant Museum at Växjö. His material was of many types: not only books, newspaper articles, manuscripts, diaries, letters, minutes, church records, maps, and brochures, but also the testimony of the descendants of emigrants in America.[25] Moberg even incorporated some of his own experiences in the novels: he was himself trapped in a blizzard and feared for his life as does Karl Oskar in *The Settlers*.[26] His aim in employing so much historically accurate detail is to create the illusion of historical authenticity so that the fictitious elements also appear to be real. A startling example of this blend of fact and pseudofact comes in the "documentary" introduction to *The Emigrants* in which the population of Ljuder parish (which does exist) is categorized down to the last "idiot" and "half-idiot" while, in fact, the population statistics provided have no basis in reality.[27]

Åkianism was a historical phenomenon, a religious revival led by Åke Svensson in Älmeboda parish in Småland in the 1780s. The Åkians held all property in common, believed that the priesthood was of the devil and that a marriage was not valid unless both parties were spiritually reborn. The sect fell foul of the authorities, and eventually eight Åkians were declared insane and sent to Danvik asylum in Stockholm where Åke Svensson died in 1788. With that the movement was crushed. Åkianism did *not* reappear in the 1840s, and the narrator's words are here deliberately ambiguous: "But in the 1840s this dangerous heresy reappeared in Ljuder parish: the events belong, however, to the story" (I, 15). The reappearance is part of the fiction. Like all the major characters, Danjel is a fictional creation, but many of his beliefs are those of the original Åkians, and his interrogation by the priests is closely based on the questions asked of the Åkians and recorded at the time and later published in *Handlingar rörande Åkianismen* (*Documents concerning Åkianism*, 1867), for example: "What is conscience? No one answered this, but they said: When one is reborn, then will he know what conscience is" (*Handlingar*, 28); "Asked Dean B.: Can you tell me: What is conscience? Answered Danjel A.: He who is reborn will know what conscience is" (*The Emigrants*, 116).[28] Danjel's belief that his disciples· will be spared seasickness and will miraculously receive the gift of tongues and speak English on arrival was that of another prophet, Erik Janson, who emigrated in 1846 and was later followed by a large group from Hälsingland to found a community at Bishop Hill, Illinois.[29] Janson is also mentioned in *Unto a Good Land* where the emigrants' guide is a former member of the sect.

In researching the sailing ships of the period Moberg conducted a

long correspondence with Captain Olof Traung of the Gothenburg
Maritime Museum; the *Charlotta* herself is based on the model of a
brig *Tre Kronor* in the museum. Moberg's questions concerned the
captain's and crew's quarters, lighting, ventilation, and sanitation
aboard ship, and a number of Traung's replies are inserted almost
verbatim in the novel; the details of sails that Robert learns from the
sailmaker are an example (I, 386). The origin of one important motif
illuminates Moberg's method. In a letter Traung depicted the burial
service at sea: the flag at half mast and the three shovelfuls of earth
cast onto the body wrapped in sailcloth which is then slipped over the
side. Moberg wrote back: "Was it the case, then, that the vessel
carried soil from land only for this purpose? Did they assume there
would be deaths on every voyage and therefore take earth along for
burial purposes?"[30] What Moberg wanted to know was not whether
ships' captains *always* carried earth aboard for burials, but whether a
particularly enterprising captain *may* have carried it. In another
letter to Traung he wrote: "Now an author should not depict what *has*
actually happened, as he is a fabulist and should depict what *could*
have happened. . . . The main thing is that he makes the story
credible."[31] This is the difference between history and the historical
novel. The detail of the earth from Sweden grew into the poignant
scene at the funeral of Inga-Lena (I, 508ff.).

Sometimes Moberg's sources are themselves presented directly in
the narrative. This is so with Robert's books on natural history and on
North America from which he so often quotes passages to astound his
fellow emigrants. His English language books are given fictional
titles, however, although they too have models in reality.[32] A historical figure who is mentioned in *Unto a Good Land* is the Swedish
pastor in Chicago, Gustaf Unonius, whose *Minnen* (*Memoirs*, 1862)
furnish several details for the narrative. These include the replace-
ment of the America chest with an oak table to eat from at the first
Christmas at Ki-Chi-Saga (II, 448), and the profound impression
made on the lonely settlers by the sound of an axe in their vicinity (III,
13f.), a sign that they would soon have neighbors in the wilderness.[33]
The priests at Chisago Lake are fictional characters, however, though
the life of Erland Törner (his surname is symbolic: "törne" means
"thorn") is based on that of Erland Carlsson who founded the first
church there in 1854.[34]

A major source of information on the life of the Swedish pioneers in
Minnesota was the diary kept by Andrew Peterson from 1854 to his
death in 1898. Peterson was born in 1818 and emigrated from Öster-

götland in 1850 to settle at Waconia in Carver County, Minnesota, and Moberg was deeply impressed by his abilities and achievements:

Peterson makes a timber house and furniture, builds fireplaces and slaughters animals; he is shoemaker, wagonmaker, roofer, fruitgrower, syrupmaker, wine cultivator, and goodness knows what else. . . . The family grows, but at the same time we can follow increases in the numbers of livestock in cowshed and pigsty. . . . Births and deaths among men and beasts, burials, weddings, church services, purchases, sales, trips to town, covering of animals, slaughtering, plowing, threshing, rain, thunderstorm, storms, snowfall—all this is part of life in the colony in Minnesota's virgin territory. . . . Peterson improves steadily but surely on his farm. Year after year the cultivated area is increased as new ground is broken and ever fatter and heavier pigs are driven to the pork market in St. Paul. The black loam soil of Minnesota gives grand harvests. The harvest yields, which he carefully notes down each autumn after threshing, clearly mirror a growing prosperity.[35]

Here we see the basis for Karl Oskar's progress at Nya Dufwemåla, and Peterson's diary also furnished Moberg with numerous details and examples of Swedish-American dialect for the narrative. In his entry for April 26, 1859, Peterson notes that he has planted apple pips, and this is one basis for the apple motif. Another is a letter from John Nelson of Parker Prairie on July 4, 1869, to his wife in Moshultamåla (Moberg's birthplace) asking her to bring with her to America "fruit seeds of as many different kinds as you can possibly get hold of." Moberg has annotated this extract with the words: "Excellent symbol to pursue: Fruit trees grow in Minnesota which come as seeds from Moshultamåla to America. Grow up into great apple trees which symbolize the move to America."[36] On November 2, 1860, Andrew Peterson writes: "Worked on a coffin until 2 o'clock at night." In the novel Karl Oskar makes three coffins, for his daughter, brother and wife. On March 30, 1881, Peterson writes: "We drove logs etc.—but I hurt my back in lifting so I could scarce walk home," and next day: "am lying in bed with a painful back."[37] It is a back injury, but from a falling oak, that leaves Karl Oskar bedridden at the end of his life.

The Swedish language newspaper *Hemlandet*, from Galesburg, Illinois, figures prominently in the last two parts of the work but also provided two important features of Robert's California trail narrative. In issue after issue of the paper from 1855 on there are appeals from people seeking lost relatives in the same way that the Nilssons advertise for news of the missing Robert (III, 228). The Indiana State

Bank, which Karl Oskar cannot find among the lists in *Hemlandet* of banks issuing worthless notes, was actually to be found there in issue No. 20 of 1856.[38]

The least successful incorporation of documentary material comes toward the end of the series, in the depiction of the Civil War and the Indian War. Despite Moberg's attempts to involve the protagonists, as when Karl Oskar volunteers for the army or Danjel dies in the Indian rising, these major upheavals stand apart from the main line of the narrative and are somewhat programmatic. Occasionally errors also creep in, the most startling of which is Moberg's location of a desert in Missouri—but on the rare occasions where Moberg deliberately departs from the historical reality it is in the interests of the narrative. At the time when the Smålanders first trek through the forest wilderness from Stillwater to Taylor Falls there was in reality a road between these places and a small township called Marine Mills,[39] but, in his desire to stress the idyllic nature of this virgin forest Moberg conveniently forgets this, and the result is a masterly depiction of the scenery of this Garden of Eden, a land of milk and honey to which the children of Sweden have been led, and where they duly give thanks to the Lord for a safe deliverance (II, 248ff.).

In the emigrant tetralogy Moberg handles a vast material which spans two continents, encompasses an epic journey and a time period of some forty-five years, as well as great movements of people. The narrative also involves a large number of characters, and initially at least takes on the form of a collective novel, a pattern abandoned already in *Unto a Good Land* as unworkable. Yet Moberg is able to dispose his material with such skill that amid the welter of detailed observation the main lines are always drawn clearly. Indeed, they are sometimes made a little too clear: the narrative becomes too didactic, for example, in the summary Moberg provides in *The Emigrants* of the Ljuder peasants' reasons for leaving their homeland (I, 258). In this first part particularly it is obvious that Moberg has a thesis or several theses that he wishes to demonstrate dramatically. One of a number of devices employed to help the reader orientate himself and to provide recapitulation is the nine letters written home to Sweden by Karl Oskar which are presented in full in the novel. These inform the folk back home of the amounts of the Nilssons' harvests, the numbers of their animals, the growing family, but also outline the developing community with the appointment of schoolmaster and priest, the arrival of the railroad in Minnesota as well as mentioning the major upheavals like the end of the Civil War and death of

Lincoln. The letters reveal Karl Oskar's growing use of Anglicisms and his peasant's predilection for understatement: the dangers, heartbreaks, and hardships are glossed over in a few words, and his account makes a fascinating contrast to the depiction of the events found elsewhere in the narrative.

The narrative is always changing, always absorbing in some new way. For example, Moberg varies the tempo: while there is great concentration upon the years 1851–1853 and 1861–1862, in the later period to 1890 there are gaps in the chronology and the events are more selective. Robert's California trail narrative is presented in a series of flashbacks resulting in a kind of counterpoint in which events on the trail become significant in Minnesota. The flow of the story is also broken by the insertion of a number of tales which at first sight may appear digressive and certainly reflect Moberg's desire to entertain his readers, but actually serve a number of functions. The thirteen tales are all found in situations where a good yarn would naturally be called for, in particular at the mill and aboard ship when the Ljuder peasants have nothing to do and the tales emphasize the slowness of time passing. They also provide further insight into the storyteller's rural culture and sometimes into his personality. The "American's" tales on *Charlotta* underline the emigrants' gullibility and prefigure the later episode when he tricks Robert out of his money, while Jonas Petter's tale of two lonely people is thinly disguised autobiography (III, 128ff.).

One of the fascinations of the tetralogy is the changing scene, from Old World to New, from New York to Minnesota, from Minnesota to Kansas. Moberg depicts a microcosm in which the small group is largely seen from within, but then is suddenly shown to represent millions of emigrants. The depiction shifts from a close-up portrayal of one settlement in the Minnesota backwoods to the broad panorama of the thousands of goldseekers off to California overland. Just as varied is Moberg's stylistic range, which covers a spectrum from harsh realism to sensitive lyricism. In just one section of *The Emigrants* we find both a stomach-turning scene in which Robert is nauseated by the seasickness of his fellow passengers below decks and the incident of the little bird which visits the ship, a biblical symbol of hope which sets the imagination of the characters alight. The novel is given a framework based on several archetypes: the journey itself is an organizing principle, familiar from the Bible and from Homer. The settlers make a life out of nothing with only their bare hands and an ingenuity evoked with the freshness of Defoe's *Robinson Crusoe*

(1719), and they make good, fulfilling the American dream; with few exceptions the pioneers make successful American citizens. Another structural feature of the work is the way in which the lives of some of the major characters describe a full circle: Robert returns to the mill stream to die, Kristina to the swing of her childhood, and Karl Oskar to Ljuder with the help of the map which is his faithful companion in his declining years.

IV   A Time on Earth

"After the emigrant novel was completed I was overcome by a great weariness, [writes Moberg] a weariness that only increased and that finally became an unendurable torment. There were times when I longed for death, which seemed to me to be the only possible deliverance. . . . The weariness could only be remedied in one way: through work. The emptiness I felt after the novel could only be fulfilled by a new project."[40] Of the strange inspiration for this new project, which grew into the novel *A Time on Earth* (1962), Moberg is later quoted as saying:

I had not been able to write anything for six months, and then I began quite suddenly one Sunday by writing a whole chapter. Some weeks earlier I had begun to think of my dead brother. My brother died when I was only eleven years old. . . . And then after all these years it was as if my brother had come back to me. I had difficulty sleeping at night; I lay thinking about him, that he had been forgotten by everyone else on earth. . . . Only in my memory did he still have life, and I felt as if he feared losing this. So I began to write, entirely without any plan. It is the only book that has come about in this way. . . . When I came to the end I felt enormously relieved.[41]

A Time on Earth is a deeply personal work in which there is a high degree of identification between author and first-person narrator. The narrator and main character is Albert Carlson, an aging Swedish emigrant living out the remainder of his days in a hotel room in a small town on the Pacific coast of California. In the midst of the Cuba Crisis of 1962, when the world teeters on the brink of a nuclear holocaust, Albert's thoughts turn to another and very different crisis, a personal tragedy which befell him some fifty years before at his childhood home in Småland—the death of his elder brother Sigfrid. The two situations are closely linked, for Sigfrid, it emerges, is a victim of militarism: he joins the army, contracts a disease, and returns home to die.

The plot centers upon Albert's search for understanding of the full circumstances surrounding his brother's death, and a search for understanding about his own life, for Albert is the unsuccessful emigrant, a close cousin to Robert Nilsson. He is a man who has failed to realize his dream of a better life and who—like Knut Toring—finds it impossible to return to the world of his youth as this world no longer exists except in his memory. The plot begins with the central incident, the scene etched in Albert's memory of his brother's deathbed in July, 1912, and proceeds via Albert's unraveling of the mystery, presented in a series of flashbacks. To begin with, Albert offers only a brief explanation: Sigfrid goes off to his barracks but returns a few months later ill. A subsequent scene, set in 1911, reveals how Sigfrid was encouraged to enlist by his father and an uncle, Corporal Nyström, and how he signs a three-year contract. Sigfrid has misgivings about the weapon training but is seduced by the offer of a free education. Shortly after Sigfrid's death, Albert's mother tells him that Sigfrid had contracted a kidney disease and fallen ill after an exercise at camp, but this does not satisfy Albert. He later finds Sigfrid's army manual in which his brother had written: "But why must I die, I who so dearly want to live?" (181). Albert feels he owes Sigfrid an answer to this question. Sigfrid hated killing, and Albert remembers when they went hunting together and shot a woodcock. The bird was only wounded and went to ground and the boys searched for it all night without success. Sigfrid never went hunting again, and Albert later discovered his gun rusting on a pile of scrap.

Twenty years are to pass after his brother's death before Albert learns the truth. He has in the meanwhile emigrated to America and is home on a visit when he meets Corporal Nyström's son, a man who served in Sigfrid's regiment. He tells Albert that on a night march Sigfrid refused to obey orders and lay down in a snow drift in the freezing cold. Soon afterward he was admitted to the hospital with damaged kidneys. Nyström discovered that Sigfrid hated handling weapons: at the firing range the cardboard figures seemed to come alive for him, and during bayonet practice he had fallen ill. Albert is deeply moved by what he learns and addresses these words to his dead brother: "You wanted to escape the service of Death—which is why you had to sacrifice your life. . . . You wanted so much to live—which is why you had to die" (270).

The search for the truth about Sigfrid is only one thread in this fascinatingly rich weave, and is linked to a number of other themes. A parallel to Sigfrid's story is that of Jesus-Jensen in the California of

1962. Jesus-Jensen's aim in life is the abolition of the motor car and
cessation of all road traffic. He too wages a war against death: "He
wished to protect and keep human life on earth. By its very transience
our existence gained its unfathomable greatness, but we had not yet
learned to value and love it" (99). Death is the great enemy, whether
it be death in war or death on the highway, and the message is
presented by a madman who is sane in the context of the insanity all
around him: the slaughter on the highways and the threat of nuclear
war represented by the warplanes thundering overhead. In Carlson's
nightmare of Jesus-Jensen's crucifixion Moberg draws the parallel
most clearly with the inherent meaning in the death of Christ and also
of Sigfrid.

The transience and fragility of human life are emphasized strongly
in the American setting of the novel. Like his creator, Albert Carlson
pursues a rootless existence, sitting in his hotel room listening to the
sounds of the vehicles on the highway by day and the waves of the
ocean at night: "I am a guest in a hotel, situated between the street
and the ocean. I live between a human creation and a timeless
element, registered from birth as a temporary phenomenon on earth.
Between the ephemeral and the eternal I have my home" (6). But this
will not always be so: some time the ocean will again be alone through
night and day. Albert feels that he has been washed up out of the
boundless waters and that he waits for the only thing left to him: "That
this same ocean which has brought me here shall take me back again,
shall wash me from my little strip of land and in its deep grant me
eternal sleep" (8–9). For Moberg the ocean is not merely a representation of eternity, however. It is also seen as a positive force in
creation. Carlson feels—as did Moberg during his periods in California—that his strength is renewed by contact with the Pacific. But
death is also an ever-present reality: while bathing he is struck by
great breakers and nearly dragged to his death. The precarious nature
of life and the insecure future of mankind itself is underlined in part
by the location in time during the Cuba Crisis but also by the physical
location in an area prone to earthquakes. The earth trembles beneath
Carlson's feet and outside the traffic roars past on the highways that
are battlefields strewn with victims. Meanwhile Carlson waits for the
great wave that will sweep him away. The sea transcends life and
death, goodness and evil, pleasure and pain, and individual existence, and Albert Carlson will soon return to the sea: "Just behind me
comes the water and fills up the holes left by my feet in the sand"
(200).

A Time on Earth may be seen as a sequel to the emigrant tetralogy a hundred years on, and Albert Carlson displays similarities with the attitudes of characters in the tetralogy, notably those of Robert and Kristina. Like Robert, Albert is a dreamer who cannot get on in the practical world. He is a failed businessman who wanted to become a historian and a man who has also failed in his personal relationships. Like Kristina, Albert feels homeless and comes to view his childhood home in Sweden as a lost paradise, building up a picture in his mind of an ideal world which does not change. He is able to return to Sweden but cannot find his dreamworld in reality. There is no return for the emigrant, just as there is no going back to childhood for the middle-aged. But the study of a man's declining years is not as harsh as in the earlier *The Clenched Hands* nor as in the picture of Karl Oskar in old age. Albert comes to a state of tranquil resignation in the face of extinction, fearing only the "Before": "Before I am back where I was previously. Before I again become unreachable. Before everything is over and transformed and has become what yesterday is today" (213).

Structurally the novel shows a development of the experimentation with time-shift technique seen in *The Settlers*, only in this work the entire narrative is based on alternations back and forth in time, revealing the story in short sweeps as if by the light of a swinging lamp. Many of the scenes from Albert's past center upon the death of Sigfrid in 1912; and the "present"—five months in 1962—from which Albert narrates his story forms the other focal point; but the story also covers in brief glimpses Albert's childhood and emigration and his life in the United States. Perhaps surprisingly, the authority of the first-person narrator is alone sufficient to create an infinitely flexible present in the work: present is where the narrator happens to be, and Albert's retelling of the past takes on the illusions of the events in real time, an illusion aided by the limitations placed on the narrator's knowledge and the use of the convention of total recall. The implications for the fiction of temporal displacement are here quite complex, and the result is again a kind of counterpoint, a pattern of association of ideas from past to present both on a personal level for Albert and on a structural level, as themes are also related in this way. The temporal displacement blurs the distinction between time present and time past and draws the whole together so that, paradoxically, time ceases to have any great significance.

A Time on Earth is primarily a moving personal document. In some ways it is a statement of belief, in others a confession, and it bears the stamp of a leave-taking and testament.

CHAPTER 8

History and Allegory

I "Something Is Rotten in the State of Sweden"

IN the early 1950s several different areas of Swedish national life were shaken by a series of legal cases which brought to light a sorry state of corruption and the misuse of authority. Moberg interrupted work on the emigrant tetralogy to throw himself into the rough and tumble of public affairs much as he had done at the beginning of the war, taking on the legal and political establishments in order, as he saw it, to defend the civil liberties of the individual in a struggle for true equality before the law. The story that emerges from these cases reads more like a piece of outrageous fiction than a well-documented sequence of events, and it is necessary to be aware of the facts of several of the cases involved—Kejne, Haijby, and Unman-Lundkvist—in order to appreciate Moberg's oblique references to them in his literary works of this period. The following account of these three cases is *based largely on Moberg's own version* in various pamphlets and articles and, where possible, verified from more objective sources.

Pastor Kejne worked at a mission in Stockholm, and in 1948–1949 he reported a pastor M. to the police for illegal homosexual activities involving minors. The police took no action against M., and instead attempted to incriminate Kejne himself. In September, 1950, they sent a young homosexual to his flat ostensibly to recover a knife he claimed to have left there on a previous visit; this is the so-called "clasp-knife trap." Luckily Kejne was entertaining the editor of *Stockholms Tidningen* at the time. Kejne was subsequently further intimidated: he was threatened with incarceration in a mental hospital and two attempts were made on his life, one by mercury poisoning. M. was eventually convicted and imprisoned for his crimes, including the slander of Kejne. Also involved was Nils Quensel, minister for the church and education, whose name figured in con-

136

nection with that of a young decorator, Hans Wallenstrand, who had been found dead in mysterious circumstances in a fire-gutted flat in Krukmakaregatan, Stockholm, on New Year's Night 1936–1937. It emerged that Quensel's name had been removed from a report into this incident. Moberg investigated the case and its consequences, and published his findings in the pamphlet *The Krukmakaregatan Case* (1951). Merely for publishing a review of this booklet, the editor of *Arbetaren* was sent to jail for a month for libeling Quensel. When a commission eventually investigated the Kejne case, it discovered that Quensel had been blackmailed for sixteen years while the police did nothing, and further that the chief of police in Stockholm had perjured himself on seven occasions in his testimony. Quensel resigned from office in October, 1951.

The Haijby affair began as far back as 1936, when Curt Haijby's wife sued him for divorce on the grounds of his "infidelity with His Majesty King Gustav V."[1] In order to prevent a scandal, officials of the royal court paid Mrs Haijby three thousand dollars to change her story. Haijby himself was packed off to America, but because the money he had been promised on arrival did not materialize, he soon returned to Sweden, receiving six thousand dollars from the court with which to furnish a 24-room castle. In November, 1938, Haijby was arrested for an alleged indecent assault on two minors. No charge was brought, but he was interned against his will for two months in Beckomberga Mental Hospital. In December, 1938, he "emigrated" to Germany. From his return in 1940 regular payments were made to him through the good offices of the chief of the Stockholm criminal police, Alvar Zetterquist. Estimates of the total payments made to him by the court range from fifty thousand to two hundred thousand dollars. In 1941 Haijby published a *roman à clef* about his alleged relationship with the king, but nearly all copies of the book were bought by the police. Having failed earlier to prosecute Haijby for "consitutional reasons," the police finally brought a prosecution in 1952—two years after the death of Gustav V—and Haijby was sentenced to six years imprisonment for blackmail. No charges resulted from the deprivation of Haijby's civil liberties or the cover-up, but Alvar Zetterquist was forced to resign. Curt Haijby killed himself in August, 1965.

During his investigation into the Haijby case Moberg was allowed to examine some documents at the Justice Department which proved that, at the time Haijby planned to bring out his book, the Stockholm police chief had suggested that he be discredited by confinement in a mental hospital. Haijby was later examined by psychiatrists who found no trace of mental illness. Moberg also discovered that in the late 1930s an officer of the Gestapo had enquired of the Swedish police whether he might help by incarcerating Haijby in a concentration camp. Moberg smuggled these documents out of the Department and photocopied them, an offense which he announced unrepentantly and for which he was prosecuted and fined.

Judge Folke Lundquist, who sat on the Stockholm bench, was on numerous occasions from 1931 onward reported to the ombudsman for embezzling funds entrusted to his care. He was first prosecuted in 1951. While administering the fortune of a ward of court, the artist Gustaf Unman, Lundquist had embezzled two hundred and fifty thousand dollars. Three men, including Unman, who had accused Lundquist of embezzlement, had all been forcibly detained in mental hospitals. The editor of *Arbetaren* served two months in prison and paid a large fine for libeling Lundquist before the judge was finally brought to book and sent to prison for a long term. As a result of this case the ombudsman resigned.

Moberg has provided detailed accounts of these and several other cases in the pamphlets *On Being Vigilant of the Authorities* (1953) and *The Conspiracies* (1956), and the cases form the background to the drama *The Judge* (1957) [2] and the novel *The Ancient Kingdom* (1953). The setting of this novel is Idyllia, "like our own country an old monarchy with a democratic system, a stable government, and an aged monarch. The two countries thus have a great deal in common" (14). Moberg's satirical technique is familiar from Swift, although Moberg's Gulliver-figure is a Swedish bureaucrat called Per Urban Secretessius who is on a fact-finding visit to the ancient kingdom to study its laws and institutions. The title of the work alludes to Strindberg's caustic satire *Det nya riket* (*The New Kingdom*, 1882).

Secretessius soon learns the darkest state secret in Idyllia, that the king prefers boys to girls. This may have dire consequences as the king is loved and emulated by all, and Secretessius's host fears that, should this become public knowledge: "Our people would cease to reproduce. They would gradually die out" (81). The effects of the secret upon the legal code of the country are significant. Blackmail is no longer a crime in Idyllia, and blackmailers are paid regular sums each month by the police. Unfortunately, catastrophe looms when Benjamin Crimson, a former friend of the king, demands to be tried for blackmail in open court. Crimson's literary works have already been purchased by the court: "The idea was only to provide economic support for the author by guaranteeing the sale of a first edition so that he would then have no need to publish any further editions" (100). Crimson has twice been deported from the kingdom and twice been interned in mental hospitals. Disaster is averted, however, by buying him off: he is elected to the Academy of Letters for his literary achievements.

There are other motifs in the novel that would have been familiar to newspaper readers of the early 1950s. In an interview with the head of the National Criminal Bureau Secretessius discovers that most crime is on the decrease in Idyllia, with a single notable exception— the libel of public servants: "The more official posts that were created, the more officials there were to libel and abuse" (50). Many of those guilty of libeling officials, and thus undermining public confidence in the administration, are writers and journalists. Crime is rapidly becoming intellectualized in Idyllia, and in order to deter the criminal there is promulgated a "Law of Protection Against Unauthorized Intrusion into the Authorities' Internal Measures," commonly known as the "Scandal Protection Law." Secretessius also reads in the newspaper of a judge, Edvard Cunning, who has been reported for embezzlement and perjury. Idyllia's ombudsman informs Secretessius that there have been hundreds of complaints against Cunning, but fifteen of his colleagues on the bench have given him character references as being honest, good-hearted, and helpful. The ombudsman adds: "These are well-founded judgments—these people know what they are talking about—Cunning has, you see, helped them all with loans" (132). And anyway, "In a number of cases mental illness has been diagnosed in the complainants or their families" (130). Mental instability is also prevalent among witnesses on behalf of Pastor Galli, who has reported a Pastor Holden for indecent behavior. Galli has produced five witnesses, but two are civil servants and are thus sworn to secrecy, two are on parole and may be rearrested with ease, and the fifth will be detained in a mental institution. Accusations have also been made against the minister for religion, and Secretessius asks his mentor, Ciceronius, whether there are any documents in the archives that might harm highly placed figures: "There *have* been, one should say, explained Doctor Ciceronius" (146).

Strindberg seems to have been an influence in the satire of state bureaucracy in this novel. Where in *The Red Room* Strindberg depicts a "Department for the Payment of Civil Servants' Salaries," Moberg evokes the horrors of a "Department for Reporting on the

Authorities' Reports." But Moberg's narrator is rather different from
Strindberg's Arvid Falk. Secretessius is more like Lemuel Gulliver,
an innocent abroad who sees only good everywhere. Idyllia is the best
of all possible worlds and our guide consequently a highly unreliable
narrator. Moberg exploits the narrative irony provided by Secretessius's innocent explanations of what is plainly a corrupt political
system. The satire derives not only from the revelations of corruption
in high places but also from the reactions of a gullible Swedish
bureaucrat. Surprisingly, many of the apparently fantastic incidents
in the novel are, as shown above, closely based on real events. Rarely
does Moberg need to exaggerate for ironic effect. Nevertheless, *The
Ancient Kingdom* is a transient work, relating to very specific events
now forgotten by the public. In order to succeed an allegory must
create an autonomous fictional world, but in this case the literal plane
of the allegory alone fails to hold our interest. What is left when the
work is shorn of its allusive elements is very limited.

II Land of Traitors

The Ancient Kingdom is a modern allegory in which many of the
characters and events possess clearly identifiable analogues in contemporary Sweden, a pattern similar to that found in *Ride This Night!*
In Moberg's last novel, *Land of Traitors* (1967), while it is possible to
find allusions to the contemporary scene, the characters and events
are essentially archetypal, and the message a timeless one.

The story is set in Värend during a dark period of its history, the
unsettled early years of King Gustav Vasa's reign in the 1520s.
Throughout the Middle Ages—in fact, from 1054 to 1658—the southern boundary of Värend also formed part of the frontier of Sweden,
bordering the Danish province of Blekinge, and as a result the border
country became a battleground whenever the two realms were at
war:

The frontier between the kingdoms in places passed right through villages,
and separated adjacent farms, thereby dividing people who were of the same
stock and family. But no boundary could eradicate their fellowship, the
relationship and friendship between them. . . . Between them a frontier had
been drawn which they had not asked for, which had been marked out against
their will by those in power. And they continued to associate across it; as
before they intermarried, traded, bought and sold cattle, bartered goods and
services. . . . Officially the people were either Swedes or Danes, but these
were labels imposed from outside. In their own eyes the border people

remained the same as they had always been down the milennia. . . . But at
the outbreak of every war before 1658 the border peasantry were turned into
enemies.[3]

In the fifteenth century the struggles within the Nordic Union (begun
in 1397) threatened the border community and the trade—especially
the export of livestock and import of salt—via the Danish port of
Ronneby in Blekinge. During periods of actual hostilities between
their countries the men on either side of the border therefore met to
negotiate separate peace treaties or "peasant peaces," and continued
to associate freely. Most of these treaties were agreed between the
men of Småland and the men of Blekinge at Furs bro, an ancient
bridge crossing the river Lyckeby whose course for six hundred years
marked the boundary between the two countries and between Vissefjärda parish in Sweden and Fridlevstad in Denmark. On this neutral
ground the peasantry met and swore not to follow their masters to
harry across the border, undertaking also to forewarn their neighbors
on the other side of impending attack. The original documents of
several such peace treaties are preserved to this day.[4]

As a punishment for the peasants' disobedience to the Swedish
crown, King Gustav Vasa (1523–1560) sent soldiers on several occasions to ravage the border country. The causes of unrest were not only
economic and political, however. The Protestant Reformation was
also a major factor, for the people of Värend held to the old religion
and resisted attempts to introduce Lutheran teachings. The king had
several times ordered the plundering of parish churches of their
precious metals, and one such desecration, in 1541, sparked off the
Dacke Rising in Småland, which came close to costing Vasa his
throne. Nils Dacke's aims were the restoration of the Catholic Mass
and the Ronneby trade. After the rising was crushed the area was
again laid waste by the king's troops.

Land of Traitors follows the events of one short period during this
time of troubles, the years around the peasant peace of 1522, and
traces the fate of a group of people who live along the border. Bengt
Sibbesson from the Swedish side marries a girl from the south,
Gertrud, and the couple have a daughter, Ingela. Mårten from the
Danish side chooses his wife from the north, and they have a son,
Lasse. Lasse develops into a giant of a man and causes his parents
much pain and heartbreak. After raping a young girl, he runs off to
join the army as a mercenary. As a young maid, Ingela tends the herds
by the Red Stone, the boundary marker in the stream that separates
the two kingdoms. There she dreams of the handsome bridegrooom

who will one day come to claim her. Lasse meanwhile fights with the
Danish army, and plunders, kills, and rapes prisoners. He is captured
by German troops fighting with the Swedes and is forced to swear
allegiance to a new banner. At home his parents await the return of
their prodigal son, prepared to kill the fatted calf. Over the years of
waiting the calf grows into a great ox.

The other important figures in the novel are clerics, natural leaders
of the local community. Pastor Nikolaus Brodde of Vissefjärda struggles valiantly to reject this earthly life and the temptations of the
flesh. In one of the most gripping scenes in the novel, Brodde
discusses his asceticism with his old friend, the Franciscan friar
Jakob, who possesses a more worldly outlook. The priest is moved to
confess to the monk his moment of weakness when, years before, he
had been seduced by one of his parishioners. For all of them he is a
spiritual father but for one, the shepherdess Ingela, he is also a
physical father.

When Brodde receives Gustav Vasa's command to urge the people
to take arms against the Danes, he burns the letter and with his
colleague, the pastor of Fridlevstad, summons the people to a meeting at Furs bro. Here, in August, 1522, they swear to maintain the
peace as hitherto and to defy their masters. But soon comes news that
German mercenaries are about to cross from the north to attack
Denmark, and Brodde and Bengt Sibbesson light the warning fire to
alarm the southern parishes and give their people time to escape into
the safety of the forests. The mercenaries leave these parishes in
ashes, and a strict guard is placed on the frontier. When Bengt and
Mårten are discovered by border guards while attempting to smuggle
an ox across the river at night, Mårten is killed by an arrow and Bengt
hauled off to a dungeon.

Lasse eventually returns home, having deserted from the army.
The ox is sold and his mother gives him the symbolic thirty pieces of
silver which she obtained for it, whereupon he disappears from the
story. Gustav Vasa is now enraged by the behavior of his subjects in
the borders:

This pack of traitors in lower Småland have sent messages and letters across
the border and warned our enemies of our army's advance over the frontier
into enemy territory. So that such treachery shall be eradicated, we shall
chastise them for their great disobedience, shown particularly by those
unheeding inhabitants of Möre and Värend, so that our subjects in lower
Småland will receive that punishment that these enemies of the Fatherland

deserve. . . . We have shown far too much patience and tolerance toward this Land of Traitors. (278)

The chastisement to follow is heralded by the arrival of soldiers at Nikolaus Brodde's church. They come upon the priest tolling the bell in alarm, and for this treachery they intend to hang him, but Brodde falls dead before they can carry out their threat. The novel ends with the symbolic violation of Ingela, the madonna figure, at the hands of an unknown soldier.

The brutality of sixteenth-century warfare is evoked in horrifying detail in *Land of Traitors*, as are its effects on the countryside and its peace-loving inhabitants. Lasse represents Man brutalized by war, an evil that grows in the midst of the peasantry: "They would have nothing to do with him. They did not recognize anything of themselves in him. Yet . . . he was born in the same district and belonged to them. He was begotten by the people themselves" (267). The murderer's evil is a timeless one, argues Moberg. It has existed in all ages from Cain himself, but nationalism is a greater evil in both Vasa's time and our own. It is nationalism that is the root cause of war, and the heavy responsibility rests squarely on the shoulders of those in power in the land: "It was kings and crowns that made war on one another; the soldiers had, according to the oath they swore to the flag, merely undertaken to keep the war going for them" (68).

The Red Stone and the frontier stream represent nationalism and its deleterious effects, and at one point the voice of the stream is heard: "I became the stream that divided them, parents from children, family from family, friend from friend. On my banks ramparts were raised and barricades built, over my surface flew arrows and spears. Blood flowed into my pure clear waters" (159–60). It is obvious that Moberg abhors all such unnatural boundaries, be they in Berlin, Korea, Ireland, or Vietnam. For the men of the borders there is no third camp to which they may belong, for the third camp is regarded as traitorous by both sides. Against nationalism Moberg sets the dream of international brotherhood represented by the bridge between peoples and the peasant peace treaties. This last is an idea long retained in folk memory in Småland, and which Moberg has recorded as being revived by a member of parliament for southern Möre as recently as 1869. At this time of international rearmament "The proposer suggests that the idea of a peasant peace could be taken up and applied by all states, which would thereby realize the dream of world peace."[5] Bengt Sibbesson, who is guilty of treason in the eyes of the state, wonders who the real traitor is, not he who warns the people of the approach of soldiers, "But those who sent out the soldiers to harry the countryside, they betrayed it, they were the traitors to their country" (157).

One does not have to look far to discover analogies in the contemporary scene to the plight of the traitor. In the mid-1960s deserters from the American army, soldiers who disagreed with the Vietnam war, sought asylum in Sweden. Moberg saw in their refusal to fight not treachery but a defiance conforming to the great tradition of freedom in America: "The United States is losing rebels, the defiant ones, men of freedom, the sort of people who laid the foundations of the American union."[6]

In its evocation of historical period and atmosphere and in the passion of its arguments, *Land of Traitors* has most in common with *Ride This Night!* and this is also true of the use Moberg makes of verifiable historical events as parallels to modern situations and as timeless symbols. But in its message the novel most closely resembles *A Time on Earth*: mankind has the possibility of creating another Eden, a kingdom of peace on earth, here represented by the poor forest area of Småland and Blekinge, but man always rejects this in favor of inflicting meaningless suffering on his own kind.

Despite its skillful presentation of historical period, its many fine set pieces, and its passages of lyrical beauty and impassioned rhetoric, the novel remains a somewhat disappointing work. The symmetry and stylization are at times too obvious, and the work suffers from structural deficiencies: there are no consistent central characters to provide a focus for the story, and even Lasse is portrayed as a symbolic figure rather than a character of flesh and blood.

III   *History and the Historical Novel*

"Among the subjects I have read other than fiction [writes Moberg] history has been my foremost love. This love embraces the subject in its widest sense: world history as much as that of Sweden, cultural history, social history, the history of ideas, of religion, of war. I have been possessed by an inquisitiveness about mankind's past, which is of course dominated by stupidity, tragic mistakes, and acts of lunacy, repeated generation after generation. World history is a gigantic crime novel, a tale of the endless crimes that mankind has perpetrated against itself."[7] Moberg's lifelong love of history reveals itself clearly in his novels which, taken together, provide a historical

review of Värend from prehistoric times (*The Brides' Spring*) to the
present day (*A Time on Earth*), pausing at the sixteenth century
(*Land of Traitors*), seventeenth century (*Ride This Night!*), and
eighteenth century (*Man's Woman*), while concentrating upon the
social changes of the past hundred years: emigration (the emigrant
tetralogy), rural depopulation and urbanization (the Knut Toring
trilogy), rural industrialization and the growing power of the working
class (*Soldier With a Broken Rifle*). To this list must be added *Raskens*, which depicts the nineteenth-century rural culture on the
verge of extinction.

A number of these novels have come to be regarded as essential
sources of information in various historical fields for researchers of
later generations: this is true of the account of the militia system in
Raskens, and, of course, of emigration in the tetralogy, of which Ulf
Beijbom writes: "It can be stated in general terms about Moberg's
significance for research into emigration, that his emigrant epic has
been a source of inspiration for the study of emigration at universities
and in study circles."[8]

Nevertheless, Swedish historians have not always greeted
Moberg's re-creations of his country's past with enthusiasm, and on
several occasions a long-running battle has followed the publication of
one of his historical novels. Typical is the controversy that surrounded *Ride This Night!* The great problem in ascertaining the
degree of accuracy of Moberg's account of seventeenth-century
Värend lies in the paucity of information about Sweden during this
period, a contentious one among historians. When the novel
appeared in 1941 Professors Henrik Munktell and Bertil Boëthius
both cast doubts on Moberg's picture of the judicial system in Sweden
during the reign of Christina, especially the use of forced labor,
sentences of outlawry, and the burial alive of captured felons,[9] and a
debate ensued in the press in the course of which Moberg cited actual
cases in refutation of these criticisms. Moberg's detailed account of an
oppressed peasantry deprived of all legal rights has in all major
respects later been verified by Gerhard Hafström from the legal
records of the period.[10] However, Professor Boëthius also argued
that the historical novelist should attempt where possible to demonstrate the normal conditions prevailing in any historical period rather
than concentrate upon a year of troubles such as 1650, an argument
ridiculed by Moberg who wondered why Boëthius did not provide a
list of the years in Swedish history that are guaranteed calm and
socially idyllic and therefore suitable for fictional treatment.[11]

The balanced overview of the historian would be neither a necessary nor a desirable attribute of the historical novelist. As Axel Strindberg has indicated, the debate over *Ride This Night!* was unsatisfactory insofar as it failed to distinguish between three possibilities, that: "(1) so and so can have happened, (2) did happen, (3) happened all the time."[12] While arguing strongly that circumstances like those found in the novel did obtain in Värend at that time, Moberg also defends a novelist's right to license: "The professors in the discipline lift an admonishing finger, of course, and say: this has demonstrably not happened! The author needs only to put forward examples from parallel events in order that he may answer: It *could* have happened!"[13] There is an important distinction to be made between literal truth and literary truth, but who is to say whether at times the latter does not provide the essential expression of a historical period, whether, for example, Karl Oskar and Kristina are not more representative of Swedish emigration than any historical emigrants. Moberg often met the historians on their own terms when he need not have done so, and the debates that resulted served often to distract attention from the important aspects of the works, their message for the contemporary reader and the presentation of this message.

On the other hand, Moberg was often unfairly harsh in his own criticisms of both the historians and the historical novelists of his homeland. In particular he attacks G. T. Odhner's classic *Fäderneslandets historia (History of the Fatherland)* for its concentration upon the decision-makers of history, the kings, nobles, and generals, to the exclusion of the peasants, soldiers, and emigrants, for glorifying war and conquest and neglecting the more constructive pursuits of farming, forestry, and building. Unfortunately, Moberg's youthful view of the narrow picture of Swedish history provided by textbook writers like Odhner remained unchanged throughout his life, long after history writing had been transformed.[14] A repeated claim made by Moberg is that of originality. Time and again he claims to be writing of Swedes whom historians and novelists have forgotten: the soldiers, the border peasants, the women in history. But, as has been shown regarding the emigrant novels, his claim is at times exaggerated. In the introduction to *A History of the Swedish People* (1970–1971) he indicates that he intends in this work primarily to "pause at those areas that the experts have hurried past" (I, 13), to write a history of all the people. But he is in fact obliged to devote a great deal of the work to accounts of the familiar figures in Swedish history—the very decision-makers upon whom Odhner concentrates—and to describe events already carefully charted by others. Here are the Folkungs, Saint Bridget, Magnus Eriksson, and the Union Queen, Margareta. In volume II in particular, social and cultural history get short shrift while Engelbrekt, Karl Knutsson Bonde, the Stures, Kristian II, and Gustav Vasa all figure prominently. Moberg's claims to originality therefore seem difficult to substantiate.

Sten Carlsson draws attention to two of Moberg's most damaging weaknesses as a historian[15]—a lack of critical discernment in his use of sources and a lack of balance which shows itself, for example, in his almost entirely negative view of Gustav Vasa (who harried Moberg's beloved Värend) and his idealization of Kristian II of Denmark (whom the border people called "The Peasants' Friend"). Moberg's argument, that the accepted view is so one-sided as to require a corrective, seems very much like special pleading.

Yet it seems that, to most of the many readers of Moberg's history, these objections are nothing more than pedantic quibbling when set against the notorious inability of most historians to present their material in an interesting and readable form. Moberg admits that he has no professional reputation to lose, and if his approach is subjective—the title of the book in Swedish means "My Swedish history, narrated for the people"—then this is what gives the work its inimitable quality. If he sees history from a particular limited vantage point, this is explicable in terms of his marked local patriotism. As he states in the foreword: "If I had been born in a different environment, among a different class, then I would also have written a different history" (I, 12). His overriding aim is to recreate a world which has long since vanished, to penetrate and illuminate the lives of dead generations, and to present these in a form which may be assimilated by a wide public.

The most effective features of *A History of the Swedish People* are often those that make it both personal and popular. One of Moberg's working principles is to move constantly to and fro between past and present, employing comparisons with past events to illumine our own age, and using contemporary illustrations to explain the past. There are many examples of this. His discussion of the pagan religion leads naturally to comments on the superstitious beliefs he encountered in his own childhood world, to a world of sprites and trolls (I, 126); medieval man's fear of the plague is compared with modern man's life in the shadow of a nuclear holocaust (I, 226); concluding his account of the Nordic Union, he cannot resist adding the thought: "One would

like to imagine that April 9, 1940, would not have been quite so
disastrous a day for Scandinavia had Sweden, Denmark, and Norway
then, as 550 years earlier, comprised one political and military unit"
(I, 307). Familiar Mobergian hobbyhorses occur frequently, notably
in volume II which is more discursive: he exposes as humbug the idea
of the monarch as God's annointed (I, 88); he ridicules the idea of the
state church (II, 251); he notes the pioneer work carried out by
Gustav Vasa on censorship (II, 258); and he laments the death of the
rural community in an account of his bicycle tour of five rural provinces in 1970 (II, 303).

Moberg delights in informing us that the Swedish tax system was
founded by King Odin, the first king of the Swedes, who decreed that
everyone possessing a nose should donate a nose-tax to the monarch,
who in return undertook to keep the peace and ensure that the crops
did not fail (I, 81). He revels in human weakness, often concentrating
upon sexual weakness, as in his account of the punishments for
adultery found in the medieval provincial laws. Here, too, he adds a
wry afterthought: "A woman condemned to death was never hanged.
For reasons of decency one sought to avoid exposing any part of her
body during her execution. This was an act of chivalry. Women were
either burned, stoned to death, or buried alive" (I, 285).

The works often provide the factual background to Moberg's
novels. When he writes of the thousands of miles of stone walls,
monuments to the patient labors of many generations of peasants (I,
58), we are reminded of Rasken or Nils and his son Karl Oskar battling
against the stone on and beneath their fields. In volume II Moberg
devotes a chapter to "The Forest and Popular Liberties" in which he
details the documentary basis for the "forest-going" motif in *Man's
Woman* and *Ride This Night!* In a chapter entitled "A Warrior People's Dreams of Peace," he provides, as we have seen above, a
thoroughly researched account of the border peaces which are the
focal point of *Land of Traitors*.

Moberg's history is a heterogeneous work, and the chapters vary
considerably in style and content. Some, like the accounts of the
Black Death and the Dacke revolt, become separate and independent essays, while others, like the many-faceted "On Medieval People," are based firmly on earlier research and are packed with detail.
Still others, like the chapters on the Folkungs and Engelbrekt are
nearer to the crime novel than the history book. The gripping opening of the chapter on Engelbrekt *in medias res* reveals the master of
narrative: "One chilly evening in April, 1436, an ax murder was

committed on a small island in Lake Hjälmaren" (II, 15). History is seen as a gigantic work of fiction and its major figures are often portrayed as protagonists in well-composed tragedy. But these figures are unfortunately not as capable of manipulation by the author as the characters of a play, for the documented facts are restricting. Several of Moberg's reviewers have expressed their wish that the master had stuck to his craft, writing novels, arguing that our picture of the past is determined more by the historical novel than by narrative history. This is certainly true of Moberg's tremendously popular historical novels, which are models of the genre.

CHAPTER 9

The Dramas

I *Moberg and Swedish Drama*

AFTER Strindberg Swedish drama was generally relegated in the world of letters to a role subordinate to the novel and poetry, and remarkably few Swedish writers of this century have devoted themselves wholeheartedly to writing works for the stage.[1] Pär Lagerkvist (1891–1974) and Hjalmar Bergman (1883–1931) are notable exceptions, but even Lagerkvist's valiant attempts to modernize Swedish drama went largely unrewarded in the 1920s and 1930s. At a time when the realism of Ibsen was still the predominant influence, Lagerkvist attempted to project the drama in a symbolist-expressionist direction along the lines of Strindberg's post-Inferno plays. But it was a long time before even the later plays of Strindberg were to prove influential, and directors showed a marked preference for foreign drama during this period. As in narrative fiction the popular forms in drama between the wars were those of bourgeois realism and folk realism. Most modern dramatists in Sweden have thought of themselves primarily as novelists, and few of the working-class writers, who dominated the 1930s and whose influence was still strong until recent years, have shown any great interest in drama as a form, although one or two have written radio plays. In this Moberg stands out as a major exception.

A difficult problem for playwrights in the first decades of the century was the limited number of professional theaters in Sweden, although the situation gradually improved with the expansion of the provincial stage and the founding of the National Touring Theater (*Riksteatern*) in 1933. Also important was the growth of radio drama in the late 1920s under the direction of Per Lindberg. Lindberg fostered radio drama in its formative years, encouraging both young dramatists like Moberg and established writers like Hjalmar Bergman and Sigfrid Siwertz (1882–1970) to write for the new medium and helping them to adapt their technique to its particular requirements.

Moberg was one of the pioneers of this new medium with plays like *Market Eve* (1930) and *The Wife* (1929), written at Lindberg's instigation. The radio play has in more recent years again attracted talented young writers: Sven Delblanc (b. 1931), Per Gunnar Evander (b. 1933), and Per Olov Enquist (b. 1934) have all made their mark in this way.

A second revolution in dramatic production came with the advent of television in the 1950s, and here too adaptations of Moberg's works, both dramas and novels, have proved highly successful. Several of Moberg's plays have also been filmed, among them *Embezzlement*, *Widower Jarl*, *Market Eve*, and *The Judge*, but none with the same acclaim as the film versions of *Ride This Night!*, directed by Gustaf Molander in 1942, and the emigrant tetralogy, directed by Jan Troell in 1971.

Literary historians have generally concentrated their attentions upon Moberg's novels to the virtual exclusion of any treatment of the dramas,[2] yet any consideration of his work which does not take them into account ignores two important features of that work. First, Moberg frequently chose to alternate between novel and drama as means of expression, often examining the same problem in two different ways and on occasion coming to different conclusions. As a result of the streamlining necessary for adapting novel into drama, several of the adaptations present the theme more effectively than do the novels on which they are based. Second, although there are comic interludes in the novels, they generally possess an underlying seriousness of purpose, whereas in a number of plays Moberg allows his considerable comic talents free reign.

Moberg wrote approximately forty dramatic works over a period of forty years. Not all of these have been published and many are now regarded as slight. Yet a number of workmanlike pieces still belong to the regular repertoire and a few stand out as dramatic masterpieces. His career as a dramatist divides approximately into three phases, each with a different focus. In the late 1920s and early 1930s his major interest lay in folk drama. The 1930s and 1940s saw a growing interest in social drama and the problem play, while in the postwar years social satire and experiments come to dominate his work.

II   *Folk Dramas*

Moberg's rural comedies and tragedies possess settings, characters, and themes similar to the early novels. In the one-act comedy *Market Eve* (1930) the reader finds himself in familiar surroundings, the kitchen of farmer Magni's cottage on the evening before the great autumn fair in Växjö. The date is not given, but the action could be imagined as taking place at any time in the fifty-year period spanning the turn of the century. The intrigue is of a simple kind, consisting of the usual love triangle: Magni, a man in his fifties, intends to leave for market after supper and promises his forty-year-old housekeeper, Lovisa, a little present on his return. Lovisa believes that this present will be the engagement ring for which she has waited patiently during long years in Magni's service. Enter Rapp, the local constable, who reveals to Lovisa that Magni is to accompany Teresia to market so that the two can buy engagement gifts. Rapp also reports a rumor that Teresia brings with her a dowry of ten thousand crowns. The cunning Rapp then makes overtures to Lovisa, believing that she has saved her wages over the years, and is mortified to discover that she has not recieved any earnings whatsoever from Magni for the last ten years. The two calculate that Lovisa is owed eight thousand crowns in all. Lovisa is quicker than the greedy Rapp and leads him on by making him think he has a chance of winning her and the pay she is owed in order to gain his help in obtaining the money from Magni.

The scene is set for a confrontation, and to complicate matters further, Lovisa informs her master that she intends to accompany him to market in the wagon. When Teresia hears of this, she loses her temper, and Magni has to ask Lovisa to stay at home. The housekeeper responds by demanding she be payed the wages she is owed, and threatens to leave Magni and sue if these are not immediately forthcoming. Teresia's dowry, it transpires, is smaller than Magni thought, some eight thousand crowns, and the disappointment at this discovery and her demand that she be allowed a full-time housekeeper when she is married upset her intended husband. Rapp returns to announce his own marriage plans: he is to wed Lovisa who will bring him a dowry of eight thousand crowns! Teresia flies into a rage at this news—Magni can afford to buy off his housekeeper, but belittles his betrothed's dowry—and she storms out in high dudgeon. Magni and Lovisa are soon reconciled when the shrewd peasant realizes that he can avoid paying his housekeeper her wages by the simple expedient of marrying her. He promptly proposes, is accepted, and the couple go off together to market.

This play was written in answer to a call from Per Lindberg for a play for radio which was entertaining and not in the least disturbing, and it has been regarded, with some justification, as one of the finest examples of modern Swedish drama, and one of Moberg's dramas that will best stand the test of time. Conforming to the dramatic unities—the play has one room, only four characters, and a limited time-period—Moberg achieves remarkable concentration. Although based on some of the traditional figures of the rustic comedy—the mean master, the cunning and resourceful servant—the play somehow transcends caricature. There is a realistic edge to the humor, too: the comic situations are in each case based on a credible premise. The rural world of the provinces is a world apart, where property—the farm—is king, and where there is little place for sentiment. It is a world like the island in the Stockholm skerries in Strindberg's *People of Hemsö* (1887) in which the plot also centers around a marriage of convenience, or the Skåne village of Ernst Ahlgren's story "Giftermål på besparing" ("Thrifty Marriage," 1884) in which an investment of only ten crowns eventually decides which of two women a mean peasant will wed. A mainspring of the plot is the rigidity of social class, the idea that marriage partners should be social and financial equals which provides a dramatic motif in *Raskens* and *Far from the Highway*—in both novels with tragic consequences.

Similar in intrigue to *Market Eve* is *Widower Jarl* (1940), a one-act "folk comedy." Again the protagonists are advanced in years and the plot revolves around marriage plans. The main character, Andreas Jarl, is an old soldier of seventy living on a pension who has had to fend for himself since losing his wife Kristina. He believes that marriage to his neighbor, the widow Gustava, would be to their mutual advantage, that is, she would wash his clothes and they would share the cost of expensive winter fuel. Gustava is in favor of the match because her son is about to marry, and could take over her cottage. It appears that Jarl's unmarried daughter Hilma also wants a say in what is decided, and a second potential suitor for Gustava, called Mandus, adds further complication. The triangle is merely the reverse of that in *Market Eve*. The climax is reached at a party to celebrate the calling of the banns for the happy couple, when they each suddenly discover the other's mercenary motives, and the nuptial plans fall through. It emerges that Jarl really wished to remain faithful to the memory of his dear departed Kristina, and the play ends with him hanging her photograph in a place of honor. The sharpness of the dialogue of *Market Eve* is lacking in *Widower Jarl*, which has a more mellow tone and a slower pace. The depiction of human relations is, however, just as down-to-earth and devoid of sentiment and brims with comic potential.

A number of critics consider that Moberg's folk comedies represent a revitalization of the whole genre, insofar as the familiar mixture of motifs like rivalry, greed, self-defeating jealousy, and certain character types are placed in the service of a portrayal of character that is essentially realistic. The comedy is thus more than just a formula—it comes alive.[3]

The three-act dramas *The Wife* and *Wedding Salute* were published in the volume Dramas of the Common People (1929), but it was some time before any interest was shown in them, and before *The Wife* was recognized as an important work and produced at the Dramatic Theater in Stockholm. The author's aim in these plays is made explicit in the preface: "Both dramatic works which are presented here are attempts to give scenic representation to the Swedish farmer and the environment in which he lives." The plays reflect the same purpose as the early novels, and the same tension is evident between the dramatic-theatrical and the realistic-depictive aspects of the works.

The setting of *The Wife* is once more a farmhouse kitchen, and the action takes place over a period of several hours one spring evening. The unities are again observed. The dramatic tension is provided by the animosity between Jakob Hjelm's young wife Helga and his mother Johanna, who are forced to live under the same roof. Johanna reproaches her daughter-in-law for being a laggard and spendthrift, and for not being her son's social equal. Helga detests her mother-in-law for interfering and trying to usurp her rightful position as mistress of the household. The play contains some barbed ironical exchanges of a rare intensity, as here in act 1, scene 3:

Johanna.	The porridge is getting cold.
Helga.	You eat. You seem to have worked for your food.
Johanna.	I have done what a mistress ought to be doing.
Helga.	But you won't need to poke your nose into everything any more. There'll be some changes here. Once in a while I shall be able to decide things in my own house.
Johanna.	Your house—you must be joking! What did you ever have before you became my daughter-in-law?
Helga.	Are we back to that again now?
Johanna.	We'll never get away from it, because it's the truth. Did you ever bring as much as a wooden spoon with you when you came here? . . .
Helga.	I know you've never liked me. I wasn't good enough for your boy, not wealthy enough. (18)[4]

There is something amiss between husband and wife, and Johanna's suspicions of her daughter-in-law prove well-founded: having failed to get Jakob to throw Johanna out of the house, Helga plans to murder her husband with the aid of the young manservant Jonas, who is under her spell. But after planning to kill his master by faking a shooting accident, Jonas begins to fear Helga's ruthlessness and gets cold feet. Then, in the second act, shots are heard and Jakob staggers in, wounded. In the third act the pattern of the play approaches the intrigue of the detective mystery: there is some doubt as to how Jakob was shot—did Jonas shoot him, or did he try to take his own life after learning of his wife's infidelity? Jonas swears to Helga that he did not pull the trigger. The suspense is sustained and finally resolved by a surprise: Jakob tells Helga their neighbor Mickel shot him, and Helga confesses that Mickel has been her lover, and that they planned his murder together. Tension mounts when the rural constable arrives, but Johanna convinces the policeman that she had been wrong in her suspicions. In the final scene, Helga, moved by her husband's good-ness to recognize her own guilt, wishes to atone for her crimes—like Lady Macbeth she imagines blood on her hands that she cannot wash away. Helga goes out to confess to the police and receive her due punishment.

The ending, with its motif of guilt and atonement, is reminiscent of Strindberg's *Miss Julie* or of Moberg's own *Far from the Highway*. The many short scenes of incisive dialogue, the use of suspense and surprise, reversals of fortune, but above all the firm basis of the rural world at the center of which is the farm, makes this the best example of Moberg's rural drama. Gunnar Brandell has suggested that the crime stories of Gustaf af Geijerstam (1858–1908), some of which are built upon trial transcripts, may be models for the plot,[5] and Moberg asserts that an actual case in Småland underlies the plot.[6]

Wedding Salute also deals with the theme of property and free-dom, and also has to do with a crime. Olof Danielsson is a rich farmer, churchwarden and respected pillar of the community. His daughter Ester has a secret lover, Bernhard, but she is unable to marry him as he is only a farm laborer. As she explains to him: "But what a farmhand earns isn't enough for us. Not for me anyway. And if I take you I won't get a scrap from home" (173). Ester is a sensible girl who agrees to her father's wishes that she marry a wealthy neighbor, someone of her own social standing. But as preparations for the wedding proceed so warnings of imposing disaster begin to appear: Bernhard is rumored to have gone mad and threatens to come unin-vited to the wedding feast. Then on the eve of the wedding Ester's bridal gown is found torn to shreds. Much is also made of the symbolism attaching to the bridal crown. The superstition runs that any girl who wears the crown but is no longer a virgin can expect a dire fate, a motif also found in Strindberg's *The Crown Bride* (1901) in which a young girl admits her disgrace—as does Ester—on her wedding day. Bernhard does appear at the wedding and threatens to carry off the bride, but is interrupted when in desperation he is about to shoot Ester and himself. He kills a servant and escapes, only to be captured. Ester is carried out unconscious, and it transpires that she has taken a lethal dose of fox poison as she is expecting Bernhard's child. Her father is crushed, perhaps more by the shame and the blow to his prestige than by any true feelings for his daughter. The theme here resembles that of *The Wife*. Though at times powerful theater, the play is flawed by the introduction of too many minor characters who tend to obscure the main figures and their development. Perhaps, also, the inexorable course of the tragedy is too unrelieved to be considered realistic.

Moberg's third rural tragedy is *The Clenched Hands* (1939), an adaptation in five acts of the novel. The work is especially suited to adaptation for the stage as all the action takes place at one location— the farm at Ulvaskog, which may indeed be considered a protagonist. It also possesses sharply defined contrasts and conflicts of character. Very little of the quality of the original has been sacrificed in the drama, which is even an improvement in some respects. There is, for example, a greater concentration upon Adolf's personal tragedy and some pruning of characters and incidents not considered central to this, including the Fate-figure, Lump-Fransen. *The Clenched Hands* is much more a drama of character than the other tragedies. The long acts, undivided into scenes, are employed to present a careful examination of the different stages in the disintegration of Adolf's personality.

Another play, written shortly after the novel *The Clenched Hands*, shares much of its social message. In the one-act drama *Between Farmers* (1933) the old peasant world of independence and self-sufficiency is set against the new ideas of interdependence and cooperation, and the generation gap is again explored. Like Adolf, Jonas at Västergårn is part of the old order, and his unmarried daughter Rut tries in vain to introduce him to newfangled notions such as electricity and milking machines. Rut's role is similar to that of Betty in *The Earth is Ours!* In this play the young agricultural improver, Henning Sjösten, plans to form a cooperative in the village, and in seeking the support of Jonas provokes a crisis in the household. There is a love story and some humor introduced by a figure resurrected from *Raskens*, the marriage broker, but these are not strong enough to counterbalance the heavily underlined social message. The play suffers from an overly pedagogic tone, a weakness in several of Moberg's plays. In comparison with *The Clenched Hands* it is a minor work, but it does show how Moberg often chose to present the same ideas in different literary forms and with a different outcome—in *The Clenched Hands* the ending is tragic while in *Between Farmers* the stubborn reactionary is finally won over into accepting change and the play ends on a concordant note.

In his folk drama Moberg intended to present the real world of the peasant farmer without lapsing into the portrayal of a gallery of rustic types, and in the preface to *Between Farmers* he feels constrained to provide explicit instructions on this point: "Everything which smacks of 'theater peasants' should be avoided. Peasants in stage representations so often become pure caricature. The dangers of exaggeration in dress, makeup, performance, etc. are very great in the case of the genuine play like the present one. In this regard moderation and care should be exercised." Moberg's low-key approach to his rural world is also seen in the way he tones down the Småland dialect in the plays—more so than the novels—using what he termed "Rikslandsmål" ("national dialect"), in some cases so as to make radio productions more easily assimilable across the country.

III   *Social Dramas and Problem Plays*

No clear dividing line separates Moberg's folk drama from the drama which focuses upon social problems. As has been shown in relation to *The Clenched Hands*, social problems of general relevance are discussed within the framework of a restricted rural setting, and because they deal with more general human problems, several plays are therefore examined in this context. As in the novels these problems are often viewed in terms of conflict between the individual and society caused by the restrictions that social conventions place upon the freedom of the individual. In the 1930s Moberg's motifs are often erotic in nature—here too the influence of the primitivists may be discerned—but when reason is abandoned in favor of instinct, the consequences are often serious for those involved. Moberg the moralist generally takes precedence over Moberg the primitivist. In the plays dealing with the problems of marriage and abortion Moberg the crusader comments upon the burning issues of the day. The settings

for the dramas are those found in the novels at the same period:
contemporary Värend, bourgeois urban milieus, and Värend in the
historical past.

Man's Woman is a wartime dramatization of the novel from 1933,
and follows the course of that novel quite closely.[7] The rewriting
presented few problems again because of the dramatic nature of the
original, but even so the result is an independent work of art. Moberg
appears to have set about the task of adaptation in much the same way
as for the more complex novel *The Clenched Hands*. Some narrative
passages have of necessity been excised, in particular the tale of
Frans-Gottfrid and the thief. Also missing from the drama is the story
of Stark-Ingel, the outlaw who lived in the forest with the woman
whom society denied him, a story which in the novel prefigures the
ending of the plot. In its place Moberg employs Herman's past
history as a parallel to the main action: he too has been forced to
choose between the girl he loved and his farm. In attempting to hold
onto his property he chose wrongly, for he finally loses both. The
sensuous depictions of the countryside—especially the use of nature
to provide atmosphere in key scenes—have had to be sacrificed, too,
but another mirror of mood, the changing seasons, is suggested by a
clever use of lighting. The set is simplified to a single room, Påvel's
kitchen, and as a result of all this the central motif—Märit's moral
dilemma—stands out in clearer relief. Her growing maturity is shown
to better advantage than in the novel, since Moberg draws her as
younger and less confident at the outset and more determined and
courageous in the final scene. The ending is more dramatic, for Märit
follows Håkan into the forest directly they are discovered by her
husband, whereas in the novel she ponders her fate for several hours
before coming to her decision.

The triangle situation is also basic to *A Vagabond* (1941), a one-act
play written at the same period as *Man's Woman*. The antipathy
between wife and mother-in-law—used to greater effect in *The
Wife*—is employed once more. A young wife has married an older
well-to-do farmer for the comforts he can provide, but is then tempted to sacrifice everything for the love of a stranger her own age. The
idea is that of *Man's Woman*, but the solution is different. In *A
Vagabond* Ragnhild decides to stay at Askebäck with her good-
natured but dull husband Linus and make the best of her lot. She has
discovered that she is expecting Linus's child, and feels she must
remain loyal to the family line whose continuity she will ensure. The

plot and its denouement are familiar, and are found in, among other works, Ernst Ahlgren's *Fru Marianne* (1887).

The four-act play *Violation* (the Swedish title *Våld* means either "violence" or "violation") from 1933 is the first of Moberg's important dramas not to be set in a rural environment. It depicts the urban middle-class Granbäck household, and examines the problems of three marriages, those of the Granbäcks themselves and their two daughters. When the curtain rises, the Granbäcks are preparing to attend the wedding of their younger daughter Betty. The husband reflects upon his own marriage and concludes that it has been a sham: the couple have stayed together for the sake of the children, and have been terribly unhappy as a consequence. He exclaims: "It is quite unnatural for two people to wear each other down like this day after day and year after year! They cannot do so without violating each other's souls! Yes . . . that's what it is really: just violation" (107). To Granbäck the sacrifice does not seem to have been worthwhile, and he now wants a divorce. In the second act the scene shifts to the home of the daughter, Margit, and her husband of two years, Gunnar. On Margit's instructions the maid has been spying on Gunnar, but Margit regrets having discovered her husband's infidelity: "One shouldn't try to discover truth, because one only suffers for it," she says (118), echoing Ibsen. In the third act the emotional strains of the bridal couple are exposed. Torsten does not believe in marriage as an institution. He has already experienced his parents' disastrous marriage, and knows how a child may become the fetter that binds a loveless couple together. Betty is pregnant, but has kept her condition a secret and nevertheless decides that she cannot compel Torsten to sacrifice his principles: "It would be like committing violence" (143)—in this case the violation of Torsten's personal integrity. But the wedding goes ahead despite these reservations, and the last act finds the Granbäcks again in the foreground. The bride and groom have left and the parents exchange confidences about their children: Gunnar's unfaithfulness, Betty's pregnancy, and Torsten's desire not to marry. The children are no longer a reason for them to stay together, and once again Granbäck announces that he will divorce Linnéa. She threatens suicide to try to force him to relent, and eventually jumps from the balcony.

In setting and ideas the play is most closely akin to the Scandinavian 1880s, not least in the motif of settling accounts with outmoded beliefs and values. The idea that compulsion is no basis for marriage is

found in Ibsen's *A Doll's House* (1879), while the terrible helplessness
of the loveless couple chained together probably owes something to
Strindberg's vision of marital hell in *The Dance of Death* (1900). Yet
Violation was written in the same year as the novel *Man's Woman*,
and provides yet another illustration of how Moberg can approach the
same problem from several different angles.

The social pressures on a couple in love to conform to contemporary notions of morality and propriety are again investigated in a later
work, the four-act drama *Woman's Man* (1965)—the choice of title
must indicate an intended association with the earlier novel and
drama. This play also has a middle-class setting, the house of Miss
Lotte Friman, fifty-eight years old. Lotte loves a young protégé, the
pianist Mikael Steiner, a man who at twenty-eight is young enough to
be her son. Her family are outwardly upset by the scandal which the
(actually Platonic) relationship is creating, but in reality they are
concerned that Lotte's inherited wealth—which they consider to be
family money—may elude their grasp and pass into Mikael's hands
should the couple marry. Lotte has sacrificed her own happiness in
order to look after elderly relatives, and now that her life is nearly
over considers that she has got very little out of it. At last she can be
carefree: "I'm going to do something that will cause a sensation.
Something *terrible*" (74). What she actually does is to donate half a
million crowns in order to establish a fund to help young composers,
thereby arousing the undying enmity of her relatives. A jealous niece
sells a choice piece of scandal about Lotte to a gossip columnist, and
Lotte attacks her betrayer and spends a night in police custody for her
pains. Finally she rejects Mikael's proposal of marriage, telling him:
"I shall die such a long time before you. . . . The great difference
between us is the distance from death, your distance and mine" (186).
Lotte feels that her body has betrayed her, and intends to give away
the rest of her fortune and take up nursing. She feels she must do
something useful with the remainder of her life.

Woman's Man brings up to date the theme of social pressures on
the individual wishing to obey her own emotions, but the play lacks
the credibility and intensity of other works on this theme. There is
also a slackness in the plot that leaves the ending hanging in limbo.

The four-act play *Our Unborn Son* (1945) is both a contribution to
the debate on abortion, and a presentation of one young woman's
moral dilemma, an idea first treated successfully in *Man's Woman* in
which the abortion motif appears. The setting is a remote village. The
time is World War II, and the story centers upon Helena, a young

schoolteacher and her boy friend Ejnar, a working-class lad who is trying hard to better himself. The couple cannot afford to get married, but then Helena discovers that she is pregnant. Rather than compel Ejnar to make a disastrous marriage which would wreck his chances of a career, she decides she must obtain an abortion. She tells Ejnar: "This is the greatest thing that has ever happened to me . . . and I shall be forced . . . to violate my conscience. But what can I do?" (26). So, undeterred by the weak and indecisive Ejnar, Helena arranges to have her pregnancy terminated. Act three begins two years later, upon the couple's engagement. Ejnar has succeeded in educating himself and in one more year is due to become an engineer. But the abortion still preys on Helena's mind. She wonders what her son would have been like, and feels guilt at having betrayed the child, blaming her own cowardice for what she has done. As a result of the operation she can now no longer have children. Ejnar, who is a dogmatic Socialist, places all the blame for what has happened on a corrupt and decadent capitalist society. The abortion was performed illegally, and the police catch up with the doctor responsible and ask to interview Helena. Ejnar's cowardice at this news proves decisive for Helena, who intends to leave him and the village for good. The message of the play is firmly underlined in act 4, when Helena asks:

Isn't it the child who redeems us, who frees us from selfishness, who delivers us from loneliness? Isn't it the child who brings out the best in all of us? And isn't it the child who finally helps us to die? We go into darkness . . . into the unknown—but we still leave something behind. Everything we have given the child. Everything of us which will live in the child when we ourselves do not exist any longer. . . . The child is our possibility. The only one we have. Our possibility of something. Of a new being. (104)

Moberg's argument against abortion is strongly emotional, relying on a firm belief in the family line and the integrity of the individual. As Helena—the author's mouthpiece—exclaims: "Oh, if they could hear me, all the women who are in the same predicament I was in on that occasion! Then I would cry to them: Don't do it! Don't kill the life within you! Just for the sake of people's respect. Because I understand now: it isn't other people's respect we need most. It is self-respect we cannot live without. It is ourselves we need to appease" (102).

Helena and Ejnar are not the whole play, however, as Moberg also introduces one of his most fascinating and original creations—Malins

Maria. Maria is one of Helena's pupils, a strange naive young orphan
who lives in a world of Bible stories and legends about Jesus and the
Virgin and often cannot distinguish between this fantasy world and
reality. She astounds the villagers gathered for the teacher's engagement party first by announcing that she, Maria, is pregnant and has
been chosen to bear the Savior, and then by condemning Helena for
murdering her own child: "You went to Herod. You let Herod
murder your son!" (79). By means of Malins Maria, Moberg injects a
lyrical element of religious mysticism into the work, and this is
associated with Helena's gradual return to her childhood faith. At the
end of the play, Helena is to take Maria away with her, for they belong
together. Maria still suffers from the fixed idea that she is to give birth
to Our Lord, and both women are thus fated to spend their lives
waiting for the same impossible event. In *Our Unborn Son* Moberg is
seen—perhaps surprisingly—to work within a framework of traditional Christian concepts: "For every child that is born, God recreates His world" (105).

In *Our Unborn Son* it is mentioned that Malins Maria will be cared
for in an old people's home, and in the short radio play *The Virgin
Mary in the Workhouse* (1954) Moberg imagines what life would be
like for her there. The play was originally intended as the final act of
Our Unborn Son.[8] The premise is simple: a group of old people sit
waiting to die and watching those around them fade away, and Malins
Maria believes that she has a calling to ease their passing by giving
them faith in the Savior. There are some fine characters among the
pensioners, but the play achieves its effect more by atmosphere than
drama, a feature of Pär Lagerkvist's earlier *Midsommardröm i
fattighuset* (*Midsummer Dream in the Workhouse*, 1941).

Ride This Night! has a complex history. There are no fewer than
four different versions of the story: Moberg's original novel from
1941, his own three-act dramatization for the stage from 1942, a radio
adaptation by Lars Levi Laestadius made in 1942, and a radio play by
Moberg from 1953. There is also a film version directed by Gustaf
Molander. But here we are concerned only with Moberg's stage
play.[9] Unlike previous dramatizations he had made of his novels, in
this play Moberg was compelled to use a number of different sets,
some of which are outdoors, but—perhaps because of the staging
problems—there are, nevertheless, few scenes depicting the hero
Ragnar Svedje's life as an outlaw in the forest. This forms a major
strand of the novel, contrasting with the life of the enslaved peasants
of the village. As a result Svedje's role is of much less significance in

the drama than in the novel. His companion in the forest, the thief Ygge, is consequently also reduced in importance, and is not seen in this version as a Robin Hood figure. An inevitable loss is that of the physical detail of nature, so effective in the novel in conveying a menacing atmosphere. Other changes include a bigger role for Alderman Stånge's wife, Alma, here a figure of imposing moral strength, in contrast to her husband. The split in the Stånge household—defiance versus appeasement—adds greatly to the contemporary relevance of the play. Annika—the sinister young woman who in the novel is responsible for Botilla's death—is in the drama a more neutral figure, undecided as to which camp to support. There are also changes in the plot. Botilla is not compelled to marry Lars Borre, and does not drown in the spring. But the recurrent images of the novel—the sun which represents justice, and the birds of ill omen—are retained and even supplemented, for a mysterious spring erupts from deep within the earth to throw up the buried "budkavle" once again, with its message of resistance.

The scene in which Svedje is captured and buried alive is muted insofar as it takes place offstage, but, despite this, the ending of the play is even more forcefully dramatic than that of the novel. The men of the village come together to swear an oath to meet oppression with armed resistance:

> *Bock*. In the lands to the south and east the peasantry are treated like serfs. But in our kingdom we still resist this German and Livonian serfdom. . . .
> *Tomasson*. We shall rise up!
> *Sibbesson*. We shall find weapons!
> *Henriksson*. We shall make our own muskets!
> *First farmer*. We can make spiked clubs!
> *Second farmer*. We can sharpen spears from our scythes!
> *First farmer*. The fiery-cross [budkavle] must be sent out [to gather the peasants]!
> *Second farmer*. Tonight it shall go forth!
> *All*. "The fiery-cross shall go forth! (195–96)

The overall effect of the modifications made is to lessen the significance of some of the minor characters who lend the novel a great deal of color, but would distract the theater audience's interest from the powerful central message of defiance to the oppressor and all those who do his errands, a message which is strongly highlighted in the play.

Of his adaptations Moberg writes: "I do not remember how many
novels I have adapted into stage plays. . . . Dramatizations are seldom successful. Personally I am only reasonably pleased with two:
Man's Woman and *A Time on Earth*."[10] The drama *A Time on Earth* is
indeed a very successful work in its own right, yet the adaptation has
been carried out with remarkably little loss of the stuff of the novel. As
Viveka Hagnell observes, all twelve scenes "on the stage of memory"
correspond to scenes in the novel, and the dialogue is often taken
directly from the novel, noticeably in the scenes depicting the deaths
of Sigfrid and Albert's father and the visit of his cousin."[11] But, then,
one third of the novel is already in the form of direct speech. In the
drama Moberg focuses almost entirely upon the events in Småland
and discards a number of the Californian characters. He links
together the twelve scenes by short monologues delivered by the
aging Albert Carlson in the solitude of his hotel beside the Pacific.
Thus the balance of the novel—"then" and "now," the stream and the
sea, Sigfrid and Jesus-Jensen—is replaced by a strong single thread:
Sigfrid's death, its precise causes and significance, as revealed to
Albert. This undeniably lends the play a greater structural unity, but
only at the cost of a subtle associative technique.[12] According to
Roland Thorstensson, Moberg wrote the play at the instigation of
Ingmar Bergman, who also provided technical advice, which may
account for the effectiveness of the flashback technique employed.[13]

A Time on Earth is at all events a powerfully moving drama of great
personal intensity. By making the tragedy more specifically individual, Moberg succeeds in conveying the antimilitarist message
with greater clarity.

IV *Satires and Experiments*

It would be wrong to assume that all Moberg's humor is born out of
a feeling of compassion for his fellowman, as is largely the case in the
folk comedies. Some of the humor is of a much bitterer kind, and
grows out of a desire to expose the flaws in human character—greed,
corruption, hypocrisy, the misuse of power and responsibility. Nor
are reason and facts the only weapons in his arsenal as a social critic,
for he frequently succeeds in making a serious statement by a skillful
use of ridicule.

Embezzlement (first published 1939), Moberg's first dramatic success, evokes the roaring Twenties, the era of dubious business
dealings and frequent bankruptcies. The embezzlers—cashiers from

several firms in a small town—join together to provide mutual aid. This is achieved by the simple expedient of rushing money to the funds of any of their number whose fraud is threatened with exposure by a sudden audit. In this way the cashiers are able to conceal deficits in their funds indefinitely. There is a little panic when the cashiers' deliberations are interrupted by the arrival of the local police chief, but it seems that he too is in need of financial assistance! It is inevitable that the tables should be turned on the embezzlers, and when their funds are in their turn stolen, they are righteously indignant at the modern lack of moral standards. The play is no masterpiece, but it did prove very popular with Swedish theaters for many years. The similarities of theme with *A. P. Rosell, Bank Director*, written some five years later, are quite striking, but *Embezzlement* deals only in terms of caricature. The wider social implications of such a corrupt society are never explored.

A more heavy-handed treatment of what Moberg saw as pernicious tendencies in modern life is to be found in the drama *Chastity* (1937). The ascetic Saint Anthony first appears as a hermit in the deserts of Egypt where he is tempted by visions of beautiful women. He is then reborn in modern times as the poet Richard, who believes passionately in the ideal relationship with woman, a union of the soul as well as the body, and thus far has lived the life of a celibate. A liberated woman, Laura Reinert, tries unsuccessfully to show him the error of his ways, but when her seduction fails, turns him over to her psychiatrist husband for treatment. At Dr. Reinert's Institute for Human Ennoblement Richard's complexes and neuroses are carefully listed and treated, and he is soon discharged only to return shortly afterward to demand that the doctor give him back his illness. After attempting suicide, Richard is taken to the Home for People Weary of Life, where he meets a group of apathetic dropouts whose every move is dictated by the nurses. But the Home is bombed (a reference to the Spanish Civil War) and Richard escapes from the devastations of war to find himself in the bosom of nature, beside a fairy spring, an eternal source with extraordinary healing properties. Out of the spring emerges a young girl, Ingun Elvira Johanna, a child of nature who cures him of his neuroses. In the final act beside the spring the lyrical qualities of the dialogue partially make up for an otherwise rather naive critique of social ills, an attempt to ridicule what Moberg believed was a growing apathy with life that he had detected in the city and which he features prominently in *Sleepless Nights*, published in the same year.

A more specific allusion to the contemporary scene is made in *The Maid's Room* (1937), a light comedy that also deals with chastity, but in the context of the controversy over indecency in literature which raged in the mid-1930s. The literary critic Dr. Konrad Tallberg is conducting a private campaign in his reviews against the modern pornographic novel. He especially takes to task a young woman writer named Brita Ljungwall, and claims in a review that the sex scenes in her latest novel must be based on personal experience. At this time Tallberg has also employed a new maid, Viola (the clue is in the Shakespearean name, for Viola is Brita Ljungwall in disguise), little knowing that, as soon as his wife is safely out of the way, the maid intends to put his own personal morality to the test. Konrad is involved in judging a competition for the best novel of sound moral content fit to be read by all the family. The prize is to go to a work entitled "The Maid's Room," written, of course, by Brita Ljungwall under a pseudonym and actually a *roman à clef* containing allusions to her relationship with her employer. The ending of the play is rather weak (Konrad's narrow-mindedness is overcome) but the play is interesting as a humorous counterweight to a rather overserious literary controversy, the scandal surrounding Agnes von Krusenstjerna's novel cycle *Fröknarna von Pahlen* (*The Misses von Pahlen*, 1930–1935).

Moberg describes *The Judge* (1957) as "a tragic comedy in six scenes" with the action taking place "in the ancient kingdom of Idyllia in our time." We are once more transported to the world of *The Ancient Kingdom*, a world of "corrupt justice" and "the corruption of friendship." In fact, the judge in question, Edvard Cunning, appears briefly in the earlier novel.[14] Both works contain a number of allusions to the Lundquist–Unman case. In the play Judge Cunning is based on Judge Folke Lundquist, the poet Krister Langton on the artist Gustaf Unman whose fortune Lundquist embezzled, the editor Lanner and his newspaper *Folk-Tribunen* on Armas Sastamoinen and *Arbetaren*, and Langton's lawyer Arnold on Unman's advocate Björn Dahlström. Moberg has indicated that the seed from which the play grew was the scene in which Krister Langton reads in a newspaper that he is suffering from *paranoia querulans*,[15] and it is Moberg's compassion for the individual so brutally treated—and even denied his most precious right of personal liberty (Unman was wrongfully incarcerated in a mental hospital)—that underlies his bitter criticism of a corrupt legal system. The ending of the play is particularly harsh: the judge, having succeeded unchecked in all his criminal enterprises, stands over the prostrate body of the poet, saying "I'm most terribly sorry" (207). The play provoked an angry reaction from legal and political circles, in which it was regarded as a gross distortion of the events. But satire depends upon concentration and caricature to achieve its effect, and anyway, on closer inspection it turns out that what appears to be poetic license in many cases is very close to what happened.[16]

Whereas *The Judge* aroused indignation among only a restricted circle, *The Fairytale Prince* (1962) provoked widespread moral outrage for its references to members of the royal family, and some "dirty tricks" were even employed in an attempt to discredit its author.[17] "The incredible events take place on a large estate in the Kingdom of Idyllia (The Ancient Kingdom)," states Moberg. The estate is owned by Madame, who believes herself to be a daughter of the late king, and it is administered by Captain Bernhard, whose plans for it include felling all the forest and opening a zoo in the grounds. Bernhard's shady business deals become known to a stranger called Max. Max blackmails Bernhard when he discovers that the prince allows Bernhard to use his royal name in order to extract money from firms. Finally the police are informed and Bernhard arrested. The play alludes to the "Huseby affair," a financial swindle in which Prince Carl Bernadotte appeared to be involved, and as such was explosive, but from this distance in time it seems ephemeral.

In the post-war years Moberg attempted to break away from the form of his earlier dramatic work and to find new forms for the themes that always obsessed him.

Wife of the God (1954) is, it is true, also set in Värend, but this is a "heathen cult comedy" whose action takes place in the tenth century. The original story comes from the Old Norse *Flateyjarbók*, although in his preface to the play Moberg states that he followed a later version of the story which locates the adventures of the Norwegian adventurer Gunnar Helming in Småland. The original episode relates to the conversion of Småland to Christianity, but Moberg places greater stress on its heathen aspects. Gunnar Helming is escaping from the king of the Goths who intends to sacrifice him. He arrives at a village where a severe drought is threatening the crops and the local inhabitants are trying to awaken the god of fertility from his winter slumbers. When this attempt fails, the priest reports that the god— Frey—demands a virgin bride, and a young girl, Ingegjär, is chosen to become the wife of the god. In order to escape from his pursuers, Gunnar hides inside the effigy of the god, and is carried into the bridal chamber where the god will spend the night with Ingegjär. She believes him to be the god incarnate, a new and more vigorous version of the Frey he has replaced. By his actions Gunnar not only succeeds in defeating the heathen god, but also overcomes old age and even death itself. The conquest of death by fertility and new life is a motif found most noticeably in *The Brides' Spring*, written at the same time as this play, the last story of which is set in prehistoric times and depicts a similar fertility ritual. Luckily for Gunnar Helming, at this juncture the skies open and the blessed rain falls, so that when morning comes he is carried round the fields in triumph and worshipped as the god Frey come to visit the people in person. The viking's luck holds, and he is quick-witted enough to exploit the situation to the full, demanding tribute of the villagers. Laden down with booty, he rides off with his new young bride.

The play is very unusual in its setting, and involves a large element of spectacle. Yet despite its broad humor, it does deal with an important theme in Moberg's work—the conquest of death.

Also based on an ancient story is *Leah and Rachel* (1954), "A drama of women," which employs the tale of Jacob and the daughters of Laban (Gen. 29ff.). Moberg's version remains close to the Bible story, though he shifts the emphasis from the problems of Jacob and Laban to the tragedy of the women. Love and fertility are prominent here too: Jacob's wife Leah gives him many children—thus fulfilling her prime function in the eyes of the society of the time—but it is the infertile wife Rachel whom Jacob loves, and for whom he labors for fourteen years. The play ends with the death of Rachel, who has stolen Laban's household god, the Teraphim, and upon whom he has brought down the wrath of Jehovah. Sigvard Mårtensson has pointed to the play's underlying character of folk drama. It deals with a people whose life is close to the earth and for whom land, beasts, and the continuation of the family line are of vital concern. In order to emphasize this Moberg employs a dialogue which juxtaposes the dignified language of the Old Testament and the folksy provincial expressions of Småland.[18]

The Night Waiter (1961) is, like *A Time on Earth*, set in the limbo of a hotel room, an anteroom to eternity, and is a very personal expression of the fear of growing old. It was written at a time when its author was at a low ebb after completing the emigrant tetralogy. The Man (none of the characters are given personal names) is an artist of sixty years and a burned-out case. Unable to complete his latest canvas entitled "Old Age," he has come to the hotel to end his life: "to live a life whose aim is only to prolong life . . . is there any meaning in that?" (28). During the day he is visited by a Friend, the Cleaning Woman, and the Mistress, who appeal to him in the name of Art, God, and Love, respectively, not to kill himself. But at night he receives another—mysterious—visitor, the Night Waiter, who offers him relief from all his fear and anguish, no less than eternal peace. The Old Man (man's old age) also comes to him at night, senile, blind, and deaf, a vision of what he himself will become if he goes on living. As a result the Man tries unsuccessfully to take his own life. An interlude when he finds he is able to help another human being, a call girl who comes to him, provides the turning point. He sits down and decides he will capture the vision of the Old Man on canvas (perhaps in much the same way that the emotionally exhausted Moberg recovered his equilibrium by writing *A Time On Earth*). The message of the play has been spelled out in other works, notably *The Clenched Hands*: "Old age is one long humiliation for Man" (28).

V *Conclusion*

Vilhelm Moberg was primarily a practitioner of drama rather than a theorist, but this is not to underestimate his contribution to drama in Sweden, which, when he began writing for the stage, was in a serious decline. His work in the organization and development of the theater and in bodies designed to aid his fellow dramatists has already been mentioned in chapter 1. He was not a great experimenter. He did not push the boundaries of the art forward in the way that, for example, Pär Lagerkvist or Stig Dagerman (1923–1954) have done, but instead drew on tradition and consolidated traditional forms. The two main fields to which he made substantial contributions are those of folk comedy and radio drama. Moberg was a pioneer of the radio play, achieving great success in the form, and although little of his output was primarily intended for the medium, much of it has since been featured on radio and has formed a reliable part of radio drama's repertoire over the years. Moberg gave folk comedy a new lease of life by employing greater realism of situation and dialogue. Many of the audience felt at home in the rural world he created, and could identify with his characters and their problems. He also put folk comedy to new use, as a vehicle for criticizing social trends. The two strands of social criticism and humor also come together in the satires, which often allude to specific events and individuals. It was through these that Moberg reached a wider audience than that which read his pamphlets or attended his meetings.

CHAPTER 10

Conclusion

NEARLY all of Vilhelm Moberg's narrative fiction and much of his drama is concerned directly or indirectly with Värend, a small area of his home country of Sweden, and yet his work in various ways manages to transcend a narrow provincialism. Several of Moberg's novels deal with the author's alter ego (called Knut, Valter, or Albert) growing up in a peasant world from which he finds himself increasingly alienated, a conservative, pious world with an unchanging, age-old cultural tradition. The young man comes into contact with more modern ideas and eventually feels that he must break out of his environment to seek a new life where he has the freedom to develop. But this process of *Bildung* and this migration do not lead him to a feeling of belonging in his new surroundings. Moberg's emigrants are always looking back wistfully to their childhood home in Värend, to a Garden of Eden which is lost for ever. They are rootless individuals, belonging nowhere and merely serving out their time on earth. Important outsider figures of this kind are Knut Toring, Albert Carlson, and even Kristina Nilsson. Uprooting is an important theme in Moberg's work. He documents and dramatizes the causes and effects of mass migration and emigration, but never loses sight of the individual human problems involved.

Flight from the community is indicative of a deeper dichotomy between the duty to contribute to the communal effort, to conform, and the desire for self-assertion, for freedom from any commitment. A number of the flights by individuals in the novels end in failure, particularly those of A. P. Rosell, Ragnar Svedje, and Robert Nilsson.

But Värend also begins to change. It was changing in the author's own childhood, and he feels he must capture something of this preindustrial culture before it is swallowed up entirely. He believes it has much that modern man may profitably emulate, in particular the stress placed on the individual and personal self-reliance. At the same time Moberg charts the course of the changes, the effects on the countryside of the new ideas, the clash of cultures.

At various points in his career Moberg attempted to find new forms in which to express his ideas. He chose historical settings or bourgeois surroundings, alternated between novel, drama, and pamphlet, and modified his natural detailed realism in the direction of myth, reportage, or symbolism. The theme of freedom gradually comes to dominate in his work, whether it be political freedom, sexual freedom, freedom from tyranny, freedom of religious belief, or freedom of speech and the press. Gradually, too, particular character types begin to emerge. One such might be called the "dreamer-liar-artist" figure. Several of his main characters are shown to be ill at ease in the practical world and at times have difficulty in distinguishing fantasy from reality. Valter Sträng and Robert Nilsson both possess this trait in large measure, but Knut Toring, Albert Carlson, and others have the same tendency. The problem of the dreamer resolves itself into an antisocial aspect (the liar) and a socially acceptable aspect (the storyteller). As children both Valter and Robert make up incredible tales and come to believe in them. But, whereas Valter is later able to control his gift of imagination and turn it to advantage as a writer of tales and eventually a novel, Robert is unable to put his overactive imagination to any good use and is finally destroyed by his dreams. Other prominent character types are the strong-willed individualist (Rasken, Adolf, Ragnar Svedje, Valter Sträng, and Karl Oskar), the diligent, pious, and fatalistic woman (Ida, Hilda Sträng, Kristina) and the sensual woman (Nergårds-Anna, Emma, Märit, Ulrika). Some characters obviously exhibit more than one of these traits, and all the traits are at times presented as forces for either good or ill.

The contrast between the dreamer and the man of action is also seen in Moberg's view of death. Moberg's philosophy is in some ways close to Buddhism, and it is not surprising to find that Schopenhauer was one of the gods of his youth.[1] There is a death wish in Moberg's works, a longing for Nirvana, to be seen in characters like Robert Nilsson and Albert Carlson. At the same time there is a strong appetite for life and a horror of growing old, found, for example, in *The Clenched Hands* and the play *The Night Waiter*. The contrast is best illustrated in *Soldier With a Broken Rifle* when Valter is in hospital with Spanish flu, enticed toward death by Schopenhauer and Nirvana but clinging to life through his desire for Ingrid. Moberg suggests that the most intense moments of life (those of procreation) are inextricably linked to death, providing "a sensation of an intensified life which ultimately bordered upon extinction" (*Soldier With a*

Broken Rifle, 593). Märit and Håkan in *Man's Woman* make their bed on decaying leaves, in *The Brides' Spring* there is lovemaking among the graves, and Valter is seduced by Ingrid in a room next to that in which he had almost died: "So he came to experience that only a thin wall separated life and death and that they came together in the union of a man and a woman" (*Soldier With a Broken Rifle*, 593).

The symbolism of spring, stream, and ocean has a similar significance. Water is both the source of life and its end, and both are linked in *The Brides' Spring*. In the novels of childhood the stream is closely linked with youth; for Adolf it is the progress that sweeps him aside and leaves him behind, while in the emigrant novels and in particular in *A Time on Earth* both stream and ocean come to represent the rejection of life: Robert fakes his suicide in the mill brook and eventually dies beside a stream, while Albert is ready to sink into the Nirvana of the Pacific Ocean. A surprising number of Moberg's characters die in water.

Moberg's narrative and dramatic techniques and his prose style have so far attracted little attention in his own country, where critics have been concerned primarily with his use of biography and carefully researched historical documentation. The materials of his novels, rather than his presentation of these materials, have seemed more important. He has wrongly been regarded as a natural storyteller rather than as a conscientious craftsman who rewrote obsessively and was never satisfied with a piece of work. This may be because he was not a major technical innovator, but he did experiment both in the narrative and drama, most notably in the use of viewpoint and chronological looping. His individual works are often carefully structured: for example, motifs recur and vary, the narrative follows a marked time-scheme or is cyclical in nature. But there is also a high degree of continuity and consistency in the *oeuvre* as a whole, in imagery, themes, characters, and incidents.

Moberg was clearly most at home in the epic third-person narrative, in which he was able to develop character and theme gradually over a long period of epic time, manipulating viewpoint and characters so as to involve the reader in depiction and action. He was generally more successful in historical settings, and in his best work there is remarkably little redundancy of detail: the characters are established with economy; the setting helps to reveal action and mood and is presented through the characters so as to enhance the interest and speed the forward movement of the plot; imagery is used to aid precision of expression, add color, and provide an extra reflection of the world of the fiction.

Over more than fifty years of writing Moberg developed a distinctive personal style in his prose, and it is one of the lasting attributes of his work. Swedish above all else, it has its roots deep in his own Småland dialect and in those Old Swedish texts he so valued, especially the pithy prose of the fourteenth-century provincial laws and the dignified language of the *Gustav Vasa Bible* of 1541. The use of the Småland dialect in the novels was part of his striving for precision of expression, but also serves to intensify the realism by locating the action firmly in Värend. The use of dialect is most marked in *Raskens*, *Ride This Night!* and the emigrant tetralogy. Here Moberg imitates dialect pronunciation in dialogue, and introduces specifically regional terms, though always in a context from which the reader may easily deduce their meaning. This results from a conscious purist aim on his part, a desire to revive indigenous words which in the standard language had fallen into disuse, and to avoid at all costs using foreign loans. The strong rhythms of the prose in certain novels are the result of the use of such rhetorical devices as assonance and alliteration, word-pairs and parallelism akin to those features of early Hebrew writing which Moberg was familiar with from the Old Testament.

Both as a man and as a writer Moberg is a complex figure, filled with ambiguities. He is a man who seemed obsessed with his home province and yet who lived most of his life in or near Stockholm or outside Sweden. In the works he constantly praises the strong individualism of the chauvinistic peasant culture, and yet was a Socialist who believed passionately in the international brotherhood of man. For most of his life he was a pacifist, although for one period was prepared to die and kill for his country, urging his fellow countrymen to do likewise. An ardent advocate of man's ability to shape his own destiny, his characters surprisingly often sink into a fatalistic rejection of the world, and flee from their responsibilities by running away or escaping into a dreamworld. An atheist from his youth, Moberg constantly employs biblical language and allusion, and reveals a remarkable insight into, and compassion for, naively pious Christians. A man very much of his own time, Moberg was also a linguistic purist who was fascinated by history. These are but some of the disharmonies and contradictions that make Vilhelm Moberg such a fascinating figure and provide his literary works with a depth and richness which amply reward the persistent reader.

Notes and References

Chapter One

1. The medieval history of Småland is outlined by Lars-Olof Larsson in *Kulturhistorisk leksikon for nordisk middelalder*, vol. 16 (Copenhagen, 1956–), pp. 303–9.
2. Moberg describes the "peasant peaces" in *Min svenska historia*, vol. 2 (Stockholm, 1971), pp. 177–96.
3. The greatest of these revolts, the Dacke Rising of 1543, is presented in ibid., pp. 325–90.
4. "Min barndoms somrar," *Svenska turistföreningens årsskrift* (Stockholm, 1968), p. 251.
5. Moberg's family background and early life are traced in both Sigvard Mårtensson, *Vilhelm Moberg. En biografi* (Stockholm, 1956) and Magnus von Platen, *Den unge Vilhelm Moberg* (Stockholm, 1978).
6. *Berättelser ur min levnad* (Stockholm, 1968), pp. 12–13.
7. See Gerhard T. Alexis, "Vilhelm Moberg: You Can Go Home Again," *Scandinavian Studies*, 40 (1968), 225–32.
8. *Berättelser ur min levnad*, pp. 55–56, 245.
9. Ibid., p. 215.
10. Ibid., pp. 20–24.
11. *Vilhelm Moberg: En biografi* (Stockholm, 1956), p. 26.
12. See Lars Furuland, *Folkhögskolan—en bildningsväg för svenska författare* (Stockholm, 1971), which contains an account of Moberg's education.
13. *Berättelser ur min levnad*, p. 105.
14. Eidevall examines the early tales and sketches for *Raskens* in his *Berättaren Vilhelm Moberg* (Stockholm, 1976), pp. 7–46. The book also contains a list of stories published between 1919 and 1927.
15. Ibid., pp. 17–18.
16. Moberg gives an account of his years in journalism in *Berättelser ur min levnad*, pp. 205–40.
17. Ibid., p. 118.
18. See *Berättaren Vilhelm Moberg* (Stockholm, 1976), pp. 41–46.
19. "Att skriva för teatern," in *Teater*, ed. G. M. Bergman and N. Beyer (Stockholm, 1954), p. 93.
20. See Sten Carlsson & Jerker Rosén, *Svensk historia*, vol. 2 (Stockholm, 1961), p. 453.

21. For an account of the reactions of Danish and Norwegian writers to the occupation of their countries, see Janet Mawby, *Writers and Politics in Modern Scandinavia* (London, 1978), pp. 5–31.

22. *I skrivande stund* (Stockholm, 1973), p. 27.

23. See Eric Wennerholm, "Vännen Ville," in *Vilhelm Moberg—en vänbok* (Stockholm, 1973), pp. 43–47.

24. The "Czech Debate" emerges from a series of articles in *Dagens Nyheter* by Eyvind Johnson (March 9, 1948); Vilhelm Moberg (March 13 and March 16, 1948); and Arnold Ljungdal (March 16, 1948).

25. *Otrons artiklar* (Stockholm, 1973), p. 28.

26. Moberg describes the background to the emigrant tetralogy in both "Romanen om utvandrarromanen," in *Berättelser ur min levnad*, pp. 291–336, and in "Sexton vandringsår: 1948–1964," *Bonniers Litterära Magasin*, 33 (1964), 430–37.

27. Moberg describes and quotes at length from Andrew Peterson's diary in *Den okända släkten*, 2d ed. (Stockholm, 1968), pp. 35–56.

28. See the pioneering work by Ingrid Wennberg, "Bönder på havet i Vilhelm Mobergs Utvandrarna. En studie i författarens material," *Svensk Litteraturtidskrift*, 25 (1962), 160–74, and Gunnar Eidevall, *Vilhelm Mobergs emigrantepos* (Stockholm, 1974), chap. 2, "Författaren och källorna."

29. *I skrivande stund*, p. 47. For a general survey of Moberg's postwar social criticism, see Armas Sastamoinen, "Vilhelm Moberg som samhällskritiker," in *Emigrationer*, ed. Magnus von Platen (Stockholm, 1968), pp. 63–82.

30. For a more detailed account of the controversy see *Berättelser ur min levnad*, pp. 317–25; *Perspektiv på Utvandrarromanen*, ed. Erland and Ulla-Britta Lagerroth (Stockholm, 1971), pp. 147–60; and Gunnar Eidevall, *Vilhelm Mobergs emigrantepos*, pp. 180–83.

31. For an account of this debate see Erik Hj. Linder, *Fem decennier av nittonhundratalet*, vol. 2 (Stockholm, 1966), pp. 603–5.

32. *Den okända släkten*, p. 133.

33. See "Nobels ofredspris," in *Otrons artiklar*, pp. 107–17, and *I skrivande stund*, pp. 24–26, 42–44.

34. *Otrons artiklar*, pp. 112–13.

35. See *Berättaren Vilhelm Moberg*, pp. 180–83.

36. *Berättelser ur min levnad*, pp. 336–37.

Chapter Two

1. *Berättelser ur min levnad*, p. 16.

2. Moberg portrays Nils Thor in the chapter "Farfarsfar" in *Berättelser ur min levnad*.

3. "Betraktelse om romanskrivning," in *Avsikter. Aderton författare om sina verk* (Stockholm, 1945), pp. 157–58.

4. See Sigvard Mårtensson, "Krönikan och dramat. En återblick på 'Raskens,' Vilhelm Mobergs stora soldatroman," *Bonniers Litterära Magasin*, 24 (1955), 531.

5. Ibid.

6. See Anders Österling's review, "En soldatfamiljs historia," in *20 romaner bedömda av samtida*, ed. Karl-Erik Rosengren & Jan Thavenius (Lund, 1967), p. 94.

7. See *Berättaren Vilhelm Moberg*, pp. 36–41 in which Eidevall compares the original tales with the episodes in the completed novel.

8. See *Berättelser ur min levnad*, pp. 155–70.

9. See *Berättaren Vilhelm Moberg*, p. 54.

10. See Sigvard Mårtensson, "Krönikan och dramat," p. 529, and Gunnar Eidevall, *Berättaren Vilhelm Moberg*, p. 49.

11. See Karl-Åke Kärnell, *Strindbergs bildspråk. En studie i prosastil* (Uppsala, 1962), p. 187.

12. See Algot Werin's review in *Ord och Bild*, 60 (1931), 393.

13. See *Berättaren Vilhelm Moberg*, pp. 92–93.

14. Mauritz Edström places the novel in its social context in *Stad och land i litteraturen* (Stockholm, 1955), pp. 5–19.

15. Vilhelm Moberg, "Nobelpriset och Vilhelm Moberg," *Veckojournalen* (1958), part 51/52, p. 54.

Chapter Three

1. Magnus von Platen claims that "the novel comes very close to the *roman à clef* " despite Moberg's denial of this. See his "Vilhelm Moberg och den självbiografiska romanen," *Svensk Litteraturtidskrift*, 41 (1978), 25.

2. Moberg depicts his own experiences as a small town journalist in *Berättelser ur min levnad*, pp. 205–229.

3. Figures cited in Stig Hadenius et al., *Sverige efter 1900* (Stockholm, 1967), p. 123.

4. Foreword to the Folkbiblioteket edition of the novel (1968).

5. See *Berättaren Vilhelm Moberg*, p. 128.

6. See my "August Strindberg: The Red Room (1879)," in *The Monster in the Mirror: Studies in Nineteenth Century Realism*, ed. D. A. Williams (Oxford, 1978), pp. 131–48.

7. *Berättelser ur min levnad*, p. 25.

8. Ibid., p. 239.

9. See *Berättaren Vilhelm Moberg*, p. 67.

10. See Magnus von Platen, "Vilhelm Moberg och den självbiografiska romanen," p. 19.

11. See *Berättelser ur min levnad*, pp. 65–66.

12. Ibid., p. 20.

13. Ibid., p. 24.

14. See, for example, *Berättaren Vilhelm Moberg*, p. 65.

178 VILHELM MOBERG

15. *Berättelser ur min levnad*, pp. 25–26.
16. For a detailed account of Swedish writers' reactions to Nazism in the 1930s, see Wolfgang Butt, *Mobilmachung des Elfenbeinturms. Reactionen auf den Faschismus in der schwedishen Literatur 1933–1939* (Neumünster, 1977).
17. Eyvind Johnson, *Nattövning* (Stockholm, 1938), p. 244.

Chapter Four

1. See "Skogen och folkfriheten" in Moberg's *Min svenska historia*, vol. 2.
2. Sven Delblanc traces this motif in "Den omöjliga flykten," *Bonniers Litterära Magasin*, 62 (1973), 264–69.
3. Letter to Maj Danelius, cited in her "Vilhelm Mobergs Mans kvinna—från roman till drama," *Svensklärarnas årsskrift* (1974–1975), 125.
4. *Atlantvind* (Stockholm, 1932), p. 223.
5. "Epikern Vilhelm Moberg," in *Vilhelm Moberg—en vänbok* (Stockholm, 1973), p. 116.
6. Erik Hj. Linder, *Fem decennier av nittonhundratalet*, II, 556.

Chapter Five

1. *Aspects of the Novel* (Harmondsworth, 1966), p. 80.
2. *Berättelser ur min levnad*, p. 131.
3. *Min svenska historia*, vol. 2: "Det dagliga barkbrödet."
4. Ivar Harrie praises Moberg's use of archaic Swedish in his *In i fyrtiotalet* (Stockholm, 1944), p. 345, while Stig Ahlgren is more critical in *Det kritiska uppdraget* (Stockholm, 1946), p. 83.
5. "Omprövning under 30-talet," *Dagens Nyheter*, January 17, 1960.
6. Ibid.
7. Vilhelm Moberg, "Författarnas uppbåd '39," *Dagens Nyheter*, January 22, 1960.
8. See Vilhelm Moberg, "Tillbaka i vapenrocken," *Dagens Nyheter*, January 27, 1960.
9. *Fem decennier av nittonhundratalet*, II, 557.
10. See Vilhelm Moberg, "När Tysklands sak var vår," in *I skrivande stund*, pp. 27–28, and *Sanningen kryper fram*, p. 36.
11. *I skrivande stund*, p. 27.
12. See "Vapnet som icke får utelämnas," in *Sanningen kryper fram*.
13. Bengt Landgren, *Hjalmar Gullberg och beredskapslitteraturen* (Uppsala, 1975), p. 65.
14. Ibid.
15. Ibid., pp. 66–67.
16. Ibid., pp. 68–69.
17. *Berättelser ur min levnad*, p. 232.

18. Moberg depicts Segerstedt's wartime stand in *Segerstedtstriden* (Stockholm, 1945).
19. *Hjalmar Gullberg och beredskapslitteraturen*, p. 70.
20. Ibid., p. 72.
21. *Ord och Bild*, 51 (1942), 418–19.
22. *Det kritiska uppdraget*, p. 85.
23. "Den omöjliga flykten," p. 266.
24. Ibid., p. 267.
25. Gunnar Eidevall, *Berättaren Vilhelm Moberg*, pp. 188–89.

Chapter Six

1. For a more detailed account of the novel, see G. K. Orton and P. A. Holmes, "Memoirs of an Idealist: Vilhelm Moberg's *Soldat med brutet gevär*," *Scandinavian Studies*, 48 (1976), 29–51.
2. See chapter 5 above.
3. See also chapter 1 above and the first two chapters of Magnus von Platen's *Den unge Vilhelm Moberg*.
4. Magnus von Platen, "Vilhelm Moberg och den självbiografiska romanen," pp. 27–31.
5. Ibid., p. 23.

Chapter Seven

1. Statistics taken from Sten Carlsson, "Chronology and Composition of Swedish Emigration to America," in *From Sweden to America, A History of the Migration*, ed. Harald Runblom and Hans Norman (Minneapolis, 1976), p. 119.
2. Ibid., p. 132.
3. Ibid., p. 133.
4. Hans Norman, "Swedes in North America," in *From Sweden to America*, p. 259.
5. Gunnar Helén, "Utvandrarland—invandrarland," in *Svenska turistföreningens årsskrift 1968*, p. 30.
6. Vilhelm Moberg, "Why I Wrote The Emigrants," in *Industria International* (1964), p. 62.
7. Ibid., p. 61.
8. *Berättelser ur min levnad*, pp. 297–98.
9. Gunnar Eidevall, *Vilhelm Mobergs emigrantepos*, pp. 15–21.
10. *Berättelser ur min levnad*, p. 295.
11. See Helmer Lång, "Moberg, utvandrarsagan och verkligheten," *Svensk litteraturtidskrift*, 32 (1969), 37, 39.
12. Lannestock describes his friend Vilhelm Moberg's stay in America in *Vilhelm Moberg i Amerika* (Stockholm, 1978).
13. For this account of the composition of the tetralogy I have drawn upon Gunnar Eidevall, *Vilhelm Mobergs emigrantepos*, pp. 27–59.

14.   See Gerhard T. Alexis, "Vilhelm Moberg's Immigrant Trilogy: A Dubious Conclusion," *Scandinavian Studies*, 38 (1966), 20–25.

15.   "Sweden to Minnesota: Vilhelm Moberg's Fictional Reconstruction," *American Quarterly*, 18 (1966), 88.

16.   See *Berättelser ur min levnad*, pp. 317–25.

17.   From a speech given in Stockholm, cited in *Perspektiv på Utvandrarromanen*, ed. Erland and Ulla-Britta Lagerroth (Stockholm, 1971), p. 153. This work contains several contributions on the "immorality debate."

18.   See also my *Vilhelm Moberg: Utvandrarna*, 2d ed., *Studies in Swedish Literature no. 6* (Hull, 1978).

19.   Roman numerals refer to volumes in the original version of the tetralogy: I: *Utvandrarna*; II: *Invandrarna*; III: *Nybyggarna*; IV: *Sista brevet till Sverige*.

20.   See also my "Symbol, Theme and Structure in Utvandrarromanen," in *Perspektiv på Utvandrarromanen*, pp. 239–48.

21.   See my *Vilhelm Moberg: Utvandrarna*, pp. 20–24, 32–46 on the language of *The Emigrants*.

22.   See Gunnar Eidevall, *Vilhelm Mobergs emigrantepos* pp. 188–96.

23.   Nils Olsson, "Vilhelm Moberg och Bibeln," III, (Ph.D. diss., University of Lund, 1966), III, 19–26.

24.   From a letter of August 1, 1949, cited in Ingrid Wennberg's "Bönder på havet," p. 161.

25.   Gunnar Eidevall provides a thorough account of the documents underlying the novels in *Vilhelm Mobergs emigrantepos*, chap. 2.

26.   See *Berättelser ur min levnad*, p. 312, and *Nybyggarna*, pp. 139–72.

27.   *Vilhelm Mobergs emigrantepos*, p. 82.

28.   Cited in Gudrun Wendel's "Åkianismen och Utvandrarromanen," in *Perspektiv på Utvandrarromanen*, p. 97.

29.   *Vilhelm Mobergs emigrantepos*, p. 82.

30.   Letter of April 30, 1949, cited in Ingrid Wennberg, "Bönder på havet," p. 171.

31.   Letter of June 7, 1949, in ibid., p. 172.

32.   See *Vilhelm Mobergs emigrantepos*, pp. 71–74, 84–88.

33.   Ibid., pp. 90–91.

34.   See Helmer Lång, "Moberg, utvandrarsagan och verkligheten," p. 31.

35.   *Den okända släkten*, pp. 40–43.

36.   Cited in Bertil Hulenvik, "Mobergsamlingen i Växjö," in *Perspektiv på Utvandrarromanen*, pp. 61–62.

37.   Ibid., p. 70.

38.   *Vilhelm Mobergs emigrantepos*, p. 105, and Moberg's *Den okända släkten*, p. 70.

39.   See Helmer Lång, "Moberg, utvandrarsagan och verkligheten," p. 35.

40. "Sexton vandringsår: 1948–1964," *Bonniers Litterära Magasin*, 33 (1964), 433–34.
41. Boel and Frederic Fleisher, "Samtal med Moberg," *Ord och Bild*, 74 (1965), 577.

Chapter Eight

1. For a detailed account of the Haijby case, see Moberg's "Haijby-affären—århundradets rättsskandal," in *Otrons artiklar*, pp. 49–66. For a study of both the Haijby and Kejne cases, see Maths Heuman, *Rättsaffärerna Kejne och Haijby*, Stockholm, 1978.
2. For an account of this play, see chapter 9 below.
3. Vilhelm Moberg, *Min svenska historia*, vol. 2, 180–81.
4. Ibid., pp. 184–88.
5. Ibid., p. 196.
6. *I skrivande stund*, p. 39.
7. *Berättelser ur min levnad*, p. 255.
8. "Forskning kring 'Den okända släkten,' " in *Emigrationer*, ed. Magnus von Platen (Stockholm, 1968), p. 86.
9. See *Svenska Dagbladet*, March 16, 23, 1942; *Dagens Nyheter*, April 8, 17, 1942.
10. "Domböckerna och Rid i natt!" in *Emigrationer*, pp. 129–51.
11. Bertil Boëthius, "Ett program för svensk historieskrivning," *Historisk tidskrift*, 62 (1942), 100, and Vilhelm Moberg in *Dagens Nyheter*, March 4, 1942.
12. "Frihetsarv och vissa hänsyn," *Tiden*, 34 (1942), 298.
13. "Om historiska romaner," *Vintergatan* (1943), 124–25.
14. *Berättelser ur min levnad*, pp. 56–58.
15. See Sten Carlsson's reviews in *Svenska Dagbladet*, August 31, 1970, October 4, 1971.

Chapter Nine

1. No comprehensive account of modern Swedish drama exists, but the reader is referred to Erik Hj. Linder, "Fem decenniers dramatik" in his *Fem decennier av nittonhundratalet*, vol. 2 (Stockholm, 1966), pp. 1007–36, and Gunnar Brandell, "Dramatik efter Strindberg," in *Svensk litteratur 1870–1970, vol. 2, Från första världskriget till 1950* (Stockholm, 1975), pp. 271–94.
2. An exception is Sigvard Mårtensson who provides a useful guide to Moberg's dramas in *Vilhelm Moberg: En biografi*, and analyzes a number of the dramas in *En bok om Vilhelm Moberg. En handledning till radioteaterns pjässerie spelåret 1953–1954* (Stockholm, 1953). See also Roland B. Thorstensson, "Vilhelm Moberg A Dramatist for the People" (Ph.D. diss., University of Washington, 1974).

3.   See Sigvard Mårtensson, *Vilhelm Moberg: En biografi*, pp. 75–77, and Gunnar Hallingberg, *Radioteatern i 40 år*. *Den svenska repertoaren belyst* (Stockholm, 1965), p. 114.

4.   Page references to *The Wife, Violation,* and *Our Unborn Son* are to the series *Vilhelm Mobergs dramatik*, 3 vols. (Stockholm, 1957).

5.   Gunnar Brandell, p. 285.

6.   *Allmogedramer* (Stockholm, 1929), pref., p. 5.

7.   Compare the account of the novel given in chapter 4 above, and see Maj Danelius, "Vilhelm Mobergs Mans kvinna—från roman till drama," *Svensklärarnas årsskrift* (1974–1975), passim.

8.   See Sigvard Mårtensson, *En bok om Vilhelm Moberg*, p. 75.

9.   For a comparison of the different versions, see Gunnar Hallingberg, *Radiodramat*. *Svensk hörspelsdiktning—bakgrund, utveckling och formvärld* (Stockholm, 1967), pp. 187ff., 200ff.

10.   Cited by Viveka Hagnell in *Att läsa litteratur och att se teater*, Skrifter för Litteraturvetenskapliga institutionen i Lund no. 3, (Lund, 1973), p. 94.

11.   Ibid., pp. 64, 84ff.

12.   Compare the account of the novel given in chapter 7 above.

13.   Roland B. Thorstensson, "Vilhelm Moberg—A Dramatist for the People," p. 35.

14.   Compare the account of the novel given in chapter 8 above.

15.   Vilhelm Moberg and I. Öhman, "Inga levande modeller i Domaren," in *Folket i Bild* (1958), 6, 47.

16.   Compare the pamphlet *Komplotterna*.

17.   See Armas Sastamoinen, "Vilhelm Moberg som samhällskritiker," in *Emigrationer*.

18.   See *Vilhelm Moberg. En biografi*, p. 205.

Chapter Ten

1.   Moberg describes the influence Schopenhauer had upon him in *Berättelser ur min levnad*, pp. 251–53.

Selected Bibliography

PRIMARY SOURCES

1. Novels (Published in Stockholm by Bonniers)
Raskens. 1926.
Långt från landsvägen (Far from the Highway). 1929.
De knutna händerna (The Clenched Hands). 1930.
A. P. Rosell, bankdirektör (A. P. Rosell, Bank Director). 1932.
Mans kvinna (Man's Woman). 1933.
Sänkt sedebetyg (Memory of Youth). 1935.
Sömnlös (Sleepless Nights). 1937.
Giv oss jorden! (The Earth is Ours!). 1939.
Rid i natt! (Ride This Night!). 1941.
Soldat med brutet gevär (Soldier With a Broken Rifle). 1944.
Brudarnas källa (The Brides' Spring). 1946.
Utvandrarna (The Emigrants). 1949.
Invandrarna (Unto a Good Land). 1952.
Det gamla riket (The Ancient Kingdom). 1953.
Nybyggarna (The Settlers). 1956.
Sista brevet till Sverige (The Last Letter to Sweden). 1959.
Din stund på jorden (A Time on Earth). 1962.
Förrädarland (Land of Traitors). 1967.

2. Plays (Published in Stockholm by Bonniers)
Hustrun (The Wife). 1929.
Bröllopssalut (Wedding Salute). 1929.
Marknadsafton (Market Eve). 1930.
Våld (Violation). 1933.
Bönder emellan (Between Farmers). 1933.
Kyskhet (Chastity). 1937.
Jungfrukammare (The Maid's Room). 1938.
Kassabrist (Embezzlement). 1939.
De knutna händerna (The Clenched Hands). 1939.
Änkeman Jarl (Widower Jarl). 1940.
En löskekarl (A Vagabond). 1941.
Rid i natt! (Ride This Night!). 1942.
Vår ofödde son (Our Unborn Son). 1945.
Mans kvinna (Man's Woman). 1953.

184   VILHELM MOBERG

Jungfru Maria på fattiggårn (The Virgin Mary in the Workhouse). 1954.
Gudens hustru (Wife of the God). 1954.
Lea och Rakel (Leah and Rachel). 1954.
Domaren (The Judge). 1957.
Nattkyparen (The Night Waiter). 1961.
Sagoprinsen (The Fairytale Prince). 1962.
Kvinnas man (Woman's Man). 1965.
Din stund på jorden (A Time on Earth). 1967.

3. Nonfiction (Published in Stockholm by Bonniers except where noted)
Svensk strävan (The Swedish Struggle). Stockholm: Försvarsstabens
    bildnings-detalj, 1941.
Sanningen kryper fram (The Truth Emerges). 1943.
Segerstedttriden (The Segerstedt Controversy). 1945.
Den okända släkten (The Unknown Relations). 1950.
Fallet Krukmakaregatan (The Krukmakaregatan Case). 1951.
Att övervaka överheten (On Being Vigilant of the Authorities). 1953.
Därför är jag republikan (Why I am a Republican). 1955.
Komplotterna (The Conspiracies). 1956.
Bondeåret (The Peasant's Year). Stockholm: Fabel, 1966.
Berättelser ur min levnad (Tales from My Life). 1968.
*Min svenska historia. Berättad för folket. Första delen. Från Oden till
    Engelbrekt (A History of the Swedish People. Part I. From Odin to
    Engelbrekt)*. Stockholm: Norstedts, 1970.
*Min svenska historia. Berättad för folket. Andra delen. Från Engelbrekt till
    och med Dacke (A History of the Swedish People. Part II. From Engel-
    brekt to Dacke)*. Stockholm: Norstedts, 1971.
I skrivande stund (At the Time of Writing). Stockholm: Federativs förlag,
    1973.
Otrons artiklar (Articles of Faithlessness). Stockholm: Författarförlaget,
    1973.

4. Articles and Essays
"Att skriva romaner" ("On writing novels"). *Bonniers Litterära Magasin*, 3
    (1934), 17–23.
"Betraktelse om romanskrivning" ("Observations on novel writing"). In
    Avsikter. Stockholm: Bonniers, 1945. Pp. 157–67.
"Att skriva för teatern" ("On writing for the theater"). In *Teater*, ed. Gösta M.
    Bergman and Nils Beyer. Stockholm: Tiden, 1954. Pp. 91–100.
"Romanen om utvandrarromanen" ("The novel about the emigrant novel").
    Svensk Litteraturtidskrift, 20 (1957), 81–100.
"Omprövning under 30-talet" ("Reappraisal in the 1930s"). *Dagens Nyheter*,
    January 17, 1960.
"Författarnas uppbåd '39" ("The authors' mobilization 1939"). *Dagens Nyhe-
    ter*, January 22, 1960.

"Tillbaka i vapenrocken" ("Back in uniform"). *Dagens Nyheter*, January 27, 1960.
"Sexton vandringsår: 1948–1964" ("Sixteen years on the move"). *Bonniers Litterära Magasin*, 33 (1964), 430–37.
"Why I Wrote The Emigrants," *Industria International* (1964), 61–64, 140–46.
"Berättarens död" ("Death of the storyteller"). *Böckernas värld* (1968), 7, 50–56.
"Min barndoms somrar" ("My childhood summers"). *Svenska turistföreningens årsskrift* (1968), 251–59.

5. English Translations
Memory of Youth [*Sänkt sedebetyg*]. Translated by E. Björkman. New York: Simon and Schuster, 1937.
The Earth is Ours! [*Sänkt sedebetyg, Sömnlös, Giv oss jorden!*]. Translated by E. Björkman. New York: Simon and Schuster, 1940.
Ride This Night! [*Rid i natt!*]. Translated by H. Alexander. New York: Doubleday and Doran, 1943.
The Emigrants [*Utvandrarna*]. Translated by G. Lannestock. New York: Simon and Schuster, 1951; London: Reinhardt, 1956.
Fulfilment [*Mans kvinna*]. Translated by M. Heron. London: Hodge, 1953.
Unto a Good Land [*Invandrarna*]. Translated by G. Lannestock. New York: Simon and Schuster; London: Reinhardt, 1957.
When I Was a Child [*Soldat med brutet gevär*]. Translated by G. Lannestock. New York: Knopf, 1956; London: Heinemann, 1957.
The Last Letter Home [*Nybyggarna, Sista brevet till Sverige*]. Translated by G. Lannestock. New York: Simon and Schuster, 1961; London: Reinhardt, 1961.
A Time on Earth [*Din stund på jorden*]. Translated by Naomi Walford. New York: Simon and Schuster, 1965; London: Heinemann, 1965.
A History of the Swedish People [*Min svenska historia*]. *Part I. From Odin to Engelbrekt*. Translated by Paul Britten Austin. London: Heinemann, 1972; New York: Pantheon, 1972.
A History of the Swedish People. *Part II. From Engelbrekt to Dacke*. Translated by Paul Britten Austin. London: Heinemann, 1973; New York: Pantheon, 1974.

SECONDARY SOURCES

AHLGREN, STIG. "Vilhelm Mobergs värld" ("Vilhelm Moberg's world"). *Ord och Bild*, 47 (1938), 598–602. A study of themes in Moberg's work before *Ride This Night!*
ALEXIS, GERHARD T. "Sweden to Minnesota: Vilhelm Moberg's Fictional Reconstruction," *American Quarterly*, 18 (Spring, 1966), 81–94. A rare view in English of the emigrant tetralogy.

DANELIUS, MAJ. "Vilhelm Mobergs Mans kvinna—från roman till drama" ("Vilhelm Moberg's Man's Woman—from novel to drama"). Svensklärarnas årsskrift (1974), 114–44. A thorough examination of Moberg's method in dramatizing one of his novels.

DELBLANC, SVEN. "Den omöjliga flykten" ("The impossible flight"). Bonniers Litterära Magasin, 62 (1973), 264–69. A thought-provoking and original study tracing an underlying theme in the works.

EIDEVALL, GUNNAR. Vilhelm Mobergs emigrantepos: Studier i verkets tillkomsthistoria, dokumentära bakgrund och konstnarliga gestaltning (Vilhelm Moberg's emigrant epic: Studies of the development of the work, its documentary background, and artistic composition). Stockholm: Norstedts, 1974. The seminal work on the documentary basis and gestation of the emigrant tetralogy.

––––––. Berättaren Vilhelm Moberg (Vilhelm Moberg the narrator). Stockholm: PAN/Norstedts, 1976. A thematic approach to the novels with much new material on the early tales.

Emigrationer: En bok till Vilhelm Moberg 20.8.1968 (Emigrations: A book for Vilhelm Moberg). Edited by Magnus von Platen. Stockholm: Bonniers, 1968. A collection of studies and views on various aspects of Moberg's work.

HOLMES, PHILIP. "Symbol, Theme and Structure in Utvandrarromanen." In Perspektiv på Utvandrarromanen, ed. Erland and Ulla-Britta Lagerroth. Stockholm: Rabén & Sjögren, 1971. Pp. 239–48. Traces various symbol complexes in the emigrant tetralogy.

––––––. Vilhelm Moberg: Utvandrarna, Studies in Swedish Literature no. 6 Hull: 1976. Examines characters and themes, narrative technique, language, and the documentary background to The Emigrants.

LÅNG, HELMER. "Moberg, utvandrarsagan och verkligheten" (Moberg, the emigrant saga, and reality"). Svensk Litteraturtidskrift. 32 (1969), 29–41. Shows where Moberg follows documented reality—and departs from it.

LUNDKVIST, ARTUR. "Epikern Vilhelm Moberg" ("Vilhelm Moberg the epic writer"). In Vilhelm Moberg—en vänbok. Stockholm: Bonniers, 1973. Pp. 110–46. An excellent brief account of Moberg's career as a novelist.

MÅRTENSSON, SIGVARD. En bok om Vilhelm Moberg: En handledning till radioteaterns pjässerie spelåret 1953–1954 (A book about Vilhelm Moberg: A guide to the radio theater's drama series for the season 1953–1954). Stockholm: Radiotjänst, 1953. A survey of a number of Moberg's important dramas.

––––––. "Krönikan och dramat: En återblick på 'Raskens,' Vilhelm Mobergs stora soldatroman" ("Chronicle and drama: A retrospective look at 'Raskens,' Vilhelm Moberg's great soldiers novel"). Bonniers Litterära Magasin, 24 (1955), 528–32. A monograph on Raskens.

––––––. Vilhelm Moberg: En biografi (Vilhelm Moberg: A Biography). Stockholm: Bonniers, 1956. A compact but informative literary biography up to 1956.

————. *Vilhelm Moberg: En bildbiografi (Vilhelm Moberg: An illustrated biography)*. Stockholm: Bonniers, 1963. An abbreviated but richly illustrated version of the above.

OLSSON, BROR. "Vilhelm Moberg: En folkloristisk studie i hans romaner" ("Vilhelm Moberg: A folkloristic study in his novels"). *Svensk Litteraturtidskrift*, 1 (1938), 63–71. Traces how Moberg employs superstition and folk belief in the early works.

ORTON, GAVIN, and HOLMES, PHILIP. "Memoirs of an Idealist: Vilhelm Moberg's *Soldat med brutet gevär.*" *Scandinavian Studies*, 48 (1976), 29–51. A monograph concentrating on the *Bildungsroman*, the autobiographical, historical, and political aspects.

Perspektiv på Utvandrarromanen (Perspective on the emigrant novel). Edited by Erland and Ulla-Britta Lagerroth. Stockholm: Rabén & Sjögren, 1971. A collection of articles on aspects of the emigrant tetralogy: especially thorough on the documentary background and the debates that followed the novel's publication.

VON PLATEN, MAGNUS. *Den unge Vilhelm Moberg (The young Vilhelm Moberg)*. Stockholm: Bonniers, 1978. The first volume of what will become the definitive literary biography; traces Moberg's life in great detail to 1935.

TORSUND, NILS. "Miljöskildringen i Mobergs utvandrarepos" ("The depiction of scene in Moberg's emigrant epic"). *Modersmålslärarnas förenings årsskrift*. (1968–1969), 148–69. A rare and original study of technique, language, and style in the emigrant tetralogy.

WENNBERG, INGRID. "Bönder på havet i Vilhelm Mobergs Utvandrarna: En studie i författarens material" ("Peasants at Sea in Vilhelm Moberg's The Emigrants: A study of the author's material"). *Svensk Litteraturtidskrift*. 25 (1962), 160–74. A pioneering study in Moberg's documentary method.

Index